SOURCE BOOK FOR LINGUISTICS

Second revised edition

WILLIAM COWAN
JAROMIRA RAKUŠAN

JOHN BENJAMINS PUBLISHING COMPANY
PHILADELPHIA/AMSTERDAM

1987

Cover illustration from: Johannes Luyken, *De Toorn van Babel*

Library of Congress Cataloging-in-Publication Data

Cowan, William & J. Rakušan
  Source book for linguistics.

(Benjamins Paperbacks; 5)
Bibliography: p.
1. Linguistics -- handbooks, manuals, etc. 2. Linguistics -- Problems, exercises, etc. I.
Rakušan, Jaromira. II. Title.
P121.C62   1985   418   85-26862
ISBN 0-915027-82-8 (U.S.)/ISBN 90 272 2105 7 (Eur.)

SOURCE BOOK FOR LINGUISTICS

BENJAMINS PAPERBACKS

5

BENJAMINS
BP
PAPERBACKS

TABLE OF CONTENTS

II. STRUCTURAL PHONOLOGY

III. PHONEMIC ALTERNATIONS

V. MORPHOLOGY

V. STRUCTURAL SYNTAX

VI. SYNTACTIC PROCESSES

VII. SOUND CHANGE

VIII. RECONSTRUCTION

INTRODUCTION

This book, as its title states, is a source book of language data to be used as exemplification and practice in introductory courses in linguistics. It contains an extensive set of illustrations and exercises in phonetics, phonology, phonemic alternations, morphology, syntax and in the historical disciplines of sound change and comparative reconstruction. The data have been drawn from a wide selection of languages, both Indo-European and non-Indo-European. The numerous exercises have been designed to provide examples of various types of language structure for instructors using any standard textbook, or using none. It is hoped that the format has enough flexibility to allow its use with a variety of different approaches to linguistics. We have found that the large number of problems allows the student to continue practice in problem solving to whatever extent is necessary to master the techniques of linguistic analysis. This large number of problems also makes it possible to continue using the book in second and higher level courses, such as phonology, grammatical analysis, historical linguistics, typology, and others.

A number of features of this book should be brought to the reader's attention:

1) In all sections the exercises are drawn mostly from languages other than English. Since the book is designed for use primarily by speakers of English, we feel that student presuppositions about English, whether from school traditions or the popular press, as well as those features of language beyond a speaker's consciousness, would obscure or impede a student's initial comprehension of many features of language structure, if those features and methodologies were introduced by examples drawn from English.

However, since we feel that no English speaking student should come away from an introductory course in linguistics without some appreciation of the linguistic structure of

English, we have included at the end of each basic section several problems demonstrating how the principles of that particular section apply to English. In effect, after the student has learned the basics of phonetics, or phonology, or syntax, we then show that these basics can also be used to analyze English, just as they can be used to analyze Spanish, or French, or Russian, or any of the other languages used earlier in the section.

2) The languages used for exemplification and exercises are, in the main, relatively accessible, well-known and well-described, with standard grammars and dictionaries, and available native speakers. We have made an effort to keep our data within this framework for two basic reasons: first, so that our data can be investigated, checked, and verified by either instructors or students. The second reason is that this gives instructors and students the opportunity to extend the data if desired. If our demonstrations and exercises are not sufficiently long to prove a point, more examples can be sought in the dictionaries or from the native speakers.

3) Most of the illustrative sets and exercises are quite short and are graded as either elementary or intermediate in difficulty. The elementary problems (and they constitute a majority of the problems) are generally limited to one point to be proven, or one feature to be discovered. For a pedagogical text of this nature, we have tried to establish a balance between maximum data and minimum features to be highlighted.

In compiling the material we tried to ensure that the instructor would feel free to use the material as he or she sees fit. However, we have the following suggestions for those who wish to know how we envision its use:

1) <u>Section I: Phonetics.</u> This section contains demonstrations, not problems to be solved. The phonetic preliminaries give the basic phonetic framework within which we present our examples, as well as the symbols we

use. The illustrations themselves are generally written in ⌐ transcription that is narrow for the feature under discussion, but broad for any other features. We do not illustrate all the sounds on our phonetic grid, but only those, and those contrasts, that are worth while pointing out to English-speaking students. All the examples have been recorded and are available on tape. After basic lectures on phonetics and presentation of the symbols used for transcription, the tapes can be played in class as demonstration of those features that we judge to be of significance to English-speaking students, with appropriate comment by the instructor. Both here and in the sections on phonemics, forms are presented in standard orthographies where feasible.

2) <u>Section II: Structural Phonology</u>. The material in the elementary exercises displays allphones of one phoneme, and the problem is to state the conditioning factors. Those instructors who wish may present the solution in distinctive feature notation. The intermediate exercises are of a more elaborate nature, consisting of a series of related problems. This material requires the student to arrange the forms in appropriate groups, determine whether the elements are in contrast or in complementary distribution, and state the results.

The English section contains a list of English consonants and vowels, along with two possible phonemic interpretations of them, and a set of exercises to assist in learning to make phonemic transcriptions of English.

3) <u>Section III: Phonemic Alternations</u>. The data of this section illustrate phonemic alternations in individual morphemes. The format is similar to that of the previous section: a series of relatively easy sets of words that can be used in class as demonstrations of phonological processes by the instructor, or as problems and exercises to be done by the students. The instructions in this section are of a very general nature to enable the instructor to use a variety of approaches to the problems.

4) <u>Section IV: Morphology</u>. The data of this section have been chosen to illustrate wide typological as well as individual differences in inflectional and derivational systems in a variety of languages. Most of the exercises require a simple analytic procedure which yields a statement on the morphemic content of words. Others require considerations of the functional aspects of the individual morphemes, thus reaching beyond the traditional descriptive analysis.

5) <u>Section V: Structural and Functional Syntax</u>. This section consists of a series of sentence sets from a variety of languages, arranged as problems. The exercises in the first part of this section illustrate various ways of expressing predication, agreement, and government. In some cases, a student is led to establish a word order pattern and compare its properties with those of English. In the second half, exercises from different languages involve descriptive analysis of constituent structures. In these sentences, appropriate morpheme divisions are indicated by hyphens, and all morphemes, bound and free, are glossed at the bottom of the page. Except for the last few exercises, there are no direct translations of the sentences. The English subsection at the end follows a similar pattern.

6) <u>Section VI: Syntactic Processes.</u> The data of this section are presented in the form of sentences designed to teach the students how to formulate phrase structure rules and simple transformations. The material from languages other than English has been chosen to highlight the contrastive features of English syntax and the syntactic properties of other languages. Exercises in English are designed for practicing the elementary transformational processes still mentioned in the majority of current introductory textbooks.

7) <u>Section VII: Sound Change</u>. The examples in this section follow the format of word sets to be used either as demonstrations or as exercises, depending on the

instructor's method of presentation. An attempt has been made to illustrate the more prevalent types of sound change by varied examples. In all cases there are presented earlier and later forms of the same item side by side. The student is shown or discovers what sound changes are responsible for the differences between the earlier and the later forms. An important feature of this section is that for every set of forms exhibiting a change under one set of conditions, a constrasting set of forms either with no change or with a different change under a different set of conditioning factors is also presented. Students are expected to determine what these conditioning factors are. A less extensive series of intermediate problems asks more complex questions and requires more complex solutions.

8) <u>Section VIII: Reconstruction</u>. The problems consist of a set of cognate forms in two or more languages. The student is required to posit and justify a single phoneme or several phonemes. Most problems are not intended to be complete enough to allow the student to reconstruct all the phonemes in all words. In fact, due to the exigencies of finding suitable forms, in many cases one has to ignore most of the word in order to satisfy the reconstruction. Again, cognate sets illustrating a proto-phoneme are folowed by other cognate sets where, under different conditions, different correspondences appear, thus providing the contrast necessary to solve the problems.

9) <u>Key to the exercises</u>. We have tried to suggest solutions for most of the exercises in order to encourage the students to work independently at home. Individual users may find different solutions, or different ways of expressing the same solution, in a number of cases. This is a typical characteristic of problems that contain a relatively small amount of data, or problems that are designed to be used with a variety of theoretical approaches. We have tried to phrase our solutions in such a way as to leave open the matter of theoretical orientation, thus allowing the instructors to use the material in the way they choose. We

hope that our solutions are flexible enough to be adapted to this variety.

We would like to thank the following persons for their help and suggestions: Alex Drahotsky, Paul Filotas, Eva Gavora, Nina and Vladimir Grebenshchikov, Kasim Korat, Angelina Levinson, Ingeborg Müller, Yuri Tambovtsev, and others.

Finally, we would like to express special gratitude to Laura Cowan, Jean-Pierre Paillet and Christina Thiele for their extensive labour and technical advice in the production of this book.

William Cowan
Jaromira Rakušan
Ottawa, February 1987

ABBREVIATIONS

A	adjective
acc	accusative
Adj	adjective
Adv	adverb
Alg	Algonquian
arch	archaic
Art	article
AS	adjectival stem
Aux	auxiliary verb
Aves	Avestan
Ban	Bantu
B-lab	bilabial
conj	conjunction
cons	consonant
dat	dative
def	definite
Def.Art	definite article
dem	demonstrative
Den	dental
Det	determinant
dial	dialectal
dim	diminutive
Dir.Ojb	direct object
-en	past participle morpheme
Eng	English
f	feminine gender
fem	feminine gender
Finn	Finnish
fut	future tense
gen	genitive
GK	Greek
Glo	glottal
Gmc	Germanic
Goth	Gothic
gramm	grammatical

I-den	interdental
IE	Indo-European
indic	indicative
Iroq	Iroquois
imp	imperfect
inan	inanimate
Ind.Obj	indirect object
indef	indefinite
inf	infinitive
infl	inflective
infl	inflectional
-ing	present participle morpheme
inst	instrumental
Lat	Latin
Latv	Latvian
L-den	labiodental
LGmc	Low Germanic
Lith	Lithuanian
loc	locative
Lt	Latin
m	masculine gender
M	modal verb
masc	masculine gender
ME	Middle English
MF	Middle French
MnE	Modern English
n	noun
n	neuter gender
N	noun
neg	negative
neut	neuter gender
NM	noun marker
Ngg	Nggela
nom	nominative
Norw	Norwegian

NP	noun phrase
Npers	noun referring to person
Nprop	proper noun
NS	noun stem
n't	negative particle
Obj	object
OCS	Old Church Slavonic
OE	Old English
OFr	Old French
OG	Old German
OHG	Old High German
OI	Old Iranian
o.m	object marker
ON	Old Norse
OPr	Old Prussian
OPruss	Old Prussian
OR	Old Russian
OS	Old Saxon
OSax	Old Saxon
P	preposition
Pal	palatal
pass	passive
perf	perfect tense
pers	personal
Pha	pharyngeal
PGmc	Proto-Germanic
PIE	Proto-Indo-European
pl	plural
p.m	person marker
PP	prepositional phrase
PP	Proto-Polynesian
PPart	past participle
prepos	prepositional
pres	present tense
Pro	pronoun
Pro	pronominal

Proneg	negative pronoun
P-Sl	Proto-Slavic
p.t.m	person-tense marker
Q	question
ques	question
Rom	Romance
Rum	Rumanian
Rus	Russian
S	sentence
Sa	Sardinian
sg	singular
Skt	Sanskrit
Sp	Spanish
Spro	pronominal subject
Subj	subject
T	Turkic
Ukr	Ukranian
Uvu	uvular
V	verb, vowel
v	verb
Vel	velar
Vinf	infinitive verb
Vit	intransitive verb
VP	verb phrase
Vpast	past tense verb
Vpro	verb with pronominal suffix
VS	verb stem
Vtr	transitive verb
Wh	what, when, where, etc.
Z3	3rd singular present tense

CHART OF CONSONANTS

	Voicing	B-lab	L-den	I-den	Den	Pal	Vel	Uvu	Pha	Glo
Stops	voiceless	p			t		k	q		ʔ
	voiced	b			d		g	ɢ		
Fricatives (Spirants)	voiceless	ɸ	f	θ	s	š,ç	x	χ	ħ	h
	voiced	β	v	ð	z	ž	ɣ	ʁ	ʕ	ɦ
Affricates	voiceless	pf			c	č				
	voiced				ʒ	ǰ				
Nasals		m			n	ñ	ŋ			
Laterals					l	λ	ɫ			
Flaps					r,ɼ					
Trills					ř			ʀ		
Glides		w,ʍ				y,ẏ				

Diacritics: Cʰ = aspiration; C̣ = retroflexion; Cʸ = palatalization; Cʷ = labialization;
C̥ = devoicing; C̹ = advanced articulation

-xxv-

CHART OF VOWELS

	Front		Central	Back	
	Unrounded	Rounded	Unrounded	Unrounded	Rounded
High	i ɪ	ü	ɨ	ɯ	u ʊ
Mid	e ɛ	ö ɔ̈	ə ʌ		o ɔ
Low	æ		a		ɒ

Diacritics: ´V = stressed; v: = long; Ṽ = nasal

I. PHONETIC ILLUSTRATIONS

1) FRENCH

The following items illustrate the unaspirated voiceless bilabial stop [p] of French:

1)	step	pa	(pas)
2)	father	pɛr	(père)
3)	louse	pu	(poux)
4)	pure	pür	(pure)
5)	worse	pir	(pire)
6)	to speak	parle	(parler)
7)	apple	pɔm	(pomme)
8)	feather	plüm	(plume)
9)	price	pri	(prix)
10)	chicken	pul	(poule)

2) CHINESE

The following items illustrate the aspirated voiceless bilabial stop [pʰ] of Chinese:

1)	slope	pʰɤ
2)	run	pʰǎo
3)	all	pʰǔ
4)	fear	pʰà
5)	known	pʰǐ
6)	plate	pʰán
7)	side	pʰáŋ
8)	rain	pʰèi
9)	store	pʰù
10)	skin	pʰí

3) CHINESE

The following items illustrate the contrast between the unaspirated voiceless bilabial stop [p] and the aspirated voiceless bilabial stop [pʰ] of Chinese:

1)	trumpet	pā
2)	strip	pʰǎ
3)	weeds	pài
4)	branch	pʰài
5)	back	pèi
6)	wear	pʰèi
7)	scatter	pàŋ
8)	collide	pʰàŋ
9)	compare	pǐ
10)	indigestion	pʰǐ

4) SPANISH

The following items illustrate the unaspirated voiceless dental stop [t] of Spanish:

1)	I have	téŋgo	(tengo)
2)	plank	táβla	(tabla)
3)	ceiling	téčo	(techo)
4)	tiger	tíɣre	(tigre)
5)	chalk	tíθa	(tiza)
6)	bull	tóro	(toro)
7)	all	tóðo	(todo)
8)	sad	tríste	(triste)
9)	you	tú	(tú)
10)	tutor	tutór	(tutor)

5) VIETNAMESE

The following items illustrate the aspirated voiceless dental stop [tʰ] of Vietnamese:

1) tower	tʰʌp
2) letter	tʰɯ
3) poetry	tʰə
4) coal	tʰan
5) autumn	tʰu
6) fragrant	tʰəm
7) tax	tʰue
8) harmony	tʰuaŋ
9) embroider	tʰeu
10) boat	tʰuien

6) HINDI

The following items illustrate the difference between the unaspirated voiceless dental stop [t] and the aspirated voiceless dental stop [tʰ] of Hindi:

1) third	tísra
2) tired	tʰáka
3) body	tán
4) station	tʰána
5) key	táli
6) dish	tʰáli
7) pluck	tórṇa
8) little	tʰóṛa
9) three	tín
10) bag	tʰéla

7) HINDI

The following items illustrate the unaspirated voiceless retroflex stop [ṭ] of Hindi:

1)	to hit	ṭakrána
2)	leg	ṭáŋ
3)	cap	ṭópi
4)	mound	ṭíla
5)	piece	ṭúkṛa
6)	broken	ṭúṭa
7)	hindrance	ṭók
8)	basket	ṭókri
9)	twig	ṭéhni
10)	support	ṭikána

8) HINDI

The following items illustrate the difference between the unaspirated voiceless retroflex stop [ṭ] and the unaspirated voiceless dental stop [t] of Hindi

1)	mark	ṭíka
2)	triangular	tikóna
3)	horsecart	ṭáŋga
4)	arrow	tír
5)	coin	ṭʌ́ka
6)	then	tʌ́b
7)	Tagore	ṭægór
8)	ready	tɛɟár
9)	cap	ṭópi
10)	parrot	tóta

-4-

9) RUSSIAN

The following items illustrate the palatalized voiceless
dental stop [tʸ] of Russian:

1)	quietly	tʸíxə	(тихо)
2)	shadow	tʸénʸ	(тень)
3)	body	tʸélə	(тело)
4)	they pull	tʸánut	(тянут)
5)	auntie	tʸótkə	(тётка)
6)	bale	tʸúk	(тюк)
7)	prison	tʸurʸmá	(тюрьма)
8)	darkness	tʸmá	(тьма)
9)	test	tʸést	(тест)
10)	draught	tʸágə	(тяга)

10) RUSSIAN

The following items illustrate the contrast between the
plain voiceless dental stop [t] and the palatalized voiceless
dental stop [tʸ] of Russian:

1)	thus	ták	(так)
2)	burden	tʸágəstʸ	(тягость)
3)	you	tí	(ты)
4)	yew tree	tʸís	(тис)
5)	here	tút	(тут)
6)	Turks	tʸúrki	(тюрки)
7)	only	tólʸkə	(только)
8)	heifer	tʸólkə	(тёлка)
9)	pumpkin	tíkvə	(тыква)
10)	to tick	tʸíkətʸ	(тикать)

11) RUSSIAN

The following items illustrate the contrast between the palatalized voiceless dental stop [tʸ] and the voiceless alveolar affricate [c] of Russian:

1)	body	tʸélə	(тело)
2)	complete	célə	(цело)
3)	undershirt	tʸélʸnʸik	(тельник)
4)	goal	celʸ	(цель)
5)	warm	tʸóplịị	(тёплый)
6)	to slap	cópətʸ	(цопать)
7)	to chop	tʸúkətʸ	(тюкать)
8)	candied peel	cukát	(цукат)
9)	chopper	tʸápkə	(тяпка)
10)	hoe	cápkə	(цапка)

12) HUNGARIAN

The following items illustrate the palatized voiced dental stop [dʸ] of Hungarian:

1)	factory	dʸá:r	(gyár)
2)	match	dʸúfa	(gyufa)
3)	quickly	dʸórš	(gyors)
4)	child	dʸérɛk	(gyerek)
5)	be cured	dʸo:dʸul	(gyógyul)
6)	lawn	dʸɛp	(gyep)
7)	coward	dʸá:va	(gyáva)
8)	win	dʸö:z	(győz)
9)	meeting	dʸü:le:š	(gyűlés)
10)	suspect	dʸánu:	(gyanú)

13) CZECH

The following items illustrate the contrast between the plain voiced dental stop [d] and the palatalized voiced dental stop [dʸ] of Czech:

1)	smoke	di:m	(dým)
2)	I say	dʸi:m	(dím)
3)	plank	deska	(deska)
4)	horrible	dʸesni:	(děsný)
5)	further	da:le	(dále)
6)	devil	dʸa:bɛl	(d'ábel)
7)	thanks	dʸi:k	(dík)
8)	porcupine	dikobras	(dikobraz)
9)	Nadja (acc.)	nadʸu	(Nad'u)
10)	I find	naj̧du	(najdu)

14) RUSSIAN

The following items illustrate the unaspirated voiceless velar stop [k] of Russian:

1)	capitalism	kapʸitʌlʸízm	(капитализм)
2)	pencil	karʌndáš	(карандаш)
3)	picture	kʌrtʸína	(картина)
4)	cemetery	kládbiščᵻ	(кладбище)
5)	circle	krúk	(круг)
6)	who	któ	(кто)
7)	whip	knút	(кнут)
8)	quartet	kvʌrtʸét	(квартет)
9)	when	kʌgdá	(когда)
10)	dwarf	kárlʸik	(карлик)

15) CHINESE

The following items illustrate the aspirated voiceless velar stop [kʰ] of Chinese:

1) wipe — kʰāi̯
2) look at — kʰàn
3) lesson — kʰə
4) but — kʰə̆ʂɯ̀
5) broad — kʰy̆ān
6) mouth — kʰə̆u̯
7) polite — kʰə̀čʰi̯
8) guest — kʰàrɛn
9) chopsticks — kʰy̆ài̯ʒɯ
10) afraid — kʰŭŋpà

16) KOREAN

The following items illustrate the contrast between the unaspirated voiceless velar stop [k] and the aspirated voiceless velar stop [kʰ] of Korean:

1) meat — kogi
2) nose — kʰo
3) fold — kɛda
4) dig out — kʰɛda
5) firmly — kuǰi
6) big — kʰɯn
7) sense — kamgak
8) loudly — kʰɯgɛ
9) study — koŋbu
10) how tall — kʰi

17) HINDI

The following items illustrate the aspirated voiced bilabial
stop [bʰ] of Hindi:

	1) devotee	bʰákt
	2) sweeper	bʰáŋgi
	3) alms	bʰíkša
	4) brown	bʰúra
	5) to forget	bʰúlna
	6) to send	bʰéɟna
	7) good	bʰʌ́la
	8) brother	bʰáį
	9) marijuana	bʰáŋg
	10) burden	bʰár

18) HINDI

The following items illustrate the contrast between the
unaspirated voiced bilabial stop [b] and the aspirated
voiced bilabial stop [bʰ] of Hindi:

1)	large	bára
2)	heavy	bʰári
3)	without	bína
4)	crowd	bʰír
5)	sackcloth	bóri
6)	disagreement	bʰéd
7)	twenty-two	baís
8)	buffalo	bʰë̃s
9)	father	báp
10)	part	bʰág

19) HINDI

The following items illustrate the contrast between the
aspirated voiceless bilabial stop [pʰ] and the aspirated
voiced bilabial stop [bʰ] of Hindi:

1)	foam	pʰén
2)	hemp	bʰáŋg
3)	month	pʰálgʊn
4)	(name)	bʰā̄l
5)	felt	pʰár̪ka
6)	bright	bʰár̪kila
7)	bird	pʰúdki
8)	god	bʰagẃan
9)	handful	pʰéŋkil
10)	nephew	bʰánʲa

20) CLASSICAL ARABIC

The following items illustrate the voiceless uvular stop [q]
of Classical Arabic:

1)	he said	qaːla	قال
2)	section	qɪsm	قسم
3)	kettle	qɪdr	قدر
4)	measurement	qiːʝaːs	قياس
5)	strength	quːɥa	قوة
6)	Koran	ʔalqurʔaːn	القران
7)	standing	qaːʔɪm	قائم
8)	law	qaːnuːn	قانون
9)	he killed	qatala	قتل
10)	judge	qaːd̪iː	قاضي

21) CLASSICAL ARABIC

The following items illustrate the contrast between the
voiceless velar stop [K] and the voiceless uvular stop [q] of
Classical Arabic:

1)	dog	Kalb	كلب
2)	heart	qalb	قلب
3)	meatloaf	Kubba	كبة
4)	dome	qubba	قبة
5)	heap	Kuds	كدس
6)	sanctity	quds	قدس
7)	noble	Kari:m	كريم
8)	near	qari:b	قريب
9)	sack	Ki:s	كيس
10)	measured	qi:sa	قيس

22) LEBANESE ARABIC

The following items illustrate the glottal stop [?] of
Lebanese Arabic:

1)	he said	?ǽ:l	قال
2)	he stayed	bí?i	بقي
3)	street	ṭarí:?	طريق
4)	apartment	ší??a	شقة
5)	apartments	šú?a?	شقق
6)	read!	?í?ra	اقرا
7)	wealth	rízı?	رزق
8)	tribes	?ará:yıb	قرايب
9)	minute	də?í:?a	دقيقة
10)	above	fáɥ?	فوق

23) LEBANESE ARABIC

The following items illustrate the contrast between the absence and the presence of the glottal stop [?] in Lebanese Arabic:

1)	there is	fí:	فيه
2)	wake up!	fí:?	فيق
3)	what	šú:	شو
4)	market	sú:?	سوق
5)	he sweetened	ḥallǽ:	حلاه
6)	barber	ḥallǽ:?	حلاق
7)	behind	wára	ورا
8)	paper	wára?	ورق
9)	evil	šar	شر
10)	east	šar?	شرق

24) GERMAN

The following items illustrate the voiceless alveolar affricate [c] of German:

1)	time	caɪt	(Zeit)
2)	room	cɪmər	(Zimmer)
3)	anger	cɔrn	(Zorn)
4)	tongue	cuŋə	(Zunge)
5)	to sit	zɪcən	(sitzen)
6)	for it	dacu:	(dazu)
7)	cat	Kacə	(Katze)
8)	complete	ganc	(ganz)
9)	wood	hɔlc	(Holz)
10)	sentence	zac	(Satz)

25) CANADIAN FRENCH

The following items illustrate the voiced alveolar affricate
[ʒ] of Canadian French:

1)	say	ʒir	(dire)
2)	God	ʒi̯ö	(Dieu)
3)	expensive	ʒɪspãʒi̯ö	(dispendieux)
4)	tithe	ʒɪm	(dîme)
5)	eighteen	ʒizɥɪt	(dix-huit)
6)	diverse	ʒivɛr	(divers)
7)	hard	ʒür	(dur)
8)	of the	ʒü	(du)
9)	quilt	ʒüvɛ	(duvet)
10)	dynamite	ʒinamɪt	(dynamite)

26) JAPANESE

The following items illustrate the voiceless bilabial spirant
[ɸ] of Japanese:

1)	wipe	ɸuku
2)	deep	ɸukai̯
3)	bathroom	ɸuroba
4)	old	ɸurui̯
5)	sliding door	ɸusuma
6)	winter	ɸuyu
7)	two	ɸutacʊ
8)	Fujiyama	ɸujiyama
9)	French	ɸuransugo
10)	couple	ɸuɸu

27) SPANISH

The following items illustrate the voiced bilabial spirant [β] of Spanish:

1)	Cuba	kúβa	(Cuba)
2)	bean	áβa	(hava)
3)	egg	ʯéβo	(huevo)
4)	wolf	lóβo	(lobo)
5)	level	niβél	(nivel)
6)	speaks	áβla	(habla)
7)	poor	póβre	(pobre)
8)	divide	dezβ̦ár	(desviar)
9)	evasive	eβasíβo	(evasivo)
10)	to move	moβér	(mover)

28) GERMAN

The following items illustrate the voiceless palatal spirant [ç] of German:

1)	I	íç	(ich)
2)	honey	hó:nɪç	(Honig)
3)	milk	mílç	(Milch)
4)	always	é:vɪç	(ewig)
5)	genuine	éçt	(echt)
6)	church	kírçə	(Kirche)
7)	dagger	dólç	(Dolch)
8)	me	míç	(mich)
9)	light	líçt	(Licht)
10)	correct	ríçtɪç	(richtig)

29) CASTILLIAN SPANISH

The following items illustrate the voiceless velar spirant
[x] of Castillian Spanish:

1)	cavalryman	xinéte	(jinete)
2)	Jesus	xesús	(Jesús)
3)	ham	xamón	(jamón)
4)	George	xórxe	(Jorge)
5)	to play	xuɣár	(jugar)
6)	judge	xμéθ	(juez)
7)	garden	xaräín	(jardin)
8)	money order	xíro	(giro)
9)	general	xenerál	(general)
10)	party	xμérya	(juerga)

30) GERMAN

The following items illustrate the contrast between the
voiceless palatal spirant [ç] and the voiceless velar spirant
[x] of German:

1)	self	zíç	(sich)
2)	oh!	áx	(ach)
3)	sight	zíçt	(sicht)
4)	eight	áxt	(acht)
5)	pike	héçt	(Hecht)
6)	high	hó:x	(hoch)
7)	justice	gəríçt	(Gericht)
8)	smoke	ráμx	(Rauch)
9)	not	níçt	(nicht)
10)	night	náxt	(Nacht)

31) SPANISH

The following items illustrate the voiced velar spirant [ɣ] of Spanish:

1)	do!	áɣa	(haga)
2)	follow!	síɣa	(siga)
3)	blind	θi̯éɣa	(ciega)
4)	rope	sóɣa	(soga)
5)	juice	xúɣo	(jugo)
6)	tiger	tíɣre	(tigre)
7)	margarine	marɣarína	(margarina)
8)	water	áɣu̯a	(agua)
9)	I go out	sálɣo	(salgo)
10)	lawyer	aβoɣáðo	(abogado)

32) EGYPTIAN ARABIC

The following items illustrate the contrast between the voiced velar stop[g] and the voiced velar spirant [ɣ] of Egyptian Arabic:

1)	he brought	gǽ:b	جاب
2)	absent	ɣǽ:b	غاب
3)	permitted	gǽ:yɪz	جايز
4)	expensive	ɣǽ:li	غالي
5)	pocket	gé:b	جيب
6)	other than	ɣé:r	غير
7)	newspaper	garí:da	جريدة
8)	strange	ɣarí:b	غريب
9)	side	gíha	جهة
10)	mistaken	ɣílɪṭ	غلط

33) CZECH

The following items illustrate the voiced glottal spirant [ɦ] of Czech:

1)	voice	ɦlás	(hlas)
2)	head	ɦláva	(hlava)
3)	brown	ɦnʸédi:	(hnědý)
4)	farmer	ɦóspoda:ř̃	(hospodář̃)
5)	castle	ɦrát	(hrad)
6)	terrible	ɦrózni:	(hrozný)
7)	pear	ɦrúška	(hruška)
8)	star	ɦvʸézda	(hvězda)
9)	disaster	póɦroma	(pohroma)
10)	Prague	práɦa	(Praha)

34) SPANISH

The following items illustrate the palatal nasal [ñ] of Spanish:

1)	year	áño	(año)
2)	little	pekéño	(pequeño)
3)	child	níño	(niño)
4)	fist	púño	(puño)
5)	vinyard	bíña	(viña)
6)	rock	péña	(peña)
7)	incompetent	ñóño	(ñoño)
8)	wedge	kúña	(cuña)
9)	kidney	riñón	(riñón)
10)	to add	añaðír	(añadir)

35) SPANISH

The following items illustrate the contrast between palatal nasal [ñ] and the sequence of alveolar nasal [n] followed by [i̯] in Spanish:

1)	(river name)	míño	(Miño)
2)	lead oxide	míni̯o	(minio)
3)	fingernail	uñón	(uñón)
4)	union	uni̯ón	(unión)
5)	aged	añóso	(añoso)
6)	negative ion	ani̯ón	(anión)
7)	canal	aθéña	(aceña)
8)	small shrub	θéni̯a	(cenia)
9)	he bathed	bañó	(bañó)
10)	handiwork	mani̯óβra	(maniobra)

36) CASTILLIAN SPANISH

The following items illustrate the palatal lateral [λ] of Castillian Spanish:

1)	key	λáβe	(llave)
2)	arrives	λéγa	(llega)
3)	cries	λóra	(llora)
4)	rain	λúβi̯a	(lluvia)
5)	full	λéno	(lleno)
6)	street	káλe	(calle)
7)	flattens	píλa	(pilla)
8)	chair	síλa	(silla)
9)	paella	paéλa	(paella)
10)	she	éλa	(ella)

37) CASTILLIAN SPANISH

The following items illustrate the contrast between the palatal lateral [λ] and the sequence of alveolar lateral [l] followed by [i̯] in Castillian Spanish:

1)	to find	aλár	(hallar)
2)	to ally	alįár	(aliar)
3)	obstacle	eskóλo	(escollo)
4)	clarification	eskólįo	(escolio)
5)	chick	póλo	(pollo)
6)	(plant name)	pólįo	(polio)
7)	open wound	λáγa	(llaga)
8)	(shrub name)	alįáγa	(aliaga)
9)	carries	λéβa	(lleva)
10	hare	lįéβre	(liebre)

38) SPANISH

The following items illustrate the voiced alveolar flap [r] of Spanish:

1)	look	míra	(mira)
2)	chorus	kóro	(coro)
3)	father	páăre	(padre)
4)	burning	arăįénte	(ardiente)
5)	clear	kláro	(claro)
6)	will be	será	(será)
7)	pure	púro	(puro)
8)	drama	dráma	(drama)
9)	crystal	kristál	(cristal)
10)	male	barón	(varón)

39) SPANISH

The following items illustrate the alveolar trill [r̃] of Spanish:

1)	branch	r̃áma	(rama)
2)	net	r̃éd	(red)
3)	rhyme	r̃íma	(rima)
4)	maple	r̃óβle	(roble)
5)	Russian	r̃úso	(ruso)
6)	land	t̪jér̃a	(tierra)
7)	saw	sjér̃a	(sierra)
8)	brown	mar̃ón	(marrón)
9)	mistake	εr̃ór̃	(error)
10)	destroy	der̃iβár̃	(derribar)

40) SPANISH

The following items illustrate the contrast between the alveolar flap [r] and alveolar trill [r̃] of Spanish:

1)	for	pára	(para)
2)	vine	pár̃a	(parra)
3)	but	péro	(pero)
4)	dog	pér̃o	(perro)
5)	dear	káro	(caro)
6)	cart	kár̃o	(carro)
7)	Moor	móro	(moro)
8)	snout	mór̃o	(morro)
9)	various	bários	(varios)
10)	districts	bár̃ios	(barrios)

41) FRENCH

The following items illustrate the voiced uvular spirant [ʁ] of French:

1)	regret	ʁagʁɛt	(regrette)
2)	bank	ʁiv	(rive)
3)	street	ʁü	(rue)
4)	rule	ʁɛgl	(règle)
5)	oar	ʁam	(rame)
6)	laugh	ʁiʁ	(rire)
7)	king	ʁµa	(roi)
8)	to break	ʁõpʁ	(rompre)
9)	red	ʁuž	(rouge)
10)	stream	ʁµiso	(ruisseau)

42) ITALIAN

The following items illustrate the contrast between single and double consonants of Italian:

1)	veil	vélo	(velo)
2)	fleece	véllo	(vello)
3)	groans	Jéme	(geme)
4)	gems	Jémme	(gemme)
5)	cheese	káčo	(cacio)
6)	I hunt	káččo	(caccio)
7)	clay	túfo	(tufo)
8)	dive	túffo	(tuffo)
9)	fate	fáto	(fato)
10)	done	fátto	(fatto)

43) CANADIAN FRENCH

The following items illustrate the high front unrounded
vowel [i] of French:

1)	yew tree	if	(if)
2)	to isolate	izɔle	(isoler)
3)	ivory	ivμar	(ivoire)
4)	book	livr	(livre)
5)	mystery	mistɛr	(mystère)
6)	worse	pir	(pire)
7)	net	filɛ	(filet)
8)	cry	kri	(cri)
9)	thanks	mɛrsi	(merci)
10)	daughter	fiĵ	(fille)

44) CANADIAN FRENCH

The following items illustrate the lower high front
unrounded vowel [ɪ] of Canadian French:

1)	Phillip	fɪlɪp	(Philippe)
2)	technique	tɛknɪk	(technique)
3)	plausible	plozɪb	(plausible)
4)	sporty	spɔrcɪf	(sportif)
5)	quickly	vɪt	(vite)
6)	maritime	marɪn	(marine)
7)	easy	fasɪl	(facile)
8)	free	lɪb	(libre)
9)	thousand	mɪl	(mille)
10)	sad	trɪs	(triste)

45) CANADIAN FRENCH

The following items illustrate the difference between the higher high front unrounded vowel [i] and the lower high front unrounded vowel [ɪ] of Canadian French:

1)	life	vi	(vie)
2)	lively	vɪf	(vif)
3)	energy	enɛrži	(énergie)
4)	energetic	enɛržɪk	(énergique)
5)	speed	vitɛs	(vitesse)
6)	fast	vɪt	(vite)
7)	Africa	afrɪk	(Afrique)
8)	African	afrikɛ̃	Africain
9)	civil	sivɪl	(civil)
10)	civility	sivilite	(civilité)

46) SPANISH

The following items illustrate the higher mid front unrounded vowel [e] of Spanish:

1)	I know	sé	(sé)
2)	chest	péčo	(pecho)
3)	cheese	késo	(queso)
4)	head	kaβéθa	(cabeza)
5)	I come	béŋgo	(vengo)
6)	fish	péska	(pesca)
7)	guest	ɥéspeθ	(huésped)
8)	to think	pensár	(pensar)
9)	extensive	esténso	(extenso)
10)	I bought	kompré	(compré)

47) SPANISH

The following items illustrate the contrast between the higher mid front unrounded vowel [e] and the diphthong [ei] of Spanish:

1)	sesame	sésamo	(sésamo)
2)	six	séįs	(seis)
3)	him	le	(le)
4)	law	léį	(ley)
5)	punishment	péna	(pena)
6)	he combs	péįna	(peina)
7)	rat trap	θépo	(cepo)
8)	plant name	θéįβo	(ceibo)
9)	reindeer	r̃éno	(reno)
10)	reign	r̃éįno	(reino)

48) HUNGARIAN

The following items illustrate the lower front unrounded vowel [ɛ] of Hungarian:

1)	you	té	(te)
2)	the east	kélɛt	(kelet)
3)	pocket	žéb	(zseb)
4)	he trains	éʒ	(edz)
5)	brush	kéfɛ	(kefe)
6)	it rains	éšik	(esik)
7)	soup	lévɛš	(leves)
8)	my hand	kézɛm	(kezem)
9)	not	šém	(sem)
10)	to eat	énni	(enni)

49) FRENCH

The following items illustrate the contrast between the higher mid front unrounded vowel [e] and lower mid front unrounded vowel [ε] of French:

1)	spoken	parle	(parlé)
2)	was speaking	parlε	(parlait)
3)	summer	ete	(été)
4)	was	etε	(était)
5)	meadow	pre	(pré)
6)	ready	prε	(prêt)
7)	house of	še	(chez)
8)	oak	šεn	(chêne)
9)	keys	kle	(clefs)
10)	salt	sεl	(sel)

50) HUNGARIAN

The following items illustrate the high front rounded vowel [ü] of Hungarian:

1)	he bakes	šüt	(süt)
2)	beech tree	bük	(bükk)
3)	dispair	čüggεd	(csügged)
4)	ear	fül	(fül)
5)	send	küld	(küld)
6)	grey	sürkε	(szürke)
7)	patience	türεlεm	(türelem)
8)	holiday	üdül	(üdül)
9)	separate	külön	(külön)
10)	parent	sülö:	(szülő)

51) FRENCH

The following items illustrate the contrast between the high back rounded vowel [u] and the high front rounded vowel [ü] of French:

1) wheel	ru	(roue)
2) street	rü	(rue)
3) crazy	fu	(fou)
4) he was	fü	(fut)
5) mouth	buš	(bouche)
6) log	büš	(bûche)
7) deaf	sur	(sourd)
8) sure	sür	(sûr)
9) mill	mulǽ	(moulin)
10) mule	mülɛ	(mulet)

52) GERMAN

The following items illustrate the higher mid front rounded vowel [ö:] of German:

1) cave	hö:lə	(Höhle)
2) nice	šö:n	(schön)
3) evil	bö:zə	(böse)
4) to drone	drö:nən	(dröhnen)
5) to kill	tö:tən	(töten)
6) King	kö:nıç	(König)
7) to loosen	lö:zən	(lösen)
8) furniture	mö:bəl	(Möbel)
9) oil	ö:l	(Öl)
10) to disturb	štö:rən	(stören)

53) FRENCH

The following items illustrate the lower mid front rounded vowel [ɔ̈] of French:

1)	fear	pɔ̈r	(peur)
2)	eye	ɔ̈i̯	(œil)
3)	beef	bɔ̈f	(bœuf)
4)	heart	kɔ̈r	(cœur)
5)	work	ɔ̈vr	(œuvre)
6)	young	žɔ̈n	(jeune)
7)	mouth	gɔ̈l	(gueule)
8)	they can	pɔ̈v	(peuvent)
9)	hour	ɔ̈r	(heure)
10)	fury	fürɔ̈r	(fureur)

54) FRENCH

The following items illustrate the difference between the higher mid front rounded vowel [ö] and the lower mid front rounded vowel [ɔ̈] of French:

1)	eggs	ö	(œufs)
2)	egg	ɔ̈f	(œuf)
3)	fast	žön	(jeûne)
4)	young	žɔ̈n	(jeune)
5)	millstone	möl	(meule)
6)	furniture	mɔ̈bl	(meuble)
7)	knot	nö	(nœud)
8)	new	nɔ̈f	(neuf)
9)	blue	blö	(bleu)
10)	their	lɔ̈r	(leur)

55) RUMANIAN

The following items illustrate the high central unrounded vowel [ɨ] of Rumanian:

1)	laugh	rɨd	(rîd)
2)	Rumanian	romɨn	(Român)
3)	close	lɨngə	(lîngă)
4)	throat	gɨt	(gît)
5)	when	kɨnd	(cînd)
6)	river	rɨu̯	(rîu)
7)	old man	bətrɨn	(bătrîn)
8)	summit	vɨrf	(vîrf)
9)	young	tɨnər	(tînăr)
10)	I eat	mənɨnk	(mănînk)

56) RUMANIAN

The following items illustrate the higher mid central unrounded vowel [ə] of Rumanian:

1)	the books	kárcile	(cărţile)
2)	we buy	kumpərám	(cumpărăm)
3)	benches	bə́nč	(bănci)
4)	apple	mə́r	(măr)
5)	pear	pə́r	(păr)
6)	without	fə́rə	(fără)
7)	bird	pásəre	(pasăre)
8)	bad	rə́u̯	(rău)
9)	puppy	kəcél	(căţel)
10)	house	kásə	(casă)

57) BRITISH ENGLISH

The following items illustrate the lower mid central unrounded vowel [ʌ] of British English:

1)	cut	kʌt
2)	son	sʌn
3)	young	yʌŋ
4)	blood	blʌd
5)	does	dʌz
6)	much	mʌč
7)	wonder	wʌndə
8)	sully	sʌlɪ
9)	tough	tʌf
10)	country	kʌntrɪ

58) RUMANIAN

The following items illustrate the low central unrounded vowel [a] of Rumanian:

1)	about	kam	(cam)
2)	I fall	kad	(cad)
3)	bed	pat	(pat)
4)	the house	kása	(casa)
5)	valley	vále	(vale)
6)	table	mása	(masă)
7)	salt	sáre	(sare)
8)	meat	kárne	(carne)
9)	large	máre	(mare)
10)	girl	fátə	(fată)

59) FRENCH

The following items illustrate the higher high back rounded vowel [u] of French:

1)	taste	gu	(goût)
2)	wolf	lu	(loup)
3)	you	vu	(vous)
4)	August	u	(août)
5)	all	tu	(tout)
6)	buckle	bukl	(boucle)
7)	to flow	kule	(couler)
8)	arch	vut	(voûte)
9)	rascal	marufl	(maroufle)
10)	fly	muš	(mouche)

60) CANADIAN FRENCH

The following items illustrate the lower high back rounded vowel [ʊ] of Canadian French:

1)	route	rʊt	(route)
2)	all	tʊt	(toute)
3)	roll	rʊl	(roule)
4)	crowd	fʊl	(foule)
5)	cup	kʊp	(coupe)
6)	pod	gʊs	(gousse)
7)	yoke	žʊg	(joug)
8)	breath	sʊf	(souffle)
9)	shower	dʊš	(douche)
10)	fly	mʊš	(mouche)

61) CANADIAN FRENCH

The following items illustrate the difference between the higher high back rounded vowel [u] and the lower high back rounded vowel [ʋ] of Canadian French:

1)	all (masc)	tu	(tout)
2)	all (fem)	tʋt	(toute)
3)	to push	puse	(pousser)
4)	thumb	pʋs	(pouce)
5)	to dine	supe	(souper)
6)	soup	sʋp	(soupe)
7)	wolf	lu	(loup)
8)	otter	lʋt	(loutre)
9)	blow	ku	(coup)
10)	cup	kʋp	(coupe)

62) SPANISH

The following items illustrate the higher mid back rounded vowel [o] of Spanish:

1)	all	tóðo	(todo)
2)	voice	bóθ	(voz)
3)	no	nó	(no)
4)	monkey	móno	(mono)
5)	he spoke	aβló	(habló)
6)	shoulder	ómbro	(hombro)
7)	eye	óxo	(ojo)
8)	sonorous	sonóro	(sonoro)
9)	elm	ólmo	(olmo)
10)	monotonous	monótono	(monótono)

63) GERMAN

The following items illustrate the lower back rounded vowel
[ɔ] of German:

1)	village	dɔrf	(Dorf)
2)	full	fɔl	(voll)
3)	gold	gɔlt	(Gold)
4)	rye	rɔgən	(Roggen)
5)	wood	hɔlc	(Holz)
6)	head	kɔpf	(Kopf)
7)	hole	lɔx	(Loch)
8)	position	pɔstən	(Posten)
9)	pate	šɔpf	(Schopf)
10)	to want	vɔlən	(wollen)

64) ITALIAN

The following items illustrate the contrast between the
higher mid back rounded vowel [o] and the lower mid back
rounded vowel [ɔ] of Italian:

1)	where	dóve	(dove)
2)	lobe	lɔ́bo	(lobo)
3)	throat	góla	(gola)
4)	throne	sɔ́λo	(soglio)
5)	hole	fóro	(foro)
6)	bull	tɔ́ro	(toro)
7)	he shows	móstra	(mostra)
8)	death	mɔ́rte	(morte)
9)	bubbles	bólle	(bolle)
10)	soft	mɔ́lle	(molle)

65) AMERICAN ENGLISH

The following items illustrate the contrast between the low
central unrounded vowel [a] and the lower mid back rounded
vowel [ɔ] of American English:

1)	cot	kat
2)	caught	kɔt
3)	Don	dan
4)	dawn	dɔn
5)	hock	hak
6)	hawk	hɔk
7)	Shah	ša
8)	Shaw	šɔ
9)	dodder	dadər
10)	daughter	dɔdər

66) BRITISH ENGLISH

The following items illustrate the low back rounded vowel
[ɒ] of British English:

1)	pot	pɒt
2)	dock	dɒk
3)	God	gɒd
4)	lodge	lɒʤ
5)	Don	dɒn
6)	stock	stɒk
7)	long	lɒŋ
8)	soft	sɒft
9)	yacht	yɒt
10)	doll	dɒl

67) JAPANESE

The following items illustrate the high back unrounded vowel [ɯ] of Japanese:

1)	pig	bɯta
2)	physics	bɯtɯri
3)	animal	dobɯtɯ
4)	warship	gɯnkan
5)	entrance	irigɯti
6)	cloud	kɯmo
7)	blind	mekɯra
8)	mouse	nezɯmi
9)	search	sagɯrɯ
10)	horn	tɯno

68) VIETNAMESE

The following items illustrate the contrast between the higher high back rounded vowel [u] and the high back unrounded vowel [ɯ] of Vietnamese:

1)	religious vow	tu
2)	fourth	tɯ
3)	to guard	tʰo
4)	to try	tʰɯ
5)	shelter	tru
6)	famous	trɯzaŋ
7)	old	ko
8)	to abstain	kɯ
9)	area	xu
10)	to hold tight	xɯ

69) FRENCH

The following items illustrate the nasal vowels of French:

1)	year	ã	(an)
2)	tooth	dã	(dent)
3)	wine	vẽ	(vin)
4)	far	lɥẽ	(loin)
5)	no	nõ	(non)
6)	good	bõ	(bon)
7)	one	œ̃	(un)
8)	brown	brœ̃	(brun)
9)	shade	õbr	(ombre)
10)	each	šakœ̃	(chacun)

70) CZECH

The following items illustrate the contrast between long and short vowels in Czech:

1)	railroad	dra:ha	(dráha)
2)	dear	draha:	(drahá)
3)	loge	lo:že	(lóže)
4)	bed	lože	(lože)
5)	he can	mu:že	(může)
6)	man (acc)	muže	(muže)
7)	Mila (name)	mi:la	(Míla)
8)	she washed	mila	(myla)
9)	summer	le:to	(léto)
10)	this year	letos	(letos)

71) CHINESE

The following items illustrate the high level tone [⌐] of Chinese:

1)	mother	mā
2)	autumn	čʰīɥ
3)	visit	kɥān
4)	drink	xə̄
5)	drive	kʰā̡i
6)	eight	pā
7)	mountain	sān
8)	he	tʰā̄
9)	to fly	fē̡i
10)	flower	xɥā

72 CHINESE

The following items illustrate the high rising tone [ʼ] of Chinese:

1)	hemp	má
2)	tea	čʰá
3)	river	xə́
4)	come	lá̡i
5)	zero	líŋ
6)	there is not	mé̡i
7)	door	mén
8)	grasp	ná
9)	person	rén
10)	chat	tʰán

73) CHINESE

The following items illustrate the low falling-rising tone
[ˇ] of Chinese:

1)	horse	mǎ
2)	pen	pǐ
3)	give	kěi̯
4)	well	xǎo
5)	how many	čǐ
6)	beautiful	měi̯
7)	you	nǐ
8)	woman	nǚ
9)	I	wɔ̌
10)	also	yɛ̌

74) CHINESE

The following items illustrate the falling tone [ˋ] of
Chinese:

1)	scold	mà
2)	newspaper	pàɒ
3)	not	pù
4)	cooked rice	fàn
5)	enough	kàу̯
6)	speech	xɥà
7)	lesson	kʰà
8)	slowly	màn
9)	meat	ràу̯
10)	ask	wèn

The following items illustrate the four tones [ˉ], [ʼ], [ˇ], and [ˋ] of Chinese:

1) mother   mā
2) hemp   má
3) horse   mǎ
4) scold   mà
5) skin   fū
6) fortune   fú
7) axe   fǔ
8) woman   fù

II. STRUCTURAL PHONOLOGY

75) CREE (elementary)

Consider the sounds [p] and [b] and determine whether they are allophones of the same phoneme, or represent two different phonemes. If allophones, state the complementary distribution; if phonemes, state the contrast. (Model solution.)

1)	pahḴi	partly
2)	ni:sosa:p	twelve
3)	ta:nispi:	when
4)	pasḴya:y	prairie
5)	asaba:p	thread
6)	wa:bame:y	he sees him
7)	na:be:y	man
8)	a:bihta:y	half
9)	nibimohta:n	I walk
10)	si:si:baḴ	ducks

76) BIBLICAL HEBREW (elementary)

Consider the sounds [p] and [f] and determine whether they are allophones of the same phoneme, or represent two different phonemes. If allophones, state the complementary distribution; if phonemes, state the contrast.

1)	pɛ	mouth	פה
2)	pol	bean	פול
3)	pil	elephant	פיל
4)	paθaḥ	to open	פתח
5)	mišpaḥa	family	משפחה
6)	af	even	אף
7)	lifnej	before	לפני
8)	sɛfɛr	book	ספר
9)	kɛsɛf	money	כסף
10)	yafɛ	beautiful	יפה

-39-

77) BIBLICAL HEBREW (elementary)

Consider the sounds [t] and [θ] and determine whether they are allophones of the same phoneme, or represent two different phonemes. If allophones, state the complementary distribution; if phonemes, state the contrast.

1)	tešaʕ	nine	תשע
2)	tafar	sew	תפר
3)	štaim	two	שתים
4)	tannur	stove	תנור
5)	tamɪd	always	תמיד
6)	baθ	daughter	בת
7)	oθax	you	אותך
8)	safoθ	languages	ספות
9)	iθɪ	with me	אתי
10)	raɪθa	you saw	ראית

78) CREE (elementary)

Consider the sounds [t] and [d] and determine whether they are allophones of the same phoneme, or represent two different phonemes. If allophones, state the complementary distribution; if phonemes, state the contrast. On the basis of the results from problems 76 and 77, what do you expect the status of [k] and [g] to be?

1)	tahkɪ	all the time
2)	mihče:t	many
3)	nisto	three
4)	tagosin	he arrives
5)	mi:bit	tooth
6)	me:daɥe:ɥ	he plays
7)	kodak	another
8)	adim	dog
9)	adihk	caribou
10)	iskode:ɥ	fire

79) BRAZILIAN PORTUGUESE (elementary)

Consider the sounds [t] and [č] and determine whether they
are allophones of the same phoneme, or represent two
different phonemes. If allophones, state the complementary
distribution; if phonemes, state the contrast.

1)	téñu	(tenho)	I have
2)	tál	(tal)	such
3)	nátu	(nato)	born
4)	kӯátru	(quatro)	four
5)	ũtár	(untar)	to anoint
6)	čívi	(tivi)	I had
7)	číӯ	(tío)	uncle
8)	pačinár	(patinar)	to skate
9)	párči	(parte)	party
10)	pē̃či	(pente)	comb

80) BRAZILIAN PORTUGUESE (elementary)

Consider the sounds [d] and [J] and determine whether they
are allophones of the same phoneme, or represent two
different phonemes. If allophones, state the complementary
distribution; if phonemes, state the contrast.

1)	dádu	(dado)	given
2)	madriña	(madrinha)	godmother
3)	modérnu	(moderno)	modern
4)	unídu	(unido)	united
5)	gӯárda	(guarda)	guard
6)	Jiñéįru	(dinheiro)	money
7)	óJįu	(odio)	hatred
8)	vérJi	(verde)	green
9)	verdáJi	(verdade)	truth
10)	grã̃Ji	(grande)	big

81) KOREAN (elementary)

Consider the sounds [s] and [š] and determine whether they
are allophones of the same phoneme, or represent two
different phonemes. If allophones, state the complementary
distribution; if phonemes, state the contrast.

1)	son	hand
2)	sɔm	sack
3)	sosəl	novel
4)	sɛk	colour
5)	us	upper
6)	šihap	game
7)	šilsu	mistake
8)	šipsam	thirteen
9)	šinho	signal
10)	maši	delicious

82) CREE (elementary)

Consider the sounds [č] and [ǰ] and determine whether they
are allophones of the same phoneme, or represent two
different phonemes. If allophones, state the complementary
distribution; if phonemes, state the contrast.

1)	či:baǰ	ghost
2)	me:g̱ya:č	meanwhile
3)	namwa:č	no way
4)	či:ma:n	canoe
5)	mi:ǰiy̱in	food
6)	wi:ǰihe:y̱	he helps him
7)	a:ǰimoy̱	he tells
8)	miǰihči:	hand
9)	koǰi:y̱	he tries
10)	ma:ǰi:y̱	he hunts

83) CREE (elementary)

Consider now the sounds [k] and [g] and form a hypothesis about their status before you examine the data of this problem (see problems 78 and 82). Then solve the problem to see whether you were correct or not. Make a generalization about the status and importance of voicing in Cree phonology as compared to English.

1)	Ki:ba	soon
2)	Ki:ja	you
3)	koJi:y	he tries
4)	maskisin	shoe
5)	maskyak	bears
6)	ma:ga	but
7)	ke:ga:č	almost
8)	či:gahigan	axe
9)	Ki:siga:y	it is day
10)	ospya:gan	pipe

84) BIBILICAL HEBREW (elementary)

Consider the sounds [k] and [x] and determine whether they are allophones of the same phoneme, or represent two different phonemes. If allophones, state the complementary distribution; if phonemes, state the contrast.

1)	kol	all	כל
2)	kɛn	yes	כן
3)	kənisa	entrance	כניסה
4)	kɛlev	dog	כלב
5)	kaf	palm of hand	כף
6)	barux	blessed	ברוך
7)	ejx	how	איך
8)	axšay	now	עכשיו
9)	bexor	first born	בכור
10)	masax	curtain	מסך

-43-

85) GERMAN (intermediate)

Consider the sounds [γ] and [g] and determine whether they are allophones of the same phoneme, or represent two different phonemes. If allophones, state the complementary distribution; if phonemes, state the contrast. (Model solution.)

1)	va:γən	(Wagen)	car
2)	ta:yə	(Tage)	days
3)	na:γən	(nagen)	nibble
4)	tayγəniçts	(Taugenichts)	idler
5)	fu:γən	(fugen)	fit together
6)	ayyən	(Augen)	eyes
7)	gɛflo:γən	(geflogen)	flown
8)	bo:γən	(Bogen)	arch
9)	zoγən	(soggen)	crystallize
10)	ja:γən	(jagen)	hunt
11)	zi:gən	(siegen)	conquer
12)	bɛrgə	(Berge)	mountains
13)	fö:glain	(Vöglein)	bird
14)	mö:gən	(mögen)	to be able
15)	re:gən	(Regen)	rain
16)	gɪŋən	(gingen)	went
17)	gaŋgɛs	(Ganges)	River Ganges
18)	uŋgarn	(Ungarn)	Hungary
19)	zɪgna:l	(Signal)	signal
20)	grɔk	(Grog)	grog

86) SERBO-CROATIAN (elementary)

Consider the sounds [ç] and [č] and determine whether they are allophones of the same phoneme, or represent two different phonemes. If allophones, state the complementary distribution; if phonemes, state the contrast.

1)	bacač	(bàcāč)	thrower
2)	čega	(čèga)	what (gen.)
3)	čaj	(ča"j)	tea

-44-

4) ručak	lunch
5) čaša	glass
6) čovek	man
7) članak	article
8) navečer	in the evening
9) čim	as soon as
10) čorba	soap
11) kuča	house
12) dača	tax
13) čača	daddy
14) čekič	hammer
15) čebe	blanket
16) čef	caprice,fancy
17) čipta	merchant
18) srečom	fortunately
19) čorda	sable
20) čurka	turkey

87) TURKISH (elementary)

Consider the sounds [r] and [ç] and determine whether they
are allophones of the same phoneme, or represent two
different phonemes. If allophones, state the complementary
distribution; if phonemes, state the contrast.

1) riǰa	request
2) čürük	spoiled
3) sürmek	to rub on
4) traš	shave
5) kıbrıt	match
6) bıç	one
7) demıç	iron
8) müdüç	director
9) hazıç	ready
10) buhaç	steam

88) KOREAN (elementary)

Consider the sounds [l] and [r] and determine whether they are allophones of the same phoneme, or represent two different phonemes. If allophones, state the complementary distribution; if phonemes, state the contrast.

1)	tal	moon
2)	talda	sweet
3)	ɔlmana	how much
4)	sul	wine
5)	solhwa	legend
6)	kirim	picture
7)	ke:ri	distance
8)	noray	song
9)	irure	reaches
10)	saram	person

89) LEBANESE ARABIC (elementary)

Consider the sounds [i] and [ɪ] and determine whether they are allophones of the same phoneme, or represent two different phonemes. If allophones, state the complementary distribution; if phonemes, state the contrast.

1)	btækli	you eat	بتاكلي
2)	kursi	chair	ثرسي
3)	ʔɪnti	you (sg.)	انت
4)	maʕi	with me	معي
5)	fi	there is/are	فيه
6)	ʔɪntu	you (pl.)	انتو
7)	bɪnt	girl	بنت
8)	mɪtɪl	like	متل
9)	ʔɪli	to me	الي
10)	bɪʔi	he stayed	بقي

90) TURKISH (elementary)

Consider the sounds [i] and [ɪ] and determine whether they
are allophones of the same phoneme, or represent two
different phonemes. If allophones, state the complementary
distribution; if phonemes, state the contrast.

1)	bilet	ticket
2)	kira	rent
3)	kitap	book
4)	sinema	movies
5)	sahife	page
6)	benɪm	mine
7)	dɪl	tongue
8)	kɪbrɪt	match
9)	ɪšte	here
10)	bɪr	one
11)	hanɪ	you know
12)	taksi	taxi
13)	efendɪ	Mr.
14)	evlɪ	married
15)	tabɪ	of course

91) POLISH (elementary)

Consider the sounds [ʒ] and [z] and determine whether they
are allophones of the same phoneme, or represent two
different phonemes. If allophones, state the complementary
distribution; if phonemes, state the contrast.

1)	odraʒačʸ	to advise
2)	saʒa	soot
3)	noʒe	foot (dat.)
4)	ʒban	jug
5)	kaʒenʸe	flattery
6)	ʒvon	bell
7)	barʒo	very

8) mozel	callus
9) vizovᵛe	audience
10) voze	reins
11) zegarek	watch
12) kazač	to command
13) i̯ẽzik	tongue
14) zvani	called
15) zator	ice
16) zbože	corn
17) groza	threat
18) łza	tear
19) egzamin	exam
20) filozof	philosopher

92) SPANISH (elementary)

Consider the sounds [e] and [ɛ] and determine whether they are allophones of the same phoneme, or represent two different phonemes. If allophones, state the complementary distribution; if phonemes, state the contrast.

1) pero	(pero)	but
2) beŋgo	(vengo)	I come
3) kompre	(compré)	I bought
4) pečo	(pecho)	chest
5) si̯empre	(siempre)	always
6) pɛr̃o	(perro)	dog
7) gɛr̃a	(guerra)	war
8) ti̯ɛr̃a	(tierra)	land
9) i̯ɛr̃o	(hierro)	iron
10) θɛr̃o	(cerro)	peak
11) lɛxos	(lejos)	far
12) oβɛxa	(oveja)	sheep
13) orɛxa	(oreja)	ear
14) ɛxe	(eje)	axle
15) dɛxo	(dejo)	I leave

93) SLOVAK (elementary)

Consider the sounds [l] and [lʸ] and determine whether they are allophones of the same phoneme, or represent two different phonemes. If allophones, state the complementary distribution; if phonemes, state the contrast.

1)	lak	varnish
2)	otstrel	blast
3)	lavica	bench
4)	uholni:	basic
5)	mul	mule
6)	za:pal	inflamation
7)	polka	polka
8)	posol	messanger
9)	lu:ka	meadow
10)	liko	fiber
11)	lʸahnu:tʸ	to lie down
12)	polʸka	Polish woman
13)	žemlʸa	bun
14)	lʸak	scare
15)	lʸu:bitʸ	to love
16)	klʸu:č	key
17)	velʸa	very
18)	hlʸadatʸ	to seek
19)	polʸe	field
20)	strelʸba	shooting

94) LEBANESE ARABIC (elementary)

Consider the sounds [u] and [ʊ] and determine whether they are allophones of the same phoneme, or represent two different phonemes. If allophones, state the complementary distribution; if phonemes, state the contrast.

1)	ʔɪžu	they came	اجو
2)	ktæbu	his book	كتابه
3)	šu	what	شو
4)	taʕu	come!	تعو
5)	ʕʊḍu	member	عضو

-49-

6) ʔʊtrʊk	leave!	اترك
7) bʊdrʊs	I study	بادرس
8) kʊtʊb	books	كتب
9) tʊšhʊr	months	تشهر
10) lʊbnæn	Lebanon	لبنان

95) TURKISH (elementary)

Consider the sounds [u] and [ʊ] and determine whether they are allophones of the same phoneme, or represent two different phonemes. If allophones, state the complementary distribution; if phonemes, state the contrast.

1) kulak	ear
2) tuhaf	strange
3) uǰʊz	cheap
4) uzak	far
5) muhakkak	sure
6) bʊz	ice
7) čoǰʊk	child
8) bʊlmak	to find
9) odʊn	firewood
10) kʊrtarmak	to save
11) bʊ	this
12) sʊ	water
13) sučlʊ	culprit
14) havlʊ	towel
15) yayrʊ	children

96) SPANISH (elementary)

Consider the sounds [b] and [β] and determine whether they are allophones of the same phoneme, or represent two different phonemes. If allophones, state the complementary distribution; if phonemes, state the contrast.

1) bráθo	(brazo)	arm
2) r̃iβéra	(ribera)	bank (of a river)
3) blokeár	(bloquear)	to blockade

-50-

4)	bíno	(vino)	he came
5)	diβíno	(divino)	divine
6)	káβo	(cabo)	end
7)	bastánte	(bastante)	enough
8)	faβór	(favor)	favour
9)	goβjérno	(gobierno)	government
10)	úβa	(uva)	grape
11)	túβo	(tuvo)	he had
12)	λáβe	(llave)	key
13)	buskár	(buscar)	to look for
14)	moβér	(mover)	to move
15)	Klaβár	(clavar)	to nail
16)	nμéβo	(nuevo)	new
17)	bólsa	(bolsa)	pocket
18)	béka	(beca)	scholarship
19)	brotár	(brotar)	to sprout
20)	proβár	(probar)	to test
21)	biλéte	(billete)	ticket
22)	báxo	(bajo)	under
23)	boKál	(vocal)	vowel
24)	bláŋKo	(blanco)	white
25)	bentána	(ventana)	window
26)	sáβjo	(sabio)	wise
27)	lóβo	(lobo)	wolf
28)	bμéstra	(vuestra)	your

97) <u>TURKISH</u> (elementary)

Consider the sounds [č] and [ǰ] and determine whether they are allophones of the same phoneme, or represent two different phonemes. If allophones, state the complementary distribution; if phonemes, state the contrast.

1)	ǰep	pocket
2)	ǰava	Java
3)	ǰami	mosque

-51-

4) aʤi	bitter
5) birinʤi	chief
6) ʤan	soul
7) finʤan	cup
8) kalinʤa	thickly
9) kiliʤ	sword
10) siʤak	hot
11) čekič	hammer
12) čoʤuk	child
13) čatal	fork
14) čekmek	to send
15) ačmak	to open
16) bahče	garden
17) ačik	deficit
18) čiček	flower
19) ač	hungry
20) učak	aeroplane

98) SPANISH (elementary)

Consider the sounds [b] and [β] again. In the light of these examples, modify the statements you made about exercise 96. In what other positions do these two sound occur? Are the allophones of the same phoneme, or represent two different phonemes?

1) aβãikár	(abdicar)	to abdicate
2) aβneɣaθ̦ón	(abnegación)	abnegation
3) ámbos	(ambos)	both
4) klúβ	(club)	club
5) álβa	(alba)	dawn
6) dóβle	(doble)	double
7) pólβo	(polvo)	dust
8) sóβra	(sobra)	excess
9) xóβ	(Job)	Job
10) lúmbre	(lumbre)	light

11) ómbre	(hombre)	man
12) oβxéto	(objeto)	object
13) oβsesjón	(obsesión)	obsession
14) oβtenér	(obtener)	obtain
15) poβréθa	(pobreza)	poverty
16) alβríθjas	(albricias)	reward
17) dezβlokár	(desblocar)	unblock
18) sómbra	(sombra)	shadow
19) simberyψénθa	(sinvergüenza)	shameless
20) sórβa	(sorba)	sip
21) áβla	(habla)	he speaks
22) dezβroθár	(desbrozar)	strip bark
23) suβteŕáneo	(subterráneo)	subterranean
24) símbolo	(símbolo)	symbol
25) ezβélto	(esbelto)	thin
26) árβol	(árbol)	tree
27) suβŕajár	(subrayar)	underline
28) imbiérno	(invierno)	winter

99) MALAY (elementary)

Observe the phonological structure of Malay words here and in other exercises, and make a statement concerning the distribution of consonants and vowels in Malay words. Note that [^{m}p], [^{n}d], etc. are prenasalized stops. In view of your statement, decide which phonemic interpretation below, A or B, is more suitable.

	A	B	
1)	baru	baru	new
2)	ha^{n}dak	handak	wish
3)	ha^{m}pir	hampir	near
4)	buroŋ	buroŋ	bird
5)	sa^{m}pir	sampir	part of the kris
6)	kain	kain	clothing
7)	li^{n}tah	lintah	leech
8)	la^{n}dak	landak	porcupine

9) anak	anak	child
10) taⁿgal	taŋgal	deep
11) biⁿkas	biŋkas	back up
12) taⁿgek	taŋgek	winnowing
13) raᵐpak	rampak	shady
14) gaⁿdar	gandar	lever
15) naᵐpak	nampak	to be visible

100) SLOVAK (intermediate)

Consider the sounds [f], [v], and [y] and determine whether they are allophones of the same phoneme, or represent two different phonemes, or three different phonemes. If allophones, state the complementary distribution; if phonemes, state the contrast.

1) vatra	camp fire
2) vedro	bucket
3) vjera	faith
4) krava	cow
5) vrx	top
6) vlk	wolf
7) zvlnʸitʸ	to make waves
8) vnada	charm
9) červi	worms
10) vdova	widow

11) frkatʸ	spatter
12) farba	paint
13) difte:rija	diphtheria
14) firma	firm
15) filozof	philosopher
16) fa:dni	monotonous
17) dofajčitʸ	to finish smoking
18) felčiar	healer
19) nafta	gas
20) nafu:kani:	conceited

21) splaɥ	sluice-gate
22) xlʸi̯eɥ	byre
23) naːzoɥ	title
24) prɥ	first
25) dʸi̯eɥča	girl
26) nʸemrɥ sa!	don't move!
27) kriɥka	curve
28) stoɥka	one hundred
29) obuɥ	footwear
30) krɥ	blood

101) <u>MALAY</u> (intermediate)

Consider the sounds [t], [tʸ], and [č] and determine
whether they are allophones of the same phoneme, or
represent two different phonemes, or three different
phonemes. If allophones, state the complementary
distribution; if phonemes, state the contrast.

1) tarek	pull
2) kətil	a pinch
3) pitər	disk
4) lawat	visit
5) čarek	rip
6) ketʸil	small
7) tʸaᵐpah	tasteless
8) kətʸut	shrivelled
9) čaᵐpah	tasteless
10) ketʸek	pampering
11) batʸa	steel
12) kəčil	small
13) čomel	cute
14) tʸarek	rip
15) tʸaŋ	pillar

102) CZECH (elementary)

Consider the sounds [a] and [a:] and determine whether
they are allophones of the same phoneme, or represent two
different phonemes. If allophones, state the complementary
distribution; if phonemes, state the contrast.

1)	kava:rna	coffee house
2)	kapat^{y}i	to drop
3)	palanda	bunk bed
4)	ran^{y}en	wounded
5)	lano	rope
6)	padafka	dropped fruit
7)	rada	advice
8)	maso	meat
9)	sedadlo	seat
10)	lavice	bench
11)	ra:no	morning
12)	la:va	lava
13)	ma:ta	mint
14)	pada:n^{y}i:	falling
15)	kra:deš	steal
16)	dobra:	good (fem.)
17)	ka:va	coffee
18)	ka:pi:	hood
19)	pa:li:	to burn (3rd.sg.)
20)	sa:dlo	lard

103) JAPANESE (intermediate)

Consider the sounds [t], [c] and [č], and determine whether
they are allophones of the same phoneme, or represent three
different phonemes. If allophones, state the complementary
distribution; if phonemes, state the contrast.

1)	tambo	paddy
2)	te	hand
3)	to	door
4)	takaj̱	high

5)	ita	board
6)	curi	fishing
7)	macu	pine tree
8)	kucu	shoe
9)	cuku	arrive
10)	cumetaj	cold
11)	či	blood
12)	čikara	strength
13)	čizu	map
14)	hači	bee
15)	cuči	earth

104) SPANISH (elementary)

Consider the sounds [d] and [ǎ] and determine whether they are allophones of the same phoneme, or represent two different phonemes. If allophones, state the complementary distribution; if phonemes, state the contrast.

1)	dráma	(drama)	drama
2)	dyeña	(dueña)	duena
3)	káǎa	(cada)	each
4)	sentíǎo	(sentido)	felt
5)	fiǎél	(Fidel)	Fidel
6)	komíǎa	(comida)	food
7)	dár	(dar)	to give
8)	dañár	(dañar)	to harm
9)	óǎjo	(odio)	hatred
10)	déxo	(dejo)	I leave
11)	durár	(durar)	to last
12)	núǎo	(nudo)	naked
13)	operaǎór	(operador)	operator
14)	dolór	(dolor)	pain
15)	crúǎo	(crudo)	raw
17)	deθír	(decir)	to say
17)	láǎo	(lado)	side
18)	keǎó	(quedó)	he stayed
19)	estuǎjánte	(estudiante)	student

-57-

20) dúlθe	(dulce)	sweet
21) díme	(dime)	tell me
22) djeθ	(diez)	ten
23) dós	(dos)	two
24) bóǎa	(boda)	wedding

105) <u>GERMAN</u> (intermediate)

Consider the sounds [ç], [š], and [x] and determine whether they are allophones of the same phoneme, or represent two different phonemes, or three different phonemes. If allophones, state the complementary distribution; if phonemes, state the contrast.

1) iç	(ich)	I
2) manç	(manch)	many
3) durç	(durch)	through
4) töçtər	(Töchter)	daughters
5) mɛ:tçɛn	(Mädchen)	girl
6) reçnən	(rechnen)	to count
7) kırça	(Kirche)	church
8) fıçtə	(Fichte)	pine
9) mɛnçən	(Männchen)	little man
10) dıç	(dich)	you
11) büšə	(Büsche)	bushes
12) tušə	(Tusche)	India ink
13) našən	(naschen)	nibble
14) kıršə	(Kirsche)	cherry
15) fıštə	(fischte)	fished
16) tıš	(Tisch)	table
17) mɛnšən	(Menschen)	people
18) špi:lən	(spielen)	play
19) šte:n	(stehen)	stand
20) šta:t	(Staat)	state
21) bu:x	(Buch)	book
22) kɔx	(Koch)	cook
23) dax	(Dach)	roof
24) naxen	(Nachen)	small boat
25) laxst	(lachst)	you laugh

-58-

26) nɔx	(noch)	still
27) tu:x	(Tuch)	scarf
28) ku:xən	(Kuchen)	cake
29) ax	(ach)	interjection
30) axa:t	(Achat)	agate

106) TURKISH (elementary)

Consider the sounds [u] and [ü] and determine whether they
are allophones of the same phoneme, or represent two
different phonemes. If allophones, state the complementary
distribution; if phonemes, state the contrast.

1) bavul	trunk
2) uyumak	to sleep
3) bozukluk	small change
4) bučuk	half
5) bu sefer	this time
6) Juma	Friday
7) usta	mechanic
8) uzak	far
9) tuz	salt
10) šu	that
11) türk	Turk
12) üč	three
13) ürkütmek	to cause
14) üst	top
15) yüzü	to refuse
16) süt	milk
17) öksürük	cough
18) üzüm	grape
19) yüzünJü	hundredth
20) ölčülü	moderate

107) MALAY (intermediate)

Consider the sounds [k], [t], and [ʔ] and determine whether
they are allophones of the same phoneme, or represent two
different phonemes, or three different phonemes. If
allophones, state the complementary distribution; if
phonemes, state the contrast.

1) kapaʔ	axle	
2) buka	open	
3) karaŋ	reef	
4) laut	sea	
5) bogoʔ	black butterfly	
6) təgoh	firm	
7) pantas	agile	
8) gəlaʔ	laugh	
9) takpi	but	
10) tapaʔ	palm of the hand	
11) kəran	small stove	
12) boŋoʔ	rough	
13) pitər	disk	
14) kətaʔ	a fold	
15) lawlat	to visit	

108) SPANISH (intermediate)

Consider now the sounds [g] and [ɣ] and formulate a
hypothesis about their status before doing the problem (see
problems 96, 98, and 104). Then examine the data of this
problem to see whether your hypothesis is correct or not.

1) seɣún	(según)	according to
2) λéɣo	(llego)	I arrive
3) gólpe	(golpe)	a blow
4) neɣóθio	(negocio)	business
5) gáto	(gato)	cat
6) míɣa	(miga)	crumb

-60-

7) áɣo	(hago)	I do
8) embrjaɣár	(embriagar)	to get drunk
9) goθár	(gozar)	to enjoy
10) galán	(galán)	galant
11) glándula	(glándula)	gland
12) gloβál	(global)	global
13) geñiλéro	(guerrillero)	guerrilla
14) gitáña	(guitarra)	guitar
15) guθmán	(Guzmán)	Guzman
16) seɣár	(segar)	to mow
17) leɣál	(legal)	legal
18) íɣaðo	(hígado)	liver
19) gísa	(guisa)	manner
20) naβeɣár	(navegar)	to navigate
21) fiɣúra	(figura)	aspect
22) santjáɣo	(Santiago)	Santiago
23) gritár	(gritar)	to shout
24) gústo	(gusto)	taste
25) gráθjas	(gracias)	thanks
26) géña	(guerra)	war
27) áɣʮa	(agua)	water
28) testíɣo	(testigo)	witness

109) <u>HUNGARIAN</u> (elementary)

Consider the sounds [n] and [nʸ] and determine whether they are allophones of the same phoneme, or represent two; different phonemes. If allophones, state the complementary distribution; if phonemes, state the contrast.

1) ne:met	German
2) se:natarto:	hack
3) nünüke	oil-beetle
4) panas	complaint
5) növel	increase
6) ra:nc	wrinkle
7) pa:nce:l	mail
8) tünde	ethereal

9)	napta:r	calendar
10)	ki:n	pain
11)	nʸom	press
12)	ra:nʸom	imprint
13)	se:panʸa	great-great grandmother
14)	nʸito:	opening
15)	tala:nʸ	riddle
16)	panʸva:z	lasso
17)	földnʸoma:š	pressure
18)	nʸugati	western
19)	nʸü:göš	peevish
20)	föle:nʸ	superior

110) **SPANISH** (intermediate)

Consider the sounds [g] and [γ] again. In what other positions do they occur? What modifications will you have to make in the statement that you made about these two sounds in exercise #108? Make a general statement about the relationship between voiced stops and voiced fricatives in Spanish.

1)	aγrikultúra	(agricultura)	agriculture
2)	anéγăota	(anecdota)	anecdote
3)	áŋgulo	(ángulo)	angle
4)	añeγlăăo	(arreglado)	arranged
5)	sáŋgre	(sangre)	blood
6)	síγlo	(siglo)	century
7)	xuăγáăo	(juzgado)	courtroom
8)	dóγma	(dogma)	dogma
9)	eγsámen	(examen)	examination
10)	eγsótiko	(exótico)	exotic
11)	gríŋgo	(gringo)	gringo
12)	kolγár	(colgar)	to hang
13)	aléγre	(alegre)	happy
14)	téŋgo	(tengo)	I have
15)	iγnoránte	(ignorante)	ignorant
16)	orγániko	(orgánico)	organic
17)	aγraăáβle	(agradable)	pleasant
18)	mayoráăγo	(mayorazgo)	primogeniture

19) póŋgo	(pongo)	I put
20) seyménto	(segment)	segment
21) álγo	(algo)	something
22) éγsito	(éxito)	success
23) téγnika	(técnica)	technique
24) léŋgᵤa	(lengua)	tongue
25) r̃ázγo	(rasgo)	trait
26) bárγas	(Vargas)	Vargas
27) beŋgánθa	(venganza)	vengeance
28) díγno	(digno)	worthy

111) RUSSIAN (intermediate)

Consider the sounds [K], [Kʷ], and [Kʸ] and determine whether they are allophones of the same phoneme, or represent two different phonemes, or three different phonemes. If allophones, state the complementary distribution; if phonemes, state the contrast.

1) kák	how
2) zʌkás	order
3) Kʷúklə	doll
4) kalʸisó	wheel
5) pʌKʷúpkə	purchase
6) Kʷóškə	cat
7) kráskə	paint
8) ʌKʷóškə	window
9) pʌklón	bow
10) rók	fate
11) Kʸít	whale
12) ruk	hand (gen.sg.)
13) Kʸɛm	whom
14) tkʸót	weaves
15) Kʷósʸtʸ	bone
16) kápʸɪlʸkə	drop
17) manʸɪkʸúr	manicure
18) Kʸáxtə	(place name)
19) skʷupój̧	stingy
20) Kʸurʸínci	Caucasian nation

-63-

112) <u>TURKISH</u> (intermediate)

Consider the sounds [k], [kʸ], [g], and [gʸ] and determine whether they are allophones of the same phoneme, or two three or four different phonemes. If allophones, state the complementary distribution; if phonemes, state the contrast.

1) Kïlïbïk   husband
2) čoJuk   child
3) Kavun   melon
4) baKan   minister
5) Kïbrïs   Cyprus
6) yoKsa   otherwise
7) koJa   husband
8) Koku   smell
9) muvafaK   successful
10) dokuzunJu   ninth

11) KʸüreKʸ   oar
12) erkʸen   early
13) čünkʸü   because
14) čičekʸ   flower
15) kʸim   who
16) Kʸöpekʸ   dog
17) tekʸlif   proposal
18) ikʸinJi   second
19) askʸerlikʸ   military service
20) Kʸömür   coal

21) gam   grief
22) tugay   brigade
23) bulgar   Bulgar
24) duygu   feeling
25) gargara   gargle
26) Kangal   coin
27) piyango   lottery
28) sargï   bandage
29) yorgun   tired
30) manga   section

31) gʸözlükʸ	eyeglasses
32) gʸüzel	beautiful
33) gʸezmekʸ	to stroll
34) gʸün	day
35) gʸöstermekʸ	to show
36) hangʸi	which
37) gʸergʸef	embroiderer's frame
38) sevgʸili	darling
39) čingʸene	gipsy
40) gʸeč	late

113) **RUSSIAN** (intermediate)

Consider the sounds [x], [xʷ] and [xʸ] and determine whether they are allophones of the same phoneme, or two or three different phonemes. If allophones, state the complementary distribution; if phonemes, state the contrast.

1) xátə	hut
2) xərʌšó	good
3) gʌróx	peas
4) xlópəti	troubles
5) pórəx	powder
6) muxá	fly
7) xʷólət	cold
8) pʌxʷót	campaign
9) ʌxʷótə	hunt
10) xʷúži	worse
11) xʷót	move
12) dúxʸɪ	spirits
13) pʸɪtuxʸí	roosters
14) v dʌxʸέ	in a fur coat
15) duxʸí	scent

114) <u>CZECH</u> (intermediate)

Consider the sounds [ř], [ɕ] and [r] and determine whether
they are allophones of the same phoneme, or represent two
or three different phonemes. If allophones, state the
complementary distribution; if phonemes, state the contrast.

1)	bři:za	birch
2)	ɦřištʸe	playground
3)	ɦřmi:	thunders
4)	řepa	beet
5)	vařbuxta	idler
6)	ɕkouce	saying
7)	tɕi	three
8)	tva:ɕ̨	face
9)	foɕ̨t	forester
10)	Kɕivi:	crooked
11)	kouɕ̨	smoke
12)	riba	fish
13)	hrop	grave
14)	brouK	beatle
15)	dort	cake
16)	dar	present
17)	Kra:l	king
18)	dra:t	wire

115) <u>HUNGARIAN</u> (elementary)

Consider the sounds [a] and [a:] and determine whether
they are allophones of the same phoneme, or represent two
different phonemes. If allophones, state the complementary
distribution; if phonemes, state the contrast.

1)	bamba:n	foolishly
2)	cafatol	tear
3)	aga:r	greyhound
4)	fɛlad	to give up
5)	cimborafa	collar beam

6)	holta	posthumously
7)	oldal	side
8)	ado:š	in debt
9)	kortina	curtain
10)	rak	to put
11)	a:g	branch
12)	a:da:z	furious
13)	ba:mul	wonder
14)	ca:pa	shark
15)	cikornʸa:š	over-ornamented
16)	fɛla:za:š	soaking up
17)	ra:k	crayfish
18)	a:bra	illustration
19)	olda:š	solution
20)	ča:	to the right

116) <u>RUSSIAN</u> (intermediate)

Consider the sounds [ɛ], [e], and [æ] and determine
whether they are allophones of the same phoneme, or two or
three different phonemes. If allophones, state the
complementary distribution; if phonemes, state the contrast.
There are two solutions possible. Which one do you favour
and why?

1)	tʸɛ	those
2)	fsʸɛ	all
3)	dʸɛlə	affaire
4)	vʸɛrə	belief
5)	yɛl	ate (masc.)
6)	yɛst	eats
7)	ɛtət	this (masc)
8)	šɛst	pole
9)	ɛrə	era
10)	žɛst	gesture
11)	yelʸ	fir-tree
12)	yesʸtʸ	there is
13)	dvʸerʸ	door

14) dʸenʸ   day
15) česʸtʸ   honour
16) etʸɪ   these
17) šesʸtʸ   six
18) celʸ   aim
19) lʸenʸ   lazyness
20) pʸetʸ   to sing

21) mʸætʸ   to crumple
22) pʸætʸ   five
23) sʸætʸ   sit down!
24) dʸædʸə   uncle
25) tʸænʸɪt   he pulls out
26) zʸætʸ   brother-in-law
27) mʸæč   ball
28) čʸæsʸtʸ   part
29) pʸɪšʸšʸætʸ   to squeak
30) nʸænʸə   nanny

117) CANADIAN FRENCH (elementary)

Consider the sounds [ü] and [ü̈] and determine whether they are allophones of the same phoneme, or represent two different phonemes. If allophones, state the complementary distribution; if phonemes, state the contrast.

1)	aküz	(accuse)	accuses
2)	brül	(brûle)	burns
3)	grüž	(gruge)	crunches
4)	küb	(cube)	cube
5)	ʒük	(duc)	duke
6)	šüt	(chute)	fall
7)	plüm	(plume)	feather
8)	füg	(fugue)	fugue
9)	bü	(but)	goal
10)	ʒür	(dur)	hard

-68-

11) büš	(bûche)	log
12) delüʒ	(déluge)	deluge
13) lün	(lune)	moon
14) mül	(mule)	mule
15) pür	(pure)	pure
16) plü	(plu)	rained
17) rüd	(rude)	rude
18) rüz	(ruse)	ruse
19) žüp	(jupe)	skirt
20) rü	(rue)	street
21) trüf	(truffe)	truffle
22) küv	(cuve)	vat
23) mür	(mur)	wall
24) cü	(tu)	you

118) CANADIAN FRENCH (elementary)

Consider the sounds [u] and [ʊ] and determine whether they are allophones of the same phoneme, or represent two different phonemes. If allophones, state the complementary distribution; if phonemes, state the contrast.

1) tʊt	(toute)	all
2) bluz	(blouse)	blouse
3) bʊk	(boucle)	buckle
4) tʊf	(touffe)	clump
5) kʊp	(coupe)	cup
6) žur	(jour)	day
7) dʊb	(double)	double
8) truv	(trouve)	find
9) guž	(gouge)	gouge
10) bʊš	(bouche)	mouth
11) bu	(boue)	mud
12) pʊd	(poudre)	powder
13) pruv	(prouve)	proves
14) ruž	(rouge)	red

15) rʊl	(roule)	rolls
16) rʊt	(route)	route
17) kʊr	(court)	runs
18) sʊp	(soupe)	soup
19) gu	(goût)	taste
20) pʊs	(pouce)	thumb
21) dʊz	(douze)	twelve
22) ru	(roue)	wheel
23) žʊg	(joug)	yoke
24) vu	(vous)	you

119) CANADIAN FRENCH (elementary)

Consider the sounds [i] and [ɪ] and determine whether they are allophones of the same phoneme, or represent two different phonemes. If allophones, state the complementary distribution; if phonemes, state the contrast.

1) abɪm	(abîme)	abyss
2) avi	(avis)	advice
3) katɔlɪk	(catholique)	Catholic
4) šɪk	(chic)	chic
5) vɪd	(vide)	empty
6) enɛrži	(énergie)	energy
7) frãsɪn	(Francine)	Francine
8) kõpri	(compris)	included
9) vi	(vie)	life
10) li	(lis)	lily
11) lɪñ	(ligne)	line
12) pɪp	(pipe)	pipe
13) plozɪb	(plausible)	plausible
14) vɪt	(vite)	quickly
15) režɪm	(régime)	regime
16) riš	(riche)	rich
17) ʒi	(dit)	said
18) si	(scie)	saw

19)	žɪg	(gigue)	shank
20)	lɪs	(lisse)	smooth
21)	spɔrcɪf	(sportif)	sporty
22)	eKɪp	(équipe)	team
23)	mɛrsi	(merci)	thanks
24)	fɪl	(fil)	wire

120) CANADIAN FRENCH (elementary)

Consider [i] and [ɪ] again, and in the light of the following examples, modify the statement you made in exercise 119. In what other positions do these sounds occur?

1)	aKcɪf	(actif)	active
2)	afrɪK	(Afrique)	Africa
3)	sɛriz	(cérise)	cherry
4)	egliz	(église)	church
5)	sɪd	(cidre)	cider
6)	aržɪl	(argile)	clay
7)	vənir	(venir)	to come
8)	riv	(rive)	bank
9)	dãcɪst	(dentiste)	dentist
10)	ẽvi	(envie)	desire
11)	ʒɪsK	(disque)	disk
12)	eKlɪps	(éclipse)	eclipse
13)	facɪg	(fatigue)	fatigue
14)	favɔri	(favori)	favorite
15)	fɪlm	(film)	film
16)	fɪlt	(filtre)	filter
17)	ami	(ami)	friend
18)	gɪd	(guide)	guide
19)	viv	(vive)	lively
20)	piž	(pige)	measures
21)	ɔbliž	(oblige)	obliges
22)	fɔtɔgrafi	(photographie)	photograph
23)	mi	(mis)	placed
24)	žoli	(jolie)	pretty

25) prẽsɪp	(princip)	principle
26) trɪst	(triste)	sad
27) abri	(abri)	shelter
28) sɪñ	(signe)	sign
29) fɪs	(fils)	son
30) espri	(esprit)	spirit
31) sɪlf	(sylphe)	sylph
32) sir	(cire)	wax

121) CANADIAN FRENCH (intermediate)

Examine [i] and [ɪ] again. Are there any modifications you must make of your previous statements? Restate a complete analysis based on this and the two previous exercises.

1) admire	(admirer)	to admire
2) bisɪKlɛt	(bicyclette)	bicycle
3) bizõ	(bison)	bison
4) sɪfle	(siffler)	to blow
5) šɪfre	(chiffrer)	calculate
6) simã	(ciment)	cement
7) sinema	(cinéma)	cinema
8) site	(cité)	city
9) sivɪl	(civil)	civil
10) livre	(livrer)	deliver
11) ʒiKtafɔn	(dictaphone)	dictaphone
12) ʒisɪpline	(discipliné)	disciplined
13) ʒizžõKcɪf	(disjonctif)	disjunctive
14) ʒɪstã	(distant)	distant
15) file	(filer)	draw out
16) fiše	(ficher)	drive in
17) eKlɪpse	(éclipser)	to eclipse
18) vide	(vider)	to empty
19) ẽfirm	(infirme)	infirm
20) bižu	(bijou)	jewel
21) vivã	(vivant)	living
22) miʒi	(midi)	noon

-72-

23) ɔbliže	(obliger)	to oblige
24) ɔbližtɛl	(oblige-t-elle)	does she oblige?
25) pɛrmisjɔ̃	(permission)	permission
26) filɪp	(Philippe)	Phillip
27) sizmɔlɔži	(sismologie)	seismology
28) sɔsjalizm	(socialisme)	socialism
29) ʒizɛn	(dizaine)	about ten
30) viržinal	(virginale)	virginal
31) brizvã	(brise-vent)	windshield
32) ivɛr	(hiver)	winter

EXERCISES IN ENGLISH TRANSCRIPTION

ENGLISH VOWELS

There are many different phonemic interpretations for the vowels of English. One of the most frequently used is the Trager-Smith system. Another system, the Fries-Pike system, does not recognize the diphthongal nature of [ij], [ej], [uw], and [ow], and transcribes these as single vowels distinct from [ɪ], [ɛ], [ʊ], and [ɔ]. The following chart shows most of the vocalic nuclei --- vowels and diphthongs --- recognized by these two analyses, and gives a characteristic word containing the nucleus.

English	Phonetic	Trager-Smith		Fries-Pike	
beat	[ij]	iy	biyt	i	bit
bit	[ɪ]	i	bit	ɪ	bɪt
bait	[ej]	ey	beyt	e	bet
bet	[ɛ]	e	bet	ɛ	bɛt
bat	[æ]	æ	bæt	æ	bæt
but	[ʌ]	ə	bət	ə	bət
god	[a]	a	gad	a	gad
boot	[uw]	uw	buwt	u	but
good	[ʊ]	u	gud	ʊ	gʊd
boat	[ow]	ow	bowt	o	bot
bought	[ɔ]	ɔ	bɔt	ɔ	bɔt
bite	[aj]	ay	bayt	aɪ	baɪt
bout	[aw]	aw	bawt	aʊ	baʊt
Boyd	[ɔj]	oy	boyd	ɔɪ	bɔɪd

Transcribe the English words in the following ten exercises using a standard phonemic transcription. (The solutions are in the Trager-Smith system.)

1)1) sought
2) hood
3) Lloyd
4) mass
5) fight
6) foam
7) retch
8) say
9) tool
10) time

11) lie
12) chick
13) lug
14) mouth
15) now
16) age
17) nod
18) does
19) put
20) leg

2)1) true
2) stick
3) pride
4) close
5) bloke
6) drive
7) stow
8) please
9) strip
10) Brill

11) cram
12) frayed
13) fluke
14) grass
15) quick
16) slime
17) twitch
18) glib
19) few
20) cream

3)1) strong
2) crimp
3) walked
4) mined
5) asks
6) etched
7) aisles
8) boast
9) lumped
10) paths

11) wives
12) pants
13) ox
14) can't
15) jogged
16) fort
17) oaks
18) lilt
19) large
20) stamps

4)1) record
2) tattle
3) going
4) city
5) houses
6) ivy
7) sofa
8) sauna
9) gallant
10) solo
11) tally
12) foible
13) liquor
14) choral
15) hussy
16) suitor
17) Swedish
18) howler
19) matches
20) hooking

5)1) stranger
2) bondage
3) punster
4) action
5) mystery
6) mortise
7) lengthy
8) gasping
9) portion
10) breastworks
11) darkness
12) Saxon
13) lightly
14) kingdom
15) priesthood
16) gangway
17) oyster
18) princely
19) masking
20) cartwheel

6)1) rely
2) emit
3) guitar
4) corral
5) remote
6) relax
7) tonight
8) Marie
9) malign
10 peruse
11) mirage
12) allowed
13) balloon
14) rejoice
15) regale
16) resent
17) collide
18) resume
19) skidoo
20) repeal

7) 1) quadrille
2) genteel
3) technique
4) endear
5) restrain
6) cartoon
7) absolve
8) despair
9) supreme
10) bespoke

11) survey
12) despoil
13) observe
14) partake
15) McLeod
16) destroy
17) curtail
18) respect
19) eclipse
20) lampoon

8) 1) correlate
2) languishing
3) proceeding
4) privateer
5) harpsichord
6) heroic
7) prediction
8) Saskatoon
9) brigadier
10) certitude

11) enchanted
12) forbearance
13) workmanship
14) universe
15) cosmetic
16) translation
17) symbolize
18) rubbery
19) punctual
20) mummify

9) 1) remarkable
2) halitosis
3) bibliophile
4) charismatic
5) decathlon
6) Rosicrucian
7) capitalize
8) repudiate
9) Calabogie
10) dramaturgy

11) salamander
12) socialistic
13) habitual
14) isometric
15) gargantuan
16) helicopter
17) innovative
18) Neanderthal
19) maladjusted
20) compensation

10)1) choreography
2) decapitation
3) qualification
4) principality
5) interrogative
6) haberdashery
7) indefatigable
8) malapropism
9) reconciliation
10) Trinitarian

11) underdeveloped
12) productivity
13) electrolysis
14) impossibility
15) unprofessional
16) dilapidated
17) monogenesis
18) auditorium
19) nationalization
20) Presbyterian

III. PHONEMIC ALTERNATIONS

122) YORUBA: NASALS (elementary)

In the following problem, separate the progressive morpheme from the verb stem. Consider the resulting variation in this progressive morpheme and account for it. What phonological process is illustrated here?

	Pres.	Prog.	
1)	bá	m̀bá	to meet
2)	bé	m̀bé	to cut off
3)	bèrù	m̀bèrù	to fear
4)	bò	m̀bò	to cover
5)	bù	m̀bù	to cut
6)	dà	ńdà	to pour
7)	dé	ńdé	to arrive
8)	dì	ńdì	to tie
9)	díkpò	ńdìkpò	to replace
10)	dúró	ńdúró	to stand
11)	ká	ŋ́ká	to fold
12)	kàn	ŋ́kàn	to touch
13)	kó	ŋ́kó	to gather
14)	kò	ŋ́kò	to reject
15)	kù	ŋ́kù	to remain

123) LATIN: FINAL OBSTRUANTS (elementary)

In the following problem, separate the morphemes meaning nominative case and genitive case from the noun stems. Consider the variation in the noun stems that are left and account for it. What phonological process is illustrated here?

	Nominative	Genitive	
1)	rēks	rēgis	king
2)	lēks	lēgis	law
3)	greks	gregis	flock

-79-

4)	conjuks	conjugis	spouse
5)	striks	strigis	groove
6)	duks	dukis	leader
7)	pāks	pāķis	peace
8)	piks	piķis	pitch
9)	neks	neķis	death
10)	lānks	lānķis	plate
11)	traps	trabis	beam
12)	urps	urbis	city
13)	hiems	hiemis	winter
14)	hērōs	hērōis	hero
15)	stirps	stirpis	root
16)	grus	gruis	crane
17)	sūs	suis	swine
18)	inops	inopis	helpless

124) ICELANDIC: VOWELS (elementary)

In the first part of the problem, separate the morphemes
meaning infinitive and past participle from the verb stems;
in the second part, separate the morphemes meaning
nominative case and dative plural case from the noun stems.
Consider the variation in the resulting verb and noun stems
and account for it. What phonological process is illustrated
here?

	Infinitive	Past Part.	
1)	taka	tekin	take
2)	draga	dregin	drag
3)	vaksa	veksin	grow
4)	aka	ekin	drive
5)	vaða	veðin	wade
6)	gefa	gefin	give
7)	vega	vegin	lift

	Nom. Sing.	Dat. Pl.	
8)	matr	mɔtum	food
9)	staǎr	stɔǎum	place
10)	harmr	hɔrmum	sorrow
11)	salr	sɔlum	hall
12)	armr	ɔrmum	arm
13)	sɔngr	sɔngum	song
14)	fjɔrǎr	fjɔrǎum	fjord

125) SPANISH: VOWELS (elementary)

In the following examples, separate the morphemes meaning infinitive and third person singular from the verb stems. Consider the alternations in the resulting stems and account for it. What phonological process is illustrated here?

	Infinitive	3rd. Sing.	
1)	debér	débe	to owe
2)	benθér	bénθe	to conquer
3)	kreθér	kréθe	to grow
4)	bebér	bébe	to drink
5)	entrár	éntra	to enter
6)	pensár	piénsa	to think
7)	kerér	kiére	to want
8)	perdér	piérde	to lose
9)	benír	biéne	to come
10)	tenér	tiéne	to have

126) SPANISH: VOWELS (elementary)

In the following examples, separate the morphemes meaning infinitive and third person singular from the verb stems. Consider the variation in the stem vowels and account for it. What phonological process is illustrated here?

	Infinitive	3rd Sing.	
1)	goθár	góθa	to enjoy
2)	korrér	kórre	to run
3)	komér	kóme	to eat
4)	kortár	kórta	to cut
5)	rompér	rómpe	to break

6)	sonár	suéna	to sound
7)	morír	muére	to die
8)	dormír	duérme	to sleep
9)	podér	puéde	to be able
10)	kontár	kuénta	to tell

127) GERMAN: FINAL OBSTRUENTS (elementary)

In the following problem, separate the various morphemes
meaning plural from the noun stems. The fact that the plural
morphemes vary is not relevant to the problem. Consider the
variation in the nouns stems that remain and account for it.
What phonological process is illustrated here?

	Singular	Plural	
1)	šulp	šulpən	cuttlebone
2)	tü:p	tü:pən	type
3)	lump	lumpən	scoundrel
4)	hi:p	hi:bə	blow
5)	di:p	di:bə	thief
6)	zi:p	zi:bə	sieve
7)	a:rt	a:rtən	kind
8)	flu:t	flu:tən	flood
9)	geštalt	geštaltən	shape
10)	felt	feldər	field
11)	gelt	geldər	coin
12)	ait	aidə	oath
13)	fink	finkən	finch
14)	flek	flekən	stain
15)	druk	drukə	hardship
16)	ta:k	ta:gə	day
17)	berk	bergə	mountain
18)	štaik	štaigə	footpath

128) TURKISH: SUFFIXING (elementary)

In the following exercise, separate the locative suffix from
the noun stem. Consider the variation in this suffix and
account for it. What phonological process is illustrated
here?

	...	in/at...	
1)	lokanta	lokantada	restaurant
2)	bina	binada	building
3)	kapi	kapida	door
4)	randevu	randevuda	appointment
5)	oda	odada	room
6)	son	sonda	end
7)	onlar	onlarda	them
8)	rakam	rakamda	number
9)	šal	šalda	shawl
10)	pul	pulda	stamp
11)	baš	bašta	head
12)	kitap	kitapta	book
13)	koltuk	koltukta	armchair
14)	ot	otta	grass
15)	taraf	tarafta	side

129) TURKISH: VOWELS (elementary)

In the following problem, separate the plural suffix from the
noun stems. Consider the variation in this suffix and
account for it. What phonological process is illustrated
here?

	Singular	Plural	
1)	baš	bašlar	head
2)	zan	zanlar	opinion
3)	dost	dostlar	friend
4)	yol	yollar	road
5)	kiz	kizlar	daughter

6) yɪl	yɪllar	year
7) but	butlar	thigh
8) suč	sučlar	crime
9) ders	dersler	lesson
10) eš	ešler	mate
11) gün	günler	day
12) yüz	yüzler	face
13) söz	sözler	word
14) göl	göller	pond
15) ip	ipler	string
16) Jin	Jinler	genie

130) CREE: STEMS (elementary)

In the following problem, separate the morphemes meaning
plural and obviative from the noun stems. Consider the
variation in the noun stems that are left and account for it.
What phonological process is illustrated here?

Sing.	Plural	
1) si:si:p	si:si:pak	duck
2) mi:kis	mi:kisak	bead
3) astis	astisak	mitten
4) asa:m	asa:mak	snowshoe
5) ayo:skan	ayo:skanak	rasberry
6) atim	atimwak	dog
7) amisk	amiskwak	beaver
8) moos	mooswak	moose
9) pi:sim	pi:simwak	sun
10) mostos	mostoswak	buffalo

Prox.	Obv.	
11) atim	atimwa	dog
12) si:si:p	si:si:pa	duck
13) amisk	amiskwa	beaver
14) mi:kis	mi:kisa	bead
15) moos	mooswa	moose

-84-

131) CREE: PREFIXING (elementary)

In the following problem, separate the possessive prefix from the noun stems; also separate the future prefix from the verb stems. Consider the variation in the possessive prefix and account for it. What phonological process is illustrated here?

	...	my...	
1)	či:ma:n	niči:ma:n	canoe
2)	so:niya:w	niso:niya:w	money
3)	wiya:š	niwiya:š	meat
4)	te:htapiwin	nite:htapiwin	chair
5)	masKisin	nimasKisin	shoe
6)	e:mihKwa:n	nite:mihKwa:n	spoon
7)	astotin	nitastotin	hat
8)	ospwa:Kan	nitospwa:Kan	pipe
9)	asapa:p	nitasapa:p	thread
10)	amisK	nitamisK	beaver

	he...	he will...	
11)	aKime:w	taaKime:w	count him
12)	apiw	taapiw	sit
13)	ohpine:w	taohpine:w	lift him
14)	ite:w	taite:w	say to him

132) AFRIKAANS: STEMS (elementary)

In the following problem, separate the morpheme meaning "one who does" from the preceding stem. Consider the variation in the resulting stems and account for it. What phonological process is illustrated here?

1)	fas	fish	fasər	fisherman
2)	baK	baKe	baKər	baKer
3)	stof	dust	stofər	duster
4)	badraix	threaten	badraixər	threatener
5)	sKets	sKetch	sKetsər	sKetcher

6)	a:nrax	cause	a:nraxtər	perpetrator
7)	a:nstəx	instigate	a:nstəxtər	instigator
8)	bɛtwəs	contest	bɛtwəstər	contestant
9)	æytrös	equip	æytröstər	outfitter
10)	Klax	complaint	Klaxtər	complainer

133) PERSIAN: STEMS (elementary)

In the following exercise, separate the morpheme meaning plural from the noun stems. Consider the variation in the resulting noun stems and account for it. What phonological process is illustrated here?

	Singular	Plural	
1)	zæn	zænan	woman
2)	læb	læban	lip
3)	hæsud	hæsudan	envious
4)	bæradær	bæradæran	brother
5)	bozorg	bozorgan	big
6)	mæleKe	mæleKean	queen
7)	valede	valedean	mother
8)	Kæbire	Kæbirean	great
9)	ahu	ahuan	gazelle
10)	hamele	hamelean	pregnant
11)	bæččе	bæččegan	child
12)	setare	setaregan	star
13)	bænde	bændegan	slave
14)	azade	azadegan	freeborn
15)	divane	divanegan	mad

134) MALTESE: STEMS (elementary)

In the following problem, separate the morpheme meaning third person plural from the verb stem. Consider the variation in the resulting stems and account for it. What phonological process is illustrated here?

	3rd Sing.	3rd Plural	
1)	Kien	Kienu	was
2)	sa:m	sa:mu	fasted
3)	die?	die?u	tasted

4)	za:r	za:ru	visited
5)	bies	biesu	kiss
6)	mes	messu	touched
7)	ʃar	ʃarru	carry
8)	sen	sennu	sharpen
9)	hak	hakku	scratch
10)	ša?	ša??u	crack

135) GREEK: STEMS (elementary)

In the following problem, separate the morphemes meaning nominative and genetive from the noun stems. Consider the variation in the resulting noun stems and account for it. In the last two examples, there is a vowel length variation that may be omitted from consideration. What phonological process is illustrated here?

	Nominative	Genitive	
1)	pʰulaks	pʰulakos	guard
2)	sarks	sarkos	flesh
3)	klo:ps	klo:pos	thief
4)	ero:s	ero:tos	love
5)	pʰo:s	pʰo:tos	light
6)	kʰaris	kʰaritos	grace
7)	elpis	elpidos	hope
8)	hellas	hellados	Greece
9)	pais	paidos	child
10)	hri:s	hri:nos	nose
11)	mela:s	melanos	black
12)	tala:s	talanos	wretched

-87-

136) <u>CLASSICAL ARABIC: STEMS</u> (elementary)

In the following problem, assume the noun to be basic and
the verb to be derived from it by the addition of a
discontinuous morpheme. Separate that morpheme from the
verb stem. Consider the variation in the resulting stem and
account for it. What phonological process is illustrated
here?

	Noun	Verb	
1)	katb	kataba	write
2)	radm	radama	fill up
3)	ḍarb	ḍaraba	hit
4)	laḥẓ	laḥaẓa	look at
5)	Jahd	Jahada	strive
6)	qawl	qaala	say
7)	mawt	maata	die
8)	xawf	xaafa	fear
9)	nawm	naama	sleep
10)	kawn	kaana	be
11)	ʕayš	ʕaaša	live
12)	qayḍ	qaaḍa	cleave
13)	bayʕ	baaʕa	sell
14)	sayr	saara	go
15)	mayl	maala	incline

137) <u>IRAQI ARABIC: NOUN STEMS</u> (elementary)

In the following problem, separate the possessive morpheme
from the noun stem. Consider the variation in the resulting
stems and account for it. What phonological process is
illustrated here?

	...	my...	
1)	walad	waladi	son
2)	qalam	qalami	pencil
3)	Jaras	Jarasi	bell
4)	balad	baladi	town
5)	tanak	tanaki	tin

-88-

6) baɣal	baɣli	mule
7) šaʕar	šaʕri	hair
8) laḥam	laḥmi	meat
9) taxat	taxti	bench
10) šaʕab	šaʕbi	people

138) IRAQI ARABIC: NOUN STEMS (elementary)

In the following problem, separate the possessive morpheme from the noun stems. Consider the variation in the resulting stems and account for it. What phonological process is illustrated here?

	...	my...	
1)	binit	binti	daughter
2)	riǰil	riǰli	leg
3)	ʔisim	ʔismi	name
4)	čiðib	čiðbi	lie
5)	siʕir	siʕri	price
6)	ʔibil	ʔibili	camels
7)	ʔuxut	ʔuxti	sister
8)	šuɣul	šuɣli	work
9)	xubuz	xubzi	bread
10)	ʕumur	ʕumri	age
11)	kušuk	kuški	cabin
12)	kutub	kutubi	books

139) FIJIAN: STEMS (elementary)

In the following problem, separate the morpheme meaning transitive aspect from the verb stems. Consider the resulting variation in the stems and account for it. What phonological process is illustrated here?

	Intransitive	Transitive	
1)	lako	lakova	fetch
2)	siŋa	siŋana	dry
3)	ndambe	ndambeða	sit

4) ðaa	ðaata	dislike
5) kila	kilaa	know
6) lewa	lewaa	decide
7) tau	taura	take
8) soli	solia	give
9) kere	kerea	ask
10) bili	biliŋa	push
11) sau	sauma	repay
12) toro	toroya	shave

140) <u>SWAHILI: NASALS</u> (elementary)

In the following problem, separate both the singular and the plural morphemes from the noun stems. Consider the variation in both these inflections and account for it. What phonological process is illustrated here?

	Singular	Plural	
1)	ubale	mbale	strip
2)	ubugu	mbugu	cord
3)	ubiši	mbiši	argument
4)	uduvi	nduvi	shrimp
5)	udago	ndago	weed
6)	udui	ndui	pustule
7)	ugimbi	ŋgimbi	beer
8)	ugono	ŋgono	intercourse
9)	ugwe	ŋgwe	string
10)	waraka	ﬁaraka	document
11)	wenzo	ñenzo	roller
12)	wimbo	ñimbo	song

141) EGYPTIAN ARABIC: VOWELS (elementary)

In the following problem, separate the morpheme meaning
"us" from the verb. Consider the variation in the shapes of
the verb and account for it. What phonological process is
illustrated here?

	he...	he...us	
1)	šaaf	šafna	saw
2)	gaab	gabna	brought
3)	ḥaaš	ḥašna	hindered
4)	zaar	zarna	visited
5)	haan	hanna	mistreated
6)	šaal	šalna	carry
7)	faad	fadna	benefited
8)	laam	lamna	rebuked
9)	saab	sabna	leave
10)	ɣaaẓ	ɣaẓna	vex

142) EGYPTIAN ARABIC: VOWELS (elementary)

In the following problem, separate the possessive morpheme
from the nouns. Consider the variation in the resulting
nouns and account for it. What phonological process is
illustrated here?

	...	our...	
1)	taag	tagna	crown
2)	baab	babna	door
3)	gaar	garna	neighbor
4)	biir	birna	well
5)	diin	dinna	religion
6)	kiis	kisna	sack
7)	nuur	nurna	light
8)	fuul	fulna	beans
9)	ruuḥ	ruḥna	soul

-91-

10) beet	bitna	house
11) deen	dinna	debt
12) seef	sifna	sword
13) door	durna	turn
14) gooz	guzna	husband
15) toom	tumna	garlic

143) HUNGARIAN: PLURAL SUFFIX (elementary)

In the following problem, separate the plural morpheme from
the nouns. Consider the variation in the shape of this plural
morpheme and account for it. What phonological process is
illustrated here?

	Singular	Plural	
1)	astal	astalok	table
2)	madᵞar	madᵞarok	Hugarian
3)	doboz	dobozok	box
4)	dob	dobok	drum
5)	kor	korok	age
6)	ember	emberek	man
7)	ez	ezek	this
8)	semüveg	semüvegek	eyeglasses
9)	iŋg	iŋgek	shirt
10)	hit	hitek	belief

144) HUNGARIAN: PLURAL SUFFIX (intermediate)

In the following problem, consider the plural morpheme once
more. On the basis of the solution of the previous problem,
account for the plural forms in this problem. What
phonological process is illustrated here?

	Singular	Plural	
1)	tanulo:	tanulo:k	pupil
2)	ayto:	ayto:k	door
3)	rigo:	rigo:k	robin

4)	fö:	fö:k	chief
5)	söllö:	söllö:k	grape
6)	ta:bla	ta:bla:k	blackboard
7)	ša:rga	ša:rga:k	yellow
8)	sürke	sürke:k	grey
9)	bögre	bögre:k	mug
10)	fa	fa:k	tree

145) SLOVAK: GENDER MORPHEMES (intermediate)

In this problem, separate the morphemes for masculine, feminine, and neuter. Consider the variation you find in the shape of these morphemes and account for it. What phonological process is illustrated here?

	Masc.	Fem.	Neuter	
1)	kruti:	kruta:	krute:	cruel
2)	slovenski:	slovenska:	slovenske:	Slovak
3)	lʸu:ti	lʸu:ta	lʸu:te	merciless
4)	zatʸati:	zatʸata:	zatʸate:	stubborn
5)	druhi:	druha:	druhe:	other
6)	tata:rski	tata:rska	tata:rske	Tartar
7)	ri:ʒi	ri:ʒa	ri:ʒe	genuine
8)	poči:taɟu:ci	poči:taɟu:ca	poči:taɟu:ce	counting
9)	tisi:ci	tisi:ca	tisi:ce	thousandth
10)	uosmi	uosma	uosme	eighth
11)	bieli	biela	biele	white
12)	buolni	buolna	buolne	painful
13)	mierni	mierna	mierne	peaceful
14)	priesvitni:	priesvitna:	priesvitne:	transparent
15)	čierni	čierna	čierne	black

146) <u>SLOVAK: PLURAL MORPHEME</u> (intermediate)

In the following problem all the forms are in the genitive plural. All the noun stems end in a consonant. Separate the genetive plural morpheme from the noun stems. Consider the variation in the genetive plural morpheme and account for it. What phonological process is illustrated here?

1)	latiek	planks
2)	čipiek	laces
3)	mariek	marks
4)	hračiek	toys
5)	tabuliek	tables
6)	plaviek	swimsuits
7)	obličiek	kidneys
8)	študentiek	students
9)	očiek	eyes
10)	boleriek	vests
11)	cediliek	strainers
12)	la:tok	materials
13)	čiapok	hats
14)	čiarok	lines
15)	hra:čok	players
16)	dialʸok	distances
17)	pla:rok	mushrooms
18)	robotni:čok	workers
19)	kuostok	pits
20)	slovi:čok	words
21)	rebierok	ribs
22)	čielok	foreheads

147) <u>CZECH: PREPOSITIONS</u> (elementary)

In the following problem, consider the final consonant of the preposition. Account for the variation in this final consonant. What phonological process is illustrated here?

1)	pod oknem	under the window
2)	z ohnʸe	out of the fire
3)	bez odmluvi	without an excuse

4) od otce	from the father
5) v oblast^yi	in the region
6) pod hlavou	under the head
7) z domu	out of the house
8) bez rod^yiču:	without parents
9) od dra:hi	from the railroad
10) v dolex	in the mines
11) pot střexou	under the roof
12) s postele	out of the bed
13) bes pen^yes	without money
14) ot sestri	from the sister
15) f pekle	in hell

143) HEBREW: PREFIXATION (elementary)

In the following problem, separate the reflexive morpheme from the verb stem in the first 10 examples. Using this as the norm, account for the forms in the second 10 examples. Variation in the vowels is not pertinent to the problem. What phonological process is illustrated here?

	Active	Reflexive	
1)	kibel	hitkabel	accept
2)	konen	hitkonen	prepare
3)	lavaš	hitlabeš	dress
4)	nigaš	hitnageš	collide
5)	gileax	hitgaleax	shave
6)	pina	hitpana	remove
7)	rašam	hitrašem	mark
8)	xipes	hitxapes	seek
9)	raxec	hitraxec	wash
10)	mina	hitmana	appoint
11)	silek	histalek	remove
12)	sipek	histapek	satisfy
13)	siyem	histayem	finish
14)	šidek	hištadex	marry

15) šina	hištana	change
16) šibeax	hištabeax	praise
17) ciref	hictaref	join
18) cideK	hictadeK	justify
19) carax	hictarex	consume
20) šigea	hištagea	crazy

149) FRENCH: STEM CONSONANTS (intermediate)

In the following problem, consider the variation of the consonants in the stems of the masculine and feminine forms. Assume that one form has at least one more morpheme than the other. Which form has the extra morpheme, and what is its shape? Account for all the forms in the problem. What phonological process is illustrated here?

	Feminine	Masculine	
1)	vɛrt	vɛr	green
2)	grãd	grã	big
3)	blãš	blã	white
4)	fɔrt	fɔr	strong
5)	gros	gro	fat
6)	bas	ba	low
7)	dus	du	sweet
8)	höröz	hörö	happy
9)	patit	pati	small
10)	tut	tu	all
11)	movɛz	movɛ	bad
12)	ẽteližãt	ẽteližã	intelligent
13)	Kurt	Kur	short
14)	almãd	almã	German
15)	ãglɛz	ãglɛ	English
16)	famöz	famö	famous
17)	fos	fo	false
18)	frɛš	frɛ	fresh
19)	ot	o	high

150) <u>WELSH: PREFIXATION</u> (intermediate)

In the following problem, separate the three different possessive morphemes from the noun stems. Consider the resulting variation and account for it. Which morpheme, noun stem or possessive suffix, will contain the conditioning factor? This takes some abstract thinking. What phonological process is illustrated here?

...	their	his	her	
1) pen	ipen	iben	ifen	head
2) porva	iporva	iborva	iforva	pasture
3) porθ	iporθ	iborθ	iforθ	door
4) pluen	ipluen	ibluen	ifluen	feather
5) tad	itad	idad	iθad	father
6) trev	itrev	idrev	iθrev	town
7) tafol	itafol	idafol	iθafol	scales
8) tal	ital	idal	iθal	forehead
9) ki	iki	igi	ixi	dog
10) kalon	ikalon	igalon	ixalon	heart
11) korn	ikorn	igorn	ixorn	horn
12) kefal	ikefal	igefal	ixefal	horse

151) <u>POLISH: NASALS</u> (intermediate)

In the following problem, separate the inflectional morphemes from the noun stems. Consider the resulting variation in the noun stems and account for it. What phonological process is illustrated here?

	Nom.sg.	Gen.sg.	Acc.sg.	Nom.pl.	
1)	dõp	dẽbu	dõp	dẽbi	oak
2)	błõt	błẽdu	błõt	błẽdi	mistake
3)	głõp	głẽba	głõp	głẽbi	stalk
4)	krõk	krẽgu	krõk	krẽgi	circle
5)	lõk	lẽgu	lõk	lẽgi	brooder
6)	obrõp	obrẽbu	obrõp	obrẽbi	border

-97-

7) rõp	rêbu	rõp	rêbi	edge
8) zõp	zêba	zõp	zêbi	tooth

9) sõšʸat	sõšʸada	sõšʸada	sõšʸedžʸi	neighbour
10) prõtek	prõtka	prõtek	prõtki	bacillus
11) rõbek	rõbka	rõbek	rõbki	veil
12) yêzik	yêzika	yêzik	yêziki	tongue
13) užêdnʸik	užêdnʸika	užêdnʸika	užêdnʸici	official
14) yêk	yêku	yêk	yêki	cry
15) kês	kêsa	kês	kêsi	piece
16) krêk	krêgu	krêk	krêgi	vertebra
17) lêk	lêku	lêk	lêki	scare
18) skrêt	skrêtu	skrêt	skrêti	braid

152) **TURKISH: VOWELS** (elementary)

In the following problem, separate the infinitive morpheme from the verb stem. Consider the variation in this morpheme and account for it. What phonological process is illustrated here?

1) yɨkamak	to wash
2) yemek	to eat
3) giyinmek	to dress
4) görünmek	to be seen
5) söylenmek	to talk to oneself
6) soymak	to undress
7) sevmek	to love
8) bulmak	to find
9) yɨkanmak	to wash oneself
10) soyunmak	to undress oneself
11) sevinmek	to be happy
12) yenmek	to be eaten
13) görmek	to see
14) bulunmak	to find oneself
15) giymek	to wear
16) dövmek	to beat
17) söylemek	to tell
18) dovunmak	to lament

153) BULGARIAN: STEM VOWELS (intermediate)

In the following problem, separate the plural morpheme from the noun. Consider the variation in the resulting noun stems and account for it. What phonological process is illustrated here?

	Singular	Plural	
1)	teátər	teátri	theatre
2)	bóbər	bóbri	beaver
3)	lávər	lávri	laurel
4)	rótmistər	rótmistri	captain
5)	žézəl	žézli	sceptre
6)	pómisəl	pómisli	intention
7)	ágəl	aglí	corner
8)	kútel	kútli	mortar
9)	stúbel	stublí	source
10)	kopén	kopní	rick
11)	ovén	ovní	ram
12)	pésen	pésni	song
13)	psalóm	psalmí	psalm
14)	begléc	beglecí	fugitive
15)	kadréc	kadrecí	curly head
16)	báncik	báncigi	band saw
17)	ízverk	ízvergi	monster
18)	prídax	prídaxi	aspiration
19)	xrabréc	xrabrecí	brave man
20)	pobóy	pobóyi	beating

154) BULGARIAN: PLURALS (intermediate)

In the following problem, separate the morphemes for the
secondary plural and the nominative plural from the noun
stems. Consider the resulting variation in the noun stems
and account for it. What phonological process is illustrated
here?

	Nom.sg.	Second. Pl.	Nom.pl.	
1)	rák	ráka	ráci	crab
2)	bélek	bélega	bélezi	mark
3)	nalók	nalóga	nalózi	tax
4)	yevnúx	yevnúxa	yevnúsi	eunuch
5)	kožúx	kožúxa	kožúsi	fur coat
6)	zádux	záduxa	zádisi	asthma
7)	znák	znáka	znáci	sign
8)	vrák	vrága	vrázi(arch.)	enemy
9)	zvúk	zvúka	zvúci	sound
10)	pódvik	pódviga	pódvizi	feat
11)	səprúk	səprúga	səprúzi	spouse
12)	siromáx	siromáxa	siromási	poor man
13)	vnúk	vnúka	vnúci	grandson
14)	almanáx	almanáxa	almanási	almanach
15)	yezík	yeziká	yezíci	language
16)	stomáx	stomáxa	stomási	stomach
17)	tebešír	tebеširá	tebešíri	chalk
18)	mólif	móliva	molívi	pencil
19)	nómer	nomerá	nómeri	number
20)	nérf	nervá	nérvi	nerve
21)	stráš	stražá	stráži	guard
22)	sərp	sərpa	sərpi	sickle
23)	stvól	stvóla	stvóli	trunk
24)	bukét	bukéta	bukéti	bouquet
25)	bukvár	bukvára	bukvári	dictionary
26)	izvár	izvára	izvári	cheese

155) <u>FINNISH: CONSONANTS</u> (intermediate)

In the following problem, separate the genetive morpheme
from the noun stems. Consider the resulting variation in
these noun stems and account for it. What phonological
process is illustrated here?

	Nominative	Genitive	
1)	kukka	kukan	flower
2)	tukki	tukin	log
3)	hoikka	hoikan	slender
4)	heikko	heikompa	weak
5)	pappi	papin	priest
6)	loppu	lopun	end
7)	kauppa	kaupan	shop
8)	oppi	opin	knowledge
9)	katto	katon	roof
10)	tüttö	tütön	girl

156) <u>FINNISH: CONSONANTS</u> (intermediate)

In the following problem, separate the first person singular
morpheme and the infinitive morpheme from the verb stems.
Consider the variation in the resulting verb stems, and also
in the infinitive morpheme and account for it. What
phonological process is illustrated here?

	1st per.sg.	Infinitive	
1)	menettelen	menetellä	to behave
2)	lämmittelen	lämmitellä	to warm oneself
3)	yuttelen	yutella	to narrate
4)	näyttelen	näytellä	to show
5)	ayattelen	ayatella	to think
6)	tavoittelen	tavoitella	to try to seize
7)	supattelen	supatella	to tattle
8)	kikattelen	kikatella	to giggle

157) FINNISH: CONSONANTS (intermediate)

In the following problem, separate the inflectional morpheme for form II from the verb stems. Consider the resulting variation in the noun stems and account for it.

	Form I	Form II	
1)	huonompa	huonomman	bad
2)	isoimpa	isoimman	great
3)	ampu	ammun	to shoot
4)	lämpö	lämmön	warmth
5)	isäntä	isännän	host
6)	kunto	kunnon	condition
7)	rakenta	rakennan	to build
8)	virta	virran	to chirp
9)	kerta	kerron	to narrate
10)	murta	murran	to break
11)	ilta	illan	evening
12)	kelta	kellan	yellow
13)	haltu	hallun	possession
14)	kuuntelen	kuunnella	to listen
15)	lavertelen	laverrella	to chatter
16)	visertelen	viserrella	to chirp
17)	piirtelen	piirrella	to draw
18)	kimaltelen	kimallella	to sparkle
19)	puhaltelen	puhallella	to blow

158) CZECH: VERB STEMS (intermediate)

In the following problem, separate the inflectional morphemes for first person, third person, and the infinitive, which is [-tʸi]. Ignore the variation in the vowel length. Consider the resulting variation in the verb stems and account for it. What is the phonological process?

	1st sg.	3rd sg.	Infin.	
1)	metu	mete	me:stʸi	sweep
2)	vedu	vede	ve:stʸi	lead
3)	pletu	plete	ple:stʸi	knit
4)	předu	přede	při:stʸi	weave
5)	svedu	svede	sve:stʸi	seduce

-102-

6) Kladu	Klade	Kla:st^{y}i	lay
7) matu	mate	ma:st^{y}i	confuse
8) hudu	hude	howst^{y}i	play
9) Kvetu	Kvete	Kve:st^{y}i	bloom
10) Kradu	Krade	Kra:st^{y}i	steal

159) MODERN GREEK: VERB STEMS (intermediate)

In the following problem, separate the prefix indicating past participle from the verb stem. Consider the variation in this morpheme and account for it. What phonological process is illustrated here?

	Infin.	Past Part.	
1)	sózo	sésoKa	save
2)	lío	léliKa	solve
3)	θío	téθiKa	sacrifice
4)	θnísKo	téθniKa	die
5)	niKó	neníKiKa	win
6)	miéo	memíiKa	initiate
7)	piéo	pepíiKa	create
8)	peráo	pepéraKa	pass
9)	fitévo	pefítefKa	plant
10)	peðévo	pepéðefKa	educate

160) ENGLISH: VOWEL ALTERNATIONS (elementary)

In the following problem, consider the vowel alternations in the following forms and account for them. What phonological process is illustrated here?

1)	vǽriyəs	(various)	vəráyətiy	(variety)
2)	Kǽnədə	(Canada)	Kənéydiyən	(Canadian)
3)	mórəl	(moral)	mərǽlətiy	(morality)
4)	fówtəgræf	(photograph)	fətágrəfiy	(photography)
5)	dəKórəm	(decorum)	déKərəs	(decorous)
6)	sówbər	(sober)	səbráyətiy	(sobriety)
7)	pə́rfəKt	(perfect)	pərféKšən	(perfection)
8)	súwpər	(super)	səpíriyər	(superior)
9)	éybəl	(able)	əbílətiy	(ability)
10)	ristór	(restore)	restəréyšən	(restoration)

161) ENGLISH: CONSONANT ALTERNATION (elementary)

In the following problem, consider the final stop in form 1 and the corresponding spirant in form 2 and account for this variation. What phonological process is illustrated here?

	Form 1	Form 2
1)	relate	relation
2)	Haiti	Haitian
3)	discreet	discretion
4)	submit	submission
5)	permit	permission
6)	elide	elision
7)	decide	decision
8)	divide	division
9)	erode	erosion
10)	corrode	corrosion

162) ENGLISH: CONSONANT ALTERNATION (elementary)

In the following problem, consider the final spirant in form 1 and the corresponding spirant in form 2. Account for this variation. What phonological process is illustrated here?

	Form 1	Form 2
1)	regress	regression
2)	race	racial
3)	office	official
4)	grace	gracious
5)	Laos	Laotian
6)	please	pleasure
7)	revise	revision
8)	enclose	enclosure
9)	expose	exposure
10)	braze	brazier

163) ENGLISH: CONSONANT CLUSTERS (elementary)

In the following problem, consider the stem final consonant clusters in form 1 and the corresponding single consonants in form 2. Account for this variation. Note that there are three different situations here, so different explanations are called for.

	Form 1	Form 2
1)	signal	sign
2)	benignant	benign
3)	malignant	malign
4)	phlegmatic	phlegm
5)	clamber	climb
6)	limber	limb
7)	crumble	crumb
8)	thimble	thumb
9)	oft	often
10)	moist	moisten
11)	soft	soften
12)	fast	fasten

164) ENGLISH: POSSESSIVE MORPHEME (elementary)

In the following problem, transcribe the forms into a phonemic representation. Consider the different shapes of the possessive morpheme and account for them. What phonological process is illustrated here?

1) sister's
2) aunt's
3) Mike's
4) nephew's
5) Garth's
6) Gibb's
7) Maud's
8) Dag's

9) Dave's
10) Dan's
11) Hal's
12) Chris's
13) lass's
14) boss's
15) wife's

165) ENGLISH: NEGATIVE PREFIX (elementary)

In the following problem, transcribe the forms into a
phonemic representation. Consider the variation in the
negative prefix and account for it. What phonological
process is illustrated here?

1) impossible
2) interminable
3) inconceivable
4) imbalance
5) independant
6) ingrate
7) illegal
8) irrational
9) irregular
10) immodest

166) ENGLISH: PLURAL (elementary)

In the following problem, transcribe the forms into a
phonemic representation. Consider the variations in the
plural suffixes and the noun stems, and account for them.
What phonological process is illustrated here?

Sg.	Pl.
1) house	houses
2) path	paths
3) wife	wives
4) knife	knives
5) oath	oaths

6) mouth	mouths
7) dwarf	dwarves
8) hoof	hooves
9) scarf	scarves
10) wharf	wharves

167) ENGLISH: PLURAL (elementary)

In the following problem, transcribe the forms into a phonemic representation. Consider the variation in the plural suffix and account for it. What phonological process is illustrated here?

1) hips
2) cats
3) ticks
4) cliffs
5) moths
6) clubs
7) dogs
8) figs
9) caves
10) clothes
11) lambs
12) cars
13) ashes
14) bruises
15) houses
16) wedges
17) garages

168) <u>ENGLISH: PAST TENSE</u> (elementary)

In the following problem, transcribe the forms into a phonemic representation. Consider the variation in the past tense suffix and account for it. What phonological process is illustrated here?

1) kept
2) walked
3) lurched
4) laughed
5) hissed
6) lobbed
7) hugged
8) lived
9) hosed
10) hummed
11) added
12) decided
13) knitted
14) fitted
15) coded

IV. MORPHOLOGY

169) EGYPTIAN ARABIC: VERBAL FORMS (elementary)

Analyse the following data into morphemes. List the morphemes and their meanings. (Model solution)

1)	xabbar	he told
2)	xabbarak	he told you (masc.)
3)	xabbarik	he told you (fem.)
4)	xabbarkum	he told you (pl.)
5)	xabbarhum	he told them
6)	ma xabbarš	he didn't tell
7)	ma xabbarakš	he didn't tell you (masc.)
8)	ma xabbarikš	he didn't tell you (fem.)
9)	ma xabbarkumš	he didn't tell you (pl.)
10)	ma xabbarhumš	he didn't tell them
11)	ḥamal	he carried
12)	ḥamalak	he carried you (masc.)
13)	ḥamalik	he carried you (fem.)
14)	ḥamalkum	he carried you (pl.)
15)	ḥamalhum	he carried them
16)	ma ḥamalš	he didn't carry
17)	ma ḥamalakš	he didn't carry you (masc.)
18)	ma ḥamalikš	he didn't carry you (fem.)
19)	ma ḥamalkumš	he didn't carry you (pl.)
20)	ma ḥamalhumš	he didn't carry them
21)	xadamak	he served you (masc.)
22)	ma šafikš	he didn't see you (fem.)
23)	tabaʕkum	he followed you (pl.)
24)	ma raggaʕhumš	he didn't bring them back

170) <u>CZECH: VERBS</u> (elementary)

Determine the morphological boundaries and state the meaning of prefixes, suffixes and roots.

1)	nesu	I carry
2)	ponese	he will carry
3)	povedete	you will lead (pl.)
4)	poplavu	I will swim
5)	plaveme	we swim
6)	připlaveš	you will swim here (sg.)
7)	přiyedou	they will drive here
8)	odvedeme	we will lead away
9)	odyede	he will drive away
10)	nese	he carries
11)	přineseme	we will bring here
12)	otplavete	you will swim away (pl.)
13)	yedu	I drive
14)	ponesu	I will carry
15)	přiyedete	you will drive here (pl.)
16)	poplaveme	we will swim
17)	vedeme	we lead
18)	odnescu	they will carry away
19)	plavou	they swim
20)	poyede	he will drive
21)	nesou	they carry
22)	přinese	he will bring (obj.) here
23)	odvedu	I will lead (obj.) away
24)	yede	he drives
25)	odneseš	you will carry away

171) <u>LEBANESE ARABIC: VERBS</u> (elementary)

What are the morphemes and their meanings?

	<u>sleep</u>	<u>say</u>	<u>love</u>	<u>slap</u>	
1)	naam	ʔuul	ḥibb	kiff	I
2)	tnaam	tʔuul	tḥibb	tkiff	you (masc.)
3)	tnaami	tʔuuli	tḥibbi	tkiffi	you (fem.)

4)	ynaam	y?uul	yhibb	ykiff	he
5)	tnaam	t?uul	thibb	tkiff	she
6)	nnaam	n?uul	nhibb	nkiff	we
7)	tnaamu	t?uulu	thibbu	tkiffu	you (pl.)
8)	ynaamu	y?uulu	yhibbu	ykiffu	they

172) <u>CREE: VERBAL AFFIXES I</u> (elementary)

Analyse the following Cree forms and find the equivalents for the English personal pronouns

1)	niwa:pahte:n	I see (it)
2)	kiwa:pahte:n	you see (it)
3)	niwa:pahte:na:n	we see (it)
4)	kiwa:pahte:na:wa:w	you (pl.) see (it)
5)	nima:čiše:n	I cut (it)
6)	kima:čiše:n	you cut (it)
7)	nima:čiše:na:n	we cut (it)
8)	kima:čiše:na:wa:w	you (pl.) cut (it)
9)	nitapin	I sit
10)	kitapin	you sit
11)	nitapina:n	we sit
12)	kitapina:wa:w	you (pl.) sit

173) <u>SWAHILI: VERBS I</u> (elementary)

Analyse the following data into morphemes. What are their meanings?

1)	ninasoma	I read
2)	unasoma	you read
3)	anasoma	he reads
4)	tunasoma	we read
5)	mnasoma	you (pl.) read
6)	wanasoma	they read

7)	nitasoma	I will read
8)	utasoma	you will read
9)	atasoma	he will read
10)	tutasoma	we will read
11)	mtasoma	you (pl.) will read
12)	watasoma	they will read
13)	ninarudi	I return
14)	unarudi	you return
15)	anarudi	he returns
16)	tutarudi	we will return
17)	mtarudi	you (pl.) will return
18)	watarudi	they will return
19)	ninaponda	I crush
20)	unatoka	you go out
21)	anakubali	he agrees
22)	tutaJibu	we will answer
23)	mtačukua	you (pl.) will carry
24)	watafika	they will arrive

174) <u>SWAHILI: VERBS II</u> (elementary)

Analyse the following data into morphemes. What are their meanings?

1)	anapenda	he likes
2)	atapenda	he will like
3)	alipenda	he liked
4)	amependa	he has liked
5)	alinipenda	he liked me
6)	alikupenda	he liked you
7)	alimpenda	he liked him
8)	alitupenda	he liked us
9)	aliwapenda	he liked you (pl.)
10)	aliwapenda	he liked them

11)	alimona	he saw him
12)	alimsaidia	he helped him
13)	alimpiga	he hit him
14)	alimčukua	he carried him
15)	alimua	he killed him

16)	ananitazama	he looks at me
17)	atakusikia	he will hear you
18)	alitupanya	he cured us
19)	amewaleta	he has brought them

175) **HEBREW: VERBS** (elementary)

Analyse the following data into morphemes. What are their meanings?

1)	higati	I arrived
2)	higata	you (masc.) arrived
3)	higat	you (fem.) arrived
4)	higanu	we arrived
5)	higatem	you (masc. pl.) arrived
6)	higaten	you (fem. pl.) arrived

7)	lamadeti	I studied
8)	lamadeta	you (masc.) studied
9)	lamadet	you (fem.) studied
10)	lamadenu	we studied
11)	lamadetem	you (masc. pl.) studied
12)	lamadeten	you (fem. pl.) studied

13)	raiti	I saw
14)	raita	you (masc.) saw
15)	rait	you (fem.) saw
16)	rainu	we saw
17)	raitem	you (masc. pl.) saw
18)	raiten	you (fem. pl.) saw

19) siparti	I told
20) siparta	you (masc.) told
21) sipart	you (fem.) told
22) siparnu	we told
23) sipartem	you (masc. pl.) told
24) siparten	you (fem. pl.) told

176) <u>HUNGARIAN: NUMERALS</u> (elementary)

a) Using the vocabulary stated below, write the English equivalents for the following Hungarian numerals.

1) harminced^y
2) hatvan
3) ötvened^y
4) ke:tsa:z
5) ti:zezer
6) ezerötsa:ztizenne:d^y
7) ned^{y}venne:d^y
8) n^{y}olcvan
9) ezern^{y}olcsa:z ned^{y}venn^{y}olc
10) husonhe:t
11) sa:zezer
12) harmincha:rom
13) tizenkilenc
14) husonkettö:
15) hatvankilenc
16) hetvenöt

b) Why is the second vowel in <u>n^{y}olcvan</u> and <u>hatvan</u> different from that in <u>ne:d^{y}ven</u> and <u>ötven</u>?

c) Translate into Hungarian:

1984

35

1245

Vocabulary

ed^Y	one
ke:t (kettö:)	two
ha:rom	three
ne:d^Y	four
öt	five
hat	six
he:t	seven
n^{Y}olc	eight
kilenc	nine
ti:z	ten
hu:s	twenty
harminc	thirty
ned^{Y}ven	forty
ötven	fifty
hetven	seventy
sa:z	hundred
ezer	thousand

177) <u>ITALIAN: VERBS</u> (elementary)

Analyse the following data into morphemes. What are their meanings?

1)	parlo	I speak
2)	parli	you speak
3)	parla	he speaks
4)	parliamo	we speak
5)	parlate	you (pl.) speak
6)	parlano	they speak
7)	porto	I carry
8)	compri	you buy
9)	usa	he uses
10)	ascoltiamo	we listen
11)	mandate	you (pl.) send
12)	trovano	they find

-115-

13) parlavo	I used to speak
14) parlavi	you used to speak
15) parlava	he used to speak
16) parlavamo	we used to speak
17) parlavate	you (pl.) used to speak
18) parlavano	they used to speak

19) trovavo	I used to find
20) mandavi	you used to send
21) ascoltava	he used to listen
22) usavamo	we used to use
23) compravate	you (pl.) used to buy
24) portavano	they used to carry

178) BULGARIAN: EXPRESSIVE NOUNS (elementary)

Identify the roots and affixes and comment on their functions.

	Nom.sg.	Nom.pl.	
1)	cvet	cvetove	flower
2)	grad	gradove	town
3)	glas	glasove	voice
4)	veter	vetrove	wind
5)	vol	volove	ox
6)	groš	grošove	coin
7)	list	listove	leaf
8)	cvetec	cvetovce	small flower
9)	gradec	gradovce	small town
10)	glasec	glasovce	thin voice
11)	vetrec	vetrovce	gentle wind
12)	volec	volovci	small ox
13)	grošec	grošovci	small coin
14)	listec	listovce	small leaf

179) **LEBANESE ARABIC: VERBS** (elementary)

Analyse the following data into morphemes. What are their meanings?

1)	šift	I saw
2)	šiftak	I saw you (masc.)
3)	šiftik	I saw you (fem.)
4)	šiftu	I saw him
5)	šifta	I saw her
6)	šiftkun	I saw you (pl.)
7)	šiftun	I saw them
8)	ḍarab	he hit
9)	ḍarabni	he hit me
10)	ḍarabak	he hit you (masc.)
11)	ḍarabik	he hit you (fem.)
12)	ḍarabu	he hit him
13)	ḍaraba	he hit her
14)	ḍarabna	he hit us
15)	ḍarabkun	he hit you (pl.)
16)	ḍarabun	he hit them

180) **CLASSICAL ARABIC: DERIVATION** (elementary)

Observe the way different words are derived from a common root in Classical Arabic. Identify the roots and the affixes. What kinds of morphological processes are demonstrated?

1)	ʕalima	he knew
2)	ʕallama	he taught
3)	taʕliim	teaching
4)	taʕallama	he learned
5)	taʕallum	learning
6)	salima	he was safe
7)	sallama	he handed over
8)	tasliim	handing over
9)	tasallama	he obtained
10)	tasallum	acquiring

-117-

11)	sallafa	he lent
12)	tasliif	lending
13)	tasallafa	he borrowed
14)	tasalluf	borrowing
15)	saruʕa	he is fast
16)	sarraʕa	he urged someone on
17)	tasriiʕ	urging
18)	tasarraʕa	he hastened
19)	tasarruʕ	haste
20)	ðakara	he remembered
21)	ðakkara	he reminded
22)	taðkiir	memento
23)	taðakkara	he kept in mind
24)	taðakkur	recollection

181) **PERSIAN: FUTURE TENSE** (elementary)

In the following Persian forms, identify the individual morphemes and their meanings.

1)	xaham xarid	I will buy
2)	xahi xarid	you will buy
3)	xahad xarid	he will buy
4)	xahim xarid	we will buy
5)	xahid xarid	you (pl.) will buy
6)	xahand xarid	they will buy
7)	xaridan	to buy
8)	naxaham xarid	I will not buy
9)	naxahi xarid	you will not buy
10)	naxahad xarid	he will not buy
11)	naxahim xarid	we will not buy
12)	naxahid xarid	you (pl.) will not buy
13)	naxahand xarid	they will not buy

Given that xahad ran means "he will paint", translate the following forms:

I will paint_____
they will paint_____
we will not paint_____

182) <u>CREE: POSSESSIVE</u> (intermediate)

Analyse the following Cree forms and find an equivalent for each English possessive pronoun. Do not overlook the distinction between singular and plural possessor.

1)	mo:hkoma:n	knife
2)	mo:hkoma:na	knives
3)	nimo:hkoma:n	my knife
4)	nimo:hkoma:na	my knives
5)	kimo:hkoma:n	your (sg)knife
6)	kimo:hkoma:na	your (sg)knives
7)	nimo:hkoma:nina:n	our knife
8)	nimo:hkoma:nina:na	our knives
9)	kimo:hkoma:niwa:w	your (pl.) knife
10)	kimo:hkoma:niwa:wa	your (pl.) knives
11)	omo:hkoma:n	his knife
12)	omo:hkoma:na	his knives
13)	omo:hkoma:niwa:w	their knife
14)	omo:hkoma:niwa:wa	their knives
15)	mi:nis	berry
16)	mi:nisa	berries
17)	nimi:nis	my berry
18)	nimi:nisa	my berries
19)	kimi:nis	your (sg)berry
20)	kimi:nisa	your (sg)berries
21)	nimi:nisina:n	our berry
22)	nimi:nisina:na	our berries
23)	kimi:nisiwa:w	your (pl.) berry
24)	kimi:nisiwa:wa	your (pl.) berries
25)	omi:nis	his berry
26)	omi:nisa	his berries
27)	omi:nisiwa:w	their berry
28)	omi:nisiwa:wa	their berries

What are the morphemes and their meanings?

1)	zurt	you (masc.) visited
2)	zurna	we visited
3)	ma zurnaaš	we didn't visit
4)	zurti	you (fem.) visited
5)	ma zurtiiš	you (fem.) didn't visit
6)	zurtu	you (pl.) visited
7)	ma zurtuuš	you (pl.) didn't visit
8)	zurnaaha	we visited her
9)	ma zurnahaaš	we didn't visit her
10)	zurtiiha	you (fem.) visited her
11)	ma zurtihaaš	you (fem.) didn't visit her
12)	zurtuuha	you (pl.) visited her
13)	ma zurtuhaaš	you (pl.) didn't visit her
14)	zurnaaki	we visited you (fem.)
15)	ma zurnakiiš	we didn't visit you (fem.)
16)	zurtiini	you (fem.) visited me
17)	ma zurtiniiš	you (fem.) didn't visit me
18)	zurtuuni	you (pl.) visited me
19)	ma zurtuniiš	you (pl.) didn't visit me
20)	šufna	we saw
21)	ma šufnakiiš	we didn't see you (fem.)
22)	ruḥtu	you (pl.) went
23)	ma ruḥtuuš	you (pl.) didn't go
24)	xufti	you (fem.) were afraid
25)	ma xuftiniiš	you (fem.) weren't afraid of me
26)	gibtiiha	you (fem.) brought her
27)	ma gibnahaaš	we didn't bring her

184) BULGARIAN: NOUNS (elementary)

Determine the stems and the inflectional patterns demonstrated by these two groups of Bulgarian nouns.

	Sg.	Pl.	
1)	trup	trupi	tree trunk
2)	štat	štati	state
3)	lač	lači	ray
4)	gost	gosti	guest
5)	glist	glisti	tapeworm
6)	pat	pati	time
7)	prast	prasti	finger
8)	stav	stavi	joint
9)	magg	magi	magician
10)	kup	kupi	heap
11)	angličanin	angličani	Englishman
12)	bakalin	bakali	grocer
13)	arapin	arapi	Black
14)	bankerin	bankeri	banker
15)	dervišin	derviši	dervish
16)	francuzin	francuzi	French
17)	stopanin	stopani	owner
18)	kalpazanin	kalpazani	good-for-nothing
19)	balgarin	balgari	Bulgarian
20)	arabin	arabi	Arab

185) PERSIAN: VERBS (elementary)

Analyse the morphemes and their meanings.

1)	xaridam	I bought
2)	xaridi	you bought
3)	xarid	he bought

4) xaridim	we bought
5) xaridid	you (pl.) bought
6) xaridand	they bought
7) mixaridam	I was buying
8) mixaaridi	you were buying
9) mixarid	he was buying
10) mixaridim	we were buying
11) mixaridid	you (pl.) were buying
12) mixaridand	they were buying
13) naxaridam	I did not buy
14) naxaridi	you did not buy
15) naxarid	he did not buy
16) naxaridim	we did not buy
17) naxaridid	you (pl.) did not buy
18) naxaridand	they did not buy
19) namixaridam	I was not buying
20) namixaridi	you were not buying
21) namixarid	he was not buying
22) namixaridim	we were not buying
23) namixaridid	you (pl.) were not buying
24) namixaridand	they were not buying

186) PERSIAN: VERBS (elementary)

Analyse the following data into morphemes and state their meanings.

1) mixaram	I am buying
2) mixari	you are buying
3) mixarad	he is buying
4) mixarim	we are buying
5) mixarid	you (pl.) are buying
6) mixarand	they are buying

7) bexaram	I may buy
8) bexari	you may buy
9) bexarad	he may buy
10) bexarim	we may buy
11) bexarid	you (pl.) may buy
12) bexarand	they may buy

13) namixaram	I am not buying
14) namixari	you are not buying
15) namixarad	he is not buying
16) namixarim	we are not buying
17) namixarid	you (pl.) are not buying
18) namixarand	they are not buying

19) naxaram	I may not buy
20) naxari	you may not buy
21) naxarad	he may not buy
22) naxarim	we may not buy
23) naxarid	you (pl.) may not buy
24) naxarand	they may not buy

187) <u>TURKISH: DERIVATION</u> (intermediate)

Isolate the derivational suffixes and determine their function.

Stems:

1) adam	man
2) ana	mother
3) asker	soldier
4) akïl	intelligence
5) bekar	bachelor
6) denis	sea
7) edep	good breeding
8) güzel	beautiful
9) hasta	sick
10) čoJuk	child
11) kapï	door

12)	kardeš	brother
13)	kara	black
14)	kìymet	value
15)	košu	race
16)	mezar	grave
17)	yol	road
18)	süt	milk
19)	sulu	moist

Derivations:

1)	yolǰu	traveller
2)	denizǰi	sailor
3)	karanlìk	blackness
4)	sütlük	dairy
5)	güzelik	beauty
6)	kardešče	brotherly
7)	čoǰukča	childish
8)	adamǰa	properly
9)	anasìz	motherless
10)	kapìǰì	gate-keeper
12)	košuǰu	runner
13)	mezarlìk	graveyard
14)	kardešlik	brotherhood
15)	analìk	motherhood
16)	bekarlìk	celibacy
17)	suluǰa	slightly moist
18)	hastalìk	sickness
19)	čoǰukluk	childhood
20)	akìlsìz	stupid
21)	kìymetsiz	valueless
22)	edepsiz	ill-bred
23)	güzelǰe	pretty fair
24)	yolsuz	irregular
25)	askerlik	military service
26)	babalìk	paternity
27)	askerǰe	militarily
28)	akìlǰa	cleverly
29)	denizǰilik	aquatic sports

30) edepče	in a good manner
31) kapiJilik	door-keeper's job
32) sütčü	milkman
33) mezarJi	gravedigger
34) hastabakiJi	trained nurse
35) čoJuksuz	childless
36) karaJi	highwayman

188) CREE: VERBAL AFFIXES II (intermediate)

Find the Cree equivalents -- single morphemes or combinations of morphemes -- for the English pronouns indicating subject and object.

1) niwa:pama:w	I see him
2) kiwa:pama:w	you (sg.) see him
3) wa:pame:w	he sees him
4) niwa:pama:na:n	we see him
5) kiwa:pama:wa:w	you (pl.) see him
6) wa:pame:wak	they see him
7) niwa:pahte:n	I see it
8) kiwa:pahte:n	you (sg.) see it
9) wa:pahtam	he sees it
10) niwa:pahte:na:n	we see it
11) kiwa:pahte:na:wa:w	you (pl.) see it
12) wa:pahtamwak	they see it
13) nikanawe:lima:w	I keep him
14) kikanawe:lima:w	you (sg.) keep him
15) kanawe:lime:w	he keeps him
16) nikanawe:lima:na:n	we keep him
17) kikanawe:lima:wa:w	you (pl.) keep him
18) kanawe:lime:wak	they keep him
19) nikaname:lihte:n	I keep it
20) kikanawe:lihte:n	you (sg.) keep it
21) kanawe:lihtam	he keeps it
22) nikanawe:lihte:na:n	we keep it
23) kikanawe:lihte:na:wa:w	you (pl.) keep it
24) kanawe:lihtamwak	they keep it

189) <u>CZECH: MASCULINE NOUNS</u> (intermediate)

The following nouns belong to four types, according to their
inflectional behaviour. Distribute the nouns according to
their inflectional types and specity the criteria used for
their distribution.

	Nom.sg	Gen.sg	Acc.sg	Nom.pl	
1)	pa:n	pa:na	pa:na	pa:nove:	Mr.
2)	muš	muže	muže	muži	man
3)	mi:č	mi:če	mi:č	mi:če	ball
4)	koš	koše	koš	koše	basket
5)	le:kař	le:kaře	le:kaře	le:kaři	doctor
6)	boy	boye	boy	boye	fight
7)	hrop	hrobu	hrop	hrobi	grave
8)	kořen	kořenu	kořen	kořeni	root
9)	sin	sina	sina	sinove:	son
10)	taksi:k	taksi:ku	taksi:k	taksi:ki	taxi
11)	da:n	da:na	da:na	da:nove:	Dane
12)	nu:š	nože	nu:š	nože	knife
13)	še:f	še:fa	še:fa	še:fove:	boss
14)	lha:ř	lha:ře	lha:ře	lha:ři	liar
15)	ku:l	ku:lu	ku:l	ku:li	post
16)	dux	duxa	duxa	duxove:	ghost
17)	tesař	tesaře	tesaře	tesaři	carpenter
18)	nerf	nervu	nerf	nervi	nerve
19)	uva:dʸeč	uva:dʸeče	uva:dʸeče	uva:dʸeči	usher
20)	stroy	stroye	stroy	stroye	machine

190) <u>TURKISH: DECLENSION</u> (elementary)

Observing the rules of vowel harmony, fill in the missing
forms.

	Nom.	Gen.	Dat.	Obj.
1)	ev	evin	_____	evi
2)	at	atın	ata	_____
3)	gül	_____	güle	gülü
4)	yol	yolun	yola	yolu

5) iČki	iČkinin	_____	iČkiyi
6) oda	odanın	odaya	odayı
7) KöprÜ	KöprÜnÜn	KöprÜye	KöprÜyÜ
8) palto	_____	paltoya	paltoyu
9) Jep	Jebin	Jebe	Jebi
10) Kitap	Kitabın	Kitaba	
11) otobÜs	otobÜsÜn	otobÜse	otobÜsÜ
12) _____	KaraKolun	KaraKola	KaraKolu
13) Kedi	_____	Kediye	Kediyi
14) para	paranın	paraya	parayı
15) sÜrÜ	sÜrÜnÜn	_____	sÜrÜyÜ
16) KoKu	KoKunun	KoKuya	_____
17) Kalem	Kalemin	Kaleme	Kalemı
18) _____	vatanın	vatana	vatanı
19) gÜn	gÜnÜn	_____	gÜnÜ
20) horoz	horozun	horoza	_____
21) mefKi	_____	mefKiye	mefKiyi
22) _____	elmanın	elmaya	elmayı
23) KöylÜ	KöylÜnÜn	KöylÜye	KöylÜyÜ
24) piyango	piyangonun	piyangoya	piyangoyu

	Abl.	Inst.	
1)	evden	evle	house
2)	attan	atla	horse
3)	gÜlden	gÜlle	rose
4)	_____	yolla	journey
5)	iČkiden	iČkiyle	drink
6)	_____	odayla	room
7)	KöprÜden	_____	bridge
8)	paltodan	paltoyla	coat
9)	Jepten	_____	pocket

10) Kitaptan	Kitapla	book
11) _____	otobüsle	bus
12) karakoldan	karakolla	station
13) kediden	kediyle	cat
14) paradan	_____	money
15) sürüden	sürüyle	herd
16) kokudan	kokuyla	smell
17) kalemden	kalemle	pencil
18) vatandan	vatanla	fatherland
19) günden	günle	day
20) horozdan	horozla	rooster
21) mefkiden	mefkiyle	class
22) elmadad	elmayla	apple
23) köylüden	_____	peasant
24) _____	piyangoyua	lottery

191) HUNGARIAN: VERBS (elementary)

Determine the verb stems and the suffixes, and comment on the distribution of their allomorphs.

1) e:rtek	I understand
2) ül	he/she sits
3) seretnek	they love
4) tudok	I know
5) repülök	I fly
6) serettek	you love (pl.)
7) tuds	you know (sg.)
8) mondotok	you say (pl.)
9) seretünk	we love
10) ülök	I sit
11) repültök	you fly (pl.)
12) e:rtünk	we understand
13) e:rtes	you understand (sg.)
14) tudnak	they know

15) üls	you sit (sg.)
16) ültök	you sit (pl.)
17) repül	he/she flies
18) seret	he/she loves
19) repülnek	they fly
20) mond	he/she says
21) ert	he/she understands
22) serets	you love (sg.)
23) mondunk	we say
24) repüls	you fly (sg.)
25) ülünk	we sit
26) tudunk	we know
27) e:rtenek	they understand
28) mondanak	they say
29) tudtok	you know (pl.)
30) tud	he/she knows
31) mondas	you say (sg.)
32) e:rtetek	you understand
33) mondok	I say
34) seretek	I love

192) <u>CZECH: AGREEMENT</u> (intermediate)

Isolate the inflectional suffixes from the stems. Classify the phrases according to the different inflectional patterns in which they occur. Observe the adjectives and try to establish what grammatical categories of their head nouns they reflect.

1) novi: du:m	a new house
2) heski: člov^yek	a handsome man
3) hloupi: xlapec	a dull boy
4) vi:koni: stroj	a productive machine
5) v^yerni: pes	a faithful dog
6) xitra: d^yifka	a clever girl
7) modra: za:st^yera	a blue apron
8) nudna: předna:ška	a boring lecture

-129-

9)	kožena: kabelka	a leather bag
10)	mila: či:šnᵛice	a pleasant waitress
11)	dobre: pero	a good pen
12)	velke: pi:smeno	a capital letter
13)	buclate: miminko	a chubby baby
14)	špičate: koleno	a pointed knee
15)	nove: slovo	a new word
16)	hesci: muži	handsome men
17)	hloupi: xlapci	dull boys
18)	vᵛernᵛi: psi	faithful dogs
19)	černi: kosi	black robins
20)	bohatᵛi: opxodnᵛi:ci	rich merchants
21)	nove: domi	new houses
22)	víkone: stroje	productive machines
23)	dlouhe: dopisi	long letters
24)	xitre: dᵛifki	clever girls
25)	modre: za:stᵛeri	blue aprons
26)	dobra: pera	good pens
27)	nova: slova	new words
28)	buclata: miminka	chubby babies
29)	špičata: kolena	pointed knees
30)	velka: pi:smena	capital letters
31)	nove:mu domu	to the new house
32)	heske:mu človᵛeku	to the handsome man
33)	hloupe:mu xlapci	to the dull boy
34)	xitre: di:fce	to the clever girl
35)	mile: či:šnᵛici	to the pleasant waitress
36)	nudne: předna:šce	to the boring lecture
37)	laskave: učitelce	to the kind teacher
38)	falešne: kamara:tce	to the faithless girlfriend
39)	dobre:mu slovu	to the good word
40)	velke:mu pismenu	to the capital letter
41)	špičate:mu peru	to the pointed knee
42)	buclate:mu kolenu	to the chubby knee

193) ENGLISH: WORD STRUCTURE (elementary)

Rewrite the following words in phonemic transcription and subdivide them into morphemes. Indicate the types of morphemes, using the following terminology: root, stem, derivational suffix, inflectional suffix, and prefix.

1) friend	27) smart
2) friendly	28) smartly
3) unfriendly	29) smartness
4) unfriendliness	30) smartaleck
5) friendship	31) smartalecky
6) friendlier	32) smartens
7) friendlily	33) smarty
8) befriends	34) smartier
9) head	35) outsmart
10) headily	36) devil
11) headache	37) devilish
12) header	38) devilkin
13) headed	39) deviltry
14) heading	40) bedevil
15) headless	41) take
16) headline	42) takable
17) headliner	43) intake
18) heady	44) taken
19) beheaded	45) take out
20) hand	46) taker
21) handbag	47) taking
22) handed	48) undertaker
23) handedness	49) undertaking
24) handful	
25) handily	
26) handiness	

194) ENGLISH: PREFIXES (intermediate)

Distribute each of the following groups of words (I, II, III) into two subgroups using the functions of their prefixes as criteria.

Group I

1) unfair
2) non-smoker
3) untie
4) insane
5) defrost
6) disloyal
7) disconnect
8) immoral
9) asymmetrical
10) deforestation
11) unhorse
12) discoloured

Group II

13) misinform
14) maltreat
15) pseudo-intellectual
16) archduke
17) subhuman
18) overdressed
19) malodorous
20) misconduct
21) superman
22) hypercritical
23) undercook
24) pseudo-patriot

Group III

25) superstructure
26) foretell
27) subway
28) pre-war
29) interpose
30) post-classical
31) ex-wife
32) pre-marital
33) transatlantic
34) subterranean
35) undercoat
36) international

195) ENGLISH: NOUN SUFFIXES (intermediate)

Indicate the functions of suffixes in the following words.

1) gangster
2) booklet
3) democracy
4) engineer
5) waitress
6) Londoner
7) daddy
8) usherette
9) teenager
10) boyhood
11) friendship
12) panelling
13) mouthful
14) auntie
15) slavery

16) princeling	21) kitchenette	26) Johnie
17) cowardly	22) kingdom	27) republican
18) machinery	23) Israelite	28) violinist
19) stardom	24) Chinese	29) communism
20) ownership	25) nunnery	30) dictatorship

196) ENGLISH: SUFFIXES (intermediate)

Suffixes which are attached to verbal stems are called
deverbatives and suffixes which are attached to the nominal
(noun or adjective) stems are called denominatives. In the
following words, find the suffixes and determine whether
they are deverbatives or denominatives.

1) driver	6) childless	11) youngish
2) useful	7) disinfectant	12) crabwise
3) cowardly	8) actor	13) dismissal
4) sanity	9) sadden	14) employee
5) drainage	10) criminal	15) inhabitant

16) violinist	21) daily	26) Darwinian
17) happiness	22) readable	27) building
18) flannelette	23) backwards	28) balconied
19) organization	24) attractive	29) spillage
20) amazement	25) idealism	30) popularize

197) ENGLISH: WORD FORMATION (intermediate)

Besides inheriting words from older stages, English uses
different word-forming processes for enrichment of its
lexicon. Some of the formations and techniques are listed
below.

Acronyms- combination of the initial sounds (letters) of the
words of an original phrase

Derivation- usage of derivational suffixes

Conversion– an item changes its word-class without the addition of an affix

Borrowings– foreign words

Compounds– words consisting of two or more words or word parts

Reduplicatives– compounds with two or more identical or slightly different elements

Clipping– subtraction of one or more syllables from a word

Observe the following words and state what type of process was used in their formation.

1) insane	11) bilateral	21) dressmaking
2) NATO	12) love	22) enslave
3) tick-tock	13) blitz	23) self-control
4) untie	14) photo	24) flu
5) misinform	15) seesaw	25) booklet
6) playboy	16) bewitch	26) robot
7) phone	17) laser	27) wishy-washy
8) doubt	18) cheat	28) bus
9) oxygen	19) radar	29) gangster
10) malodorous	20) bee-sting	30) prof

31) kingdom	41) USSR	51) walk
32) love seat	42) gladhand	52) sputnik
33) isocracy	43) vivacious	53) tip-top
34) Chinese	44) non-smoker	54) turn
35) sari	45) chutney	55) backwards
36) dorm	46) UK	56) barbecue
37) bigamy	47) youngish	57) deaf-mute
38) employee	48) lymphoma	58) crabwise
39) C.O.D.	49) wrap	59) GHQ
40) childless	50) thongs	60) baby-sit

198) ENGLISH: CONVERSION (intermediate)

In these examples, the items change their word-class without the addition of an affix. Indicate the direction of conversion for each item. E.g. release V→N (the noun release has been derived from the verb release).

1)	doubt	V N		6) comic	A N
2)	daily	N A		7) throw	V N
3)	bottle	N V		8) love	V N
4)	laugh	N V		9) calm	A V
5)	cheat	N V		10) peel	V N
11)	nurse	V N		16) walk	V N
12)	warm	A V		17) mail	N V
13)	retreat	N V		18) dirty	A V
14)	corner	N V		19) knife	N V
15)	mask	N V		20) turn	N V
21)	dry	V A		26) wet	V A
22)	bore	V N		27) married	N A
23)	cash	N V		28) hate	N V
24)	cripple	V N		29) cover	N V
25)	answer	V N		30) coat	V N

199) ENGLISH: COMPOUND NOUNS (intermediate)

Indicate the syntactic relations of the compounding elements using paraphrases according to the following example:

	sunrise	the sun rises	Subject + Verb
1)	playboy	_____	_____
2)	call-girl	_____	_____
3)	brainwashing	_____	_____
4)	earthquake	_____	_____
5)	daydreamer	_____	_____
6)	windmill	_____	_____
7)	flashlight	_____	_____
8)	bloodstain	_____	_____

9) gamekeeper   _____   _____
10) headache   _____   _____
11) sun-bathing   _____   _____
12) sleepwalking   _____   _____
13) cutpurse   _____   _____
14) hangman   _____   _____
15) homesick   _____   _____
16) loudmouth   _____   _____
17) snowflake   _____   _____
18) handwriting   _____   _____
19) dressmaking   _____   _____
20) purse-snatcher   _____   _____

V. STRUCTURAL AND FUNCTIONAL SYNTAX

200) MALAY: MORPHOSYNTAX (intermediate)

Gloss every Malay word with its English equivalent. Identify the grammatical morphemes and explain their functions. Model solution

1) dia məlihat rumah bapaña itu
   He looks at the house of his father

2) bapa itu məlihat anak ləlakiña
   The father looks at his son

3) anak ləlaki itu čintakan səoraŋ pərəmpuan yaŋ čantik
   dan miskin
   The son loves a beautiful and poor girl

4) bapa iŋin anak ləlakiña məŋkahwini səoraŋ pərəmpuan
   yaŋ kaya
   The father wants his son to marry a rich girl

5) pərəmpuan yaŋ čantik itu mənJadi marah
   The beautiful girl gets angry

6) dia bərčadaŋ untuk məŋiŋkari bapaña
   He decides to disobey his father

7) kakak ləlaki itu bərčadaŋ untuk məmbunuh pərəmpuan
   itu
   The boy's sister decides to kill the girl

8) dia mənJerit
   She screams

9) kakak yaŋ marah itu məniŋgalkan rumah itu
   The angry sister leaves the house

10) bapa itu bərčadaŋ untuk məŋampunkan anak ləlakiña
    dan pərəmpuan yaŋ miskin itu
    The father decides to forgive his son and the poor girl

201) MALAY: NOUNS (elementary)

Gloss every Malay noun with its English equivalent. Explain the formation of singular and plural. Are there any Malay equivalents for the English articles?

Singular

1) di padaŋ itu ada saekor lambu
   There is an ox in the field

2) saya ada saekor ayam
   I have a hen

3) saya bali saekor kuciŋ
   I bought a cat

4) saya ada saekor anJiŋ
   I have a dog

5) saya nampak saekor kuda
   I see a horse

6) saoraŋ murid maŋhadiri sakolah itu
   A pupil attends the school

7) saoraŋ pakerJa sadaŋ bakerJa
   A worker is working

8) saoraŋ ibu sadaŋ barihat di taman itu
   Mother is relaxing in the garden

9) ada saoraŋ pelaJar di dalam sekolah itu
   There is one student in the school

10) ada saoraŋ pelakun sadaŋ barlakun
    There is one actor performing

Plural

11) di padaŋ itu ada baŋak ləmbu
There are many oxen in the field

12) saya ada baŋak ayam
I have many hens

13) saya bəli baŋak kuciŋ
I bought some cats

14) saya ada baŋak anJin
I have some dogs

15) saya nampak baŋak kuda
I see some horses

16) ramai murid-murid məŋhadiri səkolah itu
Many pupils attend the school

17) pəkerJa-pəkerJa sədaŋ bəkerJa
Workers are working

18) ramai ibu-ibu sədaŋ barihat di taman itu
Many mothers are relaxing in the garden

19) pəlaJar-pəlaJar sədaŋ bəlaJar
Students are studying

20 ramai pəlakun-pəlakun sədaŋ bərlakun
Many actors are performing

202) LATIN: INFLECTIONS (elementary)

Identify the following morphemes: noun stems; verb stems; conjunctions; prepositions; noun suffixes; verb suffixes. State the rule for word order. Translate into English: <u>nāuta fīliam regīnae in camerās portat.</u> Translate into Latin: The sailors' daughters see the forest and the waters.

1) agricola arat
   The farmer is ploughing

2) agricola puellās terret
   The farmer frightens the girls

3) puellāē aquam portant
   The girls are carrying water

4) fēmina puellam portat
   The woman is carrying the girl

5) silvāē fēminam terrent
   The forests frighten the woman

6) fēmina et agricolāē aquam portant
   The woman and the farmers are carrying water

7) rēgīna fīliam habet
   The queen has a daughter

8) nāutāē fēminās habent
   The sailors have wives

9) habetne nāuta fīliam?
   Does the sailor have a daughter?

10) fīliāē nāutae aquam portant
    The daughters of the sailor are carrying water

11) puella nāutam vocat
    The girl is calling the sailor

12) viam vidēmus
    We see the road

13) puellāē viās vident
    The girls see the roads

14) nāuta agricolās terret
    The sailor frightens the farmers

15) rēgīnam et fīliām rēgīnāē portāmus
    We are carrying the queen and the queen's daughter

16) aratne agricola?
    Is the farmer ploughing?

17) videntne fēmināē fīliās?
    Do the women see the girls?

18) aquam in cameram portant
    They carry water into the room

19) fēmina et agricola arant
    The farmer and the woman are ploughing

20) silvāē aquam habent
    The forests have water

21) vidēmusne camerās rēgīnārum?
    Do we see the rooms of the queens?

22) fīliāē agricolārum agricolam lāudant

23) rēgīna fēminās et puellās lāudat
    The queen praises the women and the girls

24) fēmināē nāutārum aquam portant
    The wives of the sailors are carrying water

25) aqua terret fēminās et puellās
    The water frightens the women and the girls

26) vidēmusne fīliās agricolārum?
     Do we see the daughters of the farmers?

27) fēmina et agricola camerās habent
     The woman and the farmer have rooms

28) puellāē in silvās aquam portant
     The girls are carrying water into the forests

29) vocantne fīliam nāutāē?
     Are they calling the daughter of the sailor?

30) terretne rēgīnam?
     Does he frighten the queen?

203) ESTONIAN: SUFFIXES (intermediate)

Gloss every Estonian word with its English equivalent.
Identify verbal and nominal suffixes and explain their
functions. What are the three meanings of the Estonian word
on? If ütlema means "to say", what are the meanings of
ütleb and ütlevad? Translate into Estonian: the girl's doll is
in the store; the boy wants the black cover.

   1) poiss mängib klaverit
       A boy is playing the piano

   2) klaver on restoranis
       The piano is in the restaurant

   3) äri on väga suur
       The store is very large

   4) poisi onutütred mängivad nukkudega
       The boy's cousins are playing with dolls

   5) onutütrel on kaks nukku
       The cousin has two dolls

6) teisel onutütrel on üks nukk
The other cousin has one doll

7) yutu pealkiri on meie tüdruk
The title of the story is "Our Girl"

8) raamat on suur
The book is big

9) raamatu kaan on pruun
The cover of the book is brown

10) poisi onutütred on tartus
The boy's cousins are in Tartu

11) mariya ya poiss mängivad porandal
Maria and the boy are playing on the floor

12) ema loeb raamatut
Mother is reading a book

13) raamatud on klaveril
Some books are on the piano

14) siin on restoran
Here is a restaurant

15) tüdrukul on teised raamaatud
The girl has the other books

16) onutütar loeb
The cousin is reading

17) ta töötab postkontoris
She works in the post office

18) mu arve on üks kroon
My bill is one crown

19) poiss tahab Klaverit
The boy wants a piano

20) Klaver on Kohvikus
The piano is in the coffee house

21) mu arve on Kaks Krooni ja Kolm senti
My bill is two crown and three cents

22) Kaan on raamatul
The cover is on the book

23) poisil on suur must raamat
The boy has a large black book

24) Kaan on must
The cover is black

25) ta elab advoKaadiga
She lives with a lawyer

26) tema justus on Kolm poissi
There are three boys in her story

27) siin ongi mu isa äri
Here now is my father's store

28) mu Kaks venda töötavad fordi autovabrikus
My two brothers are working in the Ford automobile
plant

29) tema isa on äris
Her father is in the store

30) ta elab tartus
He lives in Tartu

204) BULGARIAN: DEFINITE ARTICLE (elementary)

Gloss every Bulgarian word with its English equivalent.
Identify grammatical morphemes and explain their functions.
State the rule for the word order. Comment on the use of the
definite article.

1) rodinata na balgarite ye balgariya.
The country of the Bulgarians is Bulgaria.

2) sofiya ye stolicata na balgariya
Sophia is the capital of Bulgaria.

3) yazovirat ye blizo do zavoda
The dam is near the plant.

4) zavodat ye do grada
The plant is in the city.

5) rozata raste v rozovata gradina
The rose grows in the rose garden.

6) balgariya ye rodinata na balgarite
Bulgaria is the country of the Bulgarians.

7) stolicata na balgariya ye sofiya
The capital of Bulgaria is Sophia.

8) zavodat ye blizo do yazovira
The plant is near the dam.

9) balgari živeyat v balgariya
Bulgarians live in Bulgaria.

10) dunavat se namira v dolinata
The Danube is situated in the valley.

11) sofiya ne ye na dunava
Sophia is not on the Danube.

12) gradət se ne namira na dunava
The city is not situated on the Danube.

13) sofiya ye grad
Sophia is a city.

14) gradət na rozite ye blizo
The city of the roses is near.

15) gradinata ye blizo
The garden is near.

16) mariya bila v golyamata gradina
Maria was in the large garden

205) <u>HEBREW: PRONOUNS</u> (elementary)

Gloss every Hebrew word with its English equivalent.
Comment on what are translated as verbs in English. What
seem to be their grammatical status in Hebrew?

1) hu gar baarec
He lives in Israel

2) ani gar baarec
I (masc.) live in Israel

3) hi gara baarec
She lives in Israel

4) ani gara baarec
I (fem.) live in Israel

5) anaxnu garim baarec
We (masc.) live in Israel

6) anaxnu garot baarec
We (fem.) live in Israel

7) hen garot baarec
   They (fem.) live in Israel

8) hem garim baarec
   They (masc.) live in Israel

9) ata gar baarec
   You (masc.) live in Israel

10) at gara baarec
    You (fem.) live in Israel

11) atem garim baarec
    You (masc.pl.) live in Israel

12) aten garot baarec
    You (fem.pl.) live in Israel

13) ani xadaš bexayfa
    I (masc.) am new in Haifa

14) at xadaša bexayfa
    You (fem.) are new in Haifa

15) atem xadašim bexayfa
    You (masc.pl.) are new in Haifa

16) hen xadašot bexayfa
    They (fem.) are new in Haifa

17) hu muxrax laruc
    He must go

18) hi muxraxa laruc
    She must go

19) aten muxraxot laruc
    You (fem.pl.) must go

20) hen muxraxim laruc
    They (masc.) must go

206) <u>HINDI: GRAMMATICAL MORPHEMES</u> (intermediate)

Gloss every Hindi word with its English equivalent. Find Hindi expressions for the following grammatical notions: progressive aspect; 3rd person singular present tense; possessive. What is the function of <u>hai/hãi</u>? Make a statement on Hindi morpheme and word order.

1) larke bāg mẽ kʰel rahe hãi
The boys are playing in the garden

2) bāg bahut barā hai
The garden is very large

3) ek larkā kitāb parʰ rahā hai
The boy is reading a book

4) vo roz kitāb parʰtā hai
He reads a book every day

5) larke aur larkiyã roz skūl jāte haĩ
The boys and girls go to school every day

6) bāg mẽ per hãi
There are trees in the garden

7) baččā dūdʰ pī rahā hai
The child is drinking milk

8) mã rām ko rotī detī hai
Mother gives Rām the bread

9) rotī rām ke lie hai
The bread is for Rām

10) larkī sī rahī hai
The girl is sewing

11) vo ek bʰāi ke lie kamīz sī rahī hai
She is sewing a shirt for one brother

12) kamīz kā kaprā lāl hai
The shirt cloth is red

13) laṛkī kā nām mālā hai
The girl's name is Mālā

14) mā bāzār se kaprā khārīditī hai
Mother buys the cloth from the bazaar

15) laṛkā lāl pataŋ khārīd rahā hai
The boy is buying a red kite

16) rām kā dost ā rahā hai
Rām's friend is coming

17) rām aur dost čāi pī rahe hãi
Rām and the friend are drinking tea

18) ve roz sāth khelte hãi
They play together every day

19) čāi bahut garam hai
The tea is very hot

20) ve garam čāi āhistā pī rahe hãi
They are drinking the hot tea slowly

21) laṛkiyã pānī rahe hãi
The girls are drinking water

22) pānī bahut thaṇḍā hai
The water is very cold

207) TURKISH: OBJECTIVE CASE (elementary)

Analyse the words into roots and suffixes. Gloss each
morpheme with its English equivalent. State the rule for the
word order.

1) čay ičtik
   We drank tea

2) bir košuJu gördüm
   I saw a runner

3) gözler gördüm
   I saw some eyes

4) kitablar sečtik
   We selected some books

5) süt ičtim
   I drank some milk

6) pasta yedim
   I ate some cakes

7) adamlar gördüm
   I saw some men

8) kahve sečtim
   I selected some coffee

9) evler baktik
   We looked for some houses

10) bir ev aldik
    We took a house

11) čayi ičtik
    We drank the tea

12) adamì gördüm
    I saw the man

13) gözleri gördüm
    I saw the eyes

14) kahveyi ičtim
    I drank the coffee

15) kitabì aldìk
    We took the book

16) pastayì yedim
    I ate the cakes

17) kapìyì sečtim
    I selected the gate

18) košuĵuyu gördük
    We saw the runner

19) sütü sečtik
    We selected the milk

20) kitablarì sevdik
    We loved the books

208) CLASSICAL ARABIC: SENTENCES I (intermediate)

Analyse the words into morphemes. Gloss each morpheme
with its English equivalent.

1) ?albaytu hinaa
   The house is here

2) huwwa fii lbayti
   He is in the house

3) raʔaytu lbayta
   I saw the house

4) baytuhu hinaa
   His house is here

5) huwwa fii baytihi
   He is in his house

6) raʔaytu baytahu
   I saw his house

7) baytuhum hinaa
   Their (masc.) house is here

8) huwwa fii baytihim
   He is in their (masc.) house

9) raʔaytu baytahum
   I saw their (masc.) house

10) baytuhunna hinaa
    Their (fem.) house is here

11) huwwa fii baytihinna
    He is in their (fem.) house

12) raʔaytu baytahunna
    I saw their (fem) house

13) ʔalkitaabu fii lJaruuri
    The book is in the drawer

14) haaðaa fii lkitaabi
    This is in the book

15) biʕtu lkitaaba
    I sold the book

16) kitaabuhu ʕalaa lmaktabi
    His book is on the desk

17) ʔalqiṣṣatu fii Kitaabihi
The story is in his book

18) xaṣartu Kitaabahu
I lost his book

19) ʔummuhum fii lmadrasati
Their (masc.) mother is in the school

20) ʔalḥaakimu maʕa ʔummihinna
The judge is with their (fem.) mother

21) sallamtu ʔummahunna
I greeted their (fem.) mother

22) zurtu madrasatahum
I visited their (masc.) school

23) ʔuxtuhunna fii lmadiinati
Their (fem.) sister is in the city

24) ðahabtu maʕa xaalihim
I went with their (masc.) uncle

209) <u>CLASSICAL ARABIC: SENTENCES II</u> (intermediate)

Analyse the words into morphemes. Gloss each morpheme
with its English equilvalent.

1) ḍarabta lwalada
You (masc.) hit the boy

2) ḍarabti lwalada
You (fem.) hit the boy

3) ḍarabaKa lwaladu
The boy hit you (masc.)

4) ḍarabaḱi lwaladu
   The boy hit you (fem.)

5) ḍaraba lwaladu lḱalba
   The boy hit the dog

6) ḍaraba lḱalbu lwalada
   The dog hit the boy

7) ḍarabnaa lwalada
   We hit the boy

8) ḍarabakumu lwaladu
   The boy hit you (masc.pl.)

9) ḍarabaka waladun
   A boy hit you (masc.)

10) ḍarabta waladan
    You (masc.) hit a boy

11) ḍarabti waladan
    You (fem.) hit a boy

12) ḍaraba waladun lḱalba
    A boy hit the dog

13) ḍaraba waladun ḱalban
    A boy hit a dog

14) ḍarabnaa ḱalban
    We hit a dog

15) ḍarabnaaka
    We hit you (masc.)

16) ḍarabnaaḱi
    We hit you (fem.)

17) ḍarabnaakum
    We hit you (masc.pl.)

18) ḍarabtum waladan
   You (masc.pl.) hit a boy

19) ḍarabtumu lkalba
   You (masc.pl.) hit the dog

20) ḍaraba kalbunu lwalada
   A dog hit the boy

210) CZECH: GENDER PATTERN (elementary)

Analyse the words into morphemes. Gloss each morpheme
with its English equivalent. Establish the agreement
pattern between noun, adjectives and verbs.

Feminine nouns

1) nova: učitelka poma:hala
   The new teacher helped

2) kovova: lampa svi:t\(^y\)ila
   The metalic lamp shined

3) mlada: d\(^y\)i:fka studovala
   The young girl studied

4) bi:la: koza b\(^y\)ežela
   The white goat ran

5) unavena: žena pracovala
   The tired woman worked

6) mlade: kozi pili
   The young goats drank

7) unavene: d\(^y\)i:fki plakali
   The tired girls cried

8) stare: ženi otpoči:vali
   The old women rested

-155-

9) zlata: harfa hra:la
   The golden harp played

10) dobre: učitelki učili
    The good teachers taught

Masculine nouns

11) novi: pracovn^{y}i:k studoval
    The new worker studied

12) kovovi: svi:cen svi:t^{y}il
    The golden candlestick shined

13) dobri: kamara:t poma:hal
    The good friend helped

14) stari: kozel pil
    The old goat drank

15) mladi: pomocn^{y}i:k hra:l
    The young worker played

16) bi:li: kozli b^{y}eželi
    The white goats ran

17) novi: kamara:d^{y}i hra:li
    The new friends played

18) kovove: svi:cni svi:t^{y}ili
    The metalic candlesticks shined

19) stare: obleki otpoči:vali
    The old suits rested

20) unaven^{y}i: pracovn^{y}i:ci pracovali
    The tired workers worked

21) nove: motori b^{y}eželi
    The new engines ran

211) CZECH: PARTICIPLES (elementary)

Observe the influence of the subject on the inflectional
properties of the present participle and the 1-participle
(past tense). State the pattern.

1) žena piyi:c čay psala dopis
   The woman wrote a letter while drinking tea

2) matka ukli:zeyi:c yi:delnu poslouxala ra:diyo
   The mother listened to the radio while cleaning the
   dining room

3) dʸi:fka studuyi:c yeho tva:ř přetstʸi:rala klit
   The girl pretended to be calm while studying his face

4) dʸelnʸice pracuyi:c u stavu mislela na dʸi:tʸe
   The woman worker thought about her child while
   working at the loom

5) helena leži:c f tra:vʸe hluboce spala
   Helena slept deeply while lying on the grass

6) dʸelnʸi:k poslouxaye ra:diyo zametal halu
   The worker swept the hall while listening to the radio

7) xlapec hledaye knʸihu pobi:hal
   The boy ran around while looking for a book

8) student připravuye se ke skoušce přečetl pʸet knʸix
   The student read five books while preparing for the
   exam

9) muš hledaye dʸi:tʸe prošel celi: park
   The man went through the whole park while looking for
   his child

10) pavel leže f tra:vʸe studoval
    Pavel studied while lying on the grass

11) ženi a muži piyi:ce čay hovořili
    The women and men talked while drinking tea

12) dʸelnʸi:ci pracuyi:ce misleli na sta:fku
    The workers thought about the strike while working

13) studentʸi hovoři:ce o marksizmu pili vodku
    The students drank vodka while talking about Marxism

14) dʸi:fki misli:ce na pavla plakali
    The girls cried while thinking of Paul

15) matki tuši:ce neštʸestʸi: vibi:hali na ulici
    The mothers ran out on the street expecting an
    accident

212) <u>RUSSIAN: DIRECT OBJECT</u> (elementary)

Explain the difference in the inflection of the Russian nouns
functioning as objects. The Russian sentences are presented
in a standard transliteration.

1) on nayelsya saxaru
   He ate a lot of sugar

2) devočka syela vesʸ saxar
   The girl ate all the sugar

3) ivan napilsya čayu
   Ivan drank some tea

4) kolxozniki viraščivali čay
   The farmers grew tea

5) rabočiye privezli pesku
   The workers brought some sand

6) mi nasipali pesok v yaščik
   We filled the box with sand

7) sevodnya nasipalo snegu
   Today it snowed a lot

8) včera vipal sneg
   Yesterday it snowed

213) <u>GERMAN: ARTICLES</u> (elementary)

Observe the underlined noun phrases and explain what causes the differences in the forms of their articles. Formulate the pertinent grammatical rules. Notice that the German sentences are presented in standard orthography.

1) Während <u>des Krieges</u> schliefen wir in Bunkern
   During the war we used to sleep in bunkers

2) Anstelle <u>des Hutes</u> trug ich eine Mütze
   Instead of the hat I put on a cap

3) Ausserhalb <u>des Kreises</u> liegen Steine
   Outside of the circle lay stones

4) <u>Der Hund</u> rennt aus <u>dem Haus</u>
   The dog ran from the house

5) Heute is <u>die Mutter</u> bei <u>dem Onkel</u>
   Today my mother is at my uncle's house

6) <u>Die Katze</u> streitet mit <u>dem Hund</u>
   The cat fought with the dog

7) <u>Der Garten</u> sieht besser aus ohne <u>den Baum</u>
   The garden looks better without the tree

8) Die Frau wäscht für den Mann
The woman does the laundry for her husband

9) Wir pflanzen die Blumen um den Tisch
We are planting the flowers around the table

10) Zugunsten des Professors wird die Bücherei mehr
Bücher Kaufen
The library will buy more books because of the
professor

11) Anstatt des Traumes bevorzugen wir die Wirklichkeit
Instead of the dream we prefer reality

12) Die Familie geht durch den Wald
The family goes through the forest

13) Die Kinder rennen gegen den Schnee
The children run against the snow

14) Wir trocknen uns nach dem Sturm
We are drying ourselves after the storm

15) Der Fahrer fährt zu dem Bahnhof
The driver drives to the railway station

214) TURKISH: WORD ORDER (intermediate)

Classify each Turkish word as either subject, object, verb, or
adverbial. Comment on the behaviour of verbs from the point
of view of their transitivity.

1) hasan öküzü aldı
Hasan bought the ox

2) köpek dišlerini gösterdi
The dog showed his teeth

3) denizaltı gemiyi batırdı
The submarine sank the ship

4) müdür odasìnda dir
   The director is in his room

5) bakan ingiltereye gitti
   The minister has gone to England

6) sultan sarayda šerbet ičti
   The sultan drank sherbert in his palace

7) kizkardešim evlerini almak istedi
   My sister wanted to buy their houses

8) ahmed dün ankaraya gitti
   Yesterday Ahmed went to Ankara

9) kìzlara čay verdim
   I gave the girls tea

10) čoJuklara elmalarì verdim
    I gave the children the apples

11) kìzlarì gördüm
    I saw the girls

12) bu kitabì arkadašìnìz ahmetten aldìm
    I bought this book from your friend Ahmet

13) bu otomobili babanìzdan aldìm
    I bought this car from your father

14) evde čay ičtik
    We drank tea in the house

15) vapuru gördük
    We saw the steamer

16) işimize başladık
We began our work

17) sigara almak istedi
He wanted to buy cigarettes

18) dün akşam sinemaya gitti
He went to the cinema yesterday evening

215) <u>BASQUE: ERGATIVITY</u> (elementary)

Find the nouns functioning as subjects and explain the differences in their forms. Notice that the Basque sentences are presented in standard orthography.

1) Aitak bazuen fabrike aundi
The father had a big factory

2) Gizonak ikasten du
The man sees it

3) Semeak badu zaldia
The sons have the horses

4) Joanesek etxe bat erosi du
John has bought a house

5) Mikelek duro bat amari kendu dio
Michael has taken a coin from his mother

6) Aite izango da
Father will be (there)

7) Gizona oihanean galdu da
The man is lost in the forest

8) Semea handia da
The son is tall

9) Joanes ettoriko da
   John will come

10) Mikel ona da
    Michael is good

216) <u>RUSSIAN: REFLEXIVE VERBS</u> (intermediate)

The reflexive suffix in Russian is represented by two forms: -sya and -s^y. Comparing the Russian examples with their English translations, state what functions are preformed by the reflexive suffix. Group the sentences according to their functions. The Russian sentences are presented in a standard transliteration.

1) stariki vsyo branyatsya
   The old men quarrel all the time

2) devuška moyetsya
   The girl is washing herself

3) ti odevayešsya
   You are dressing yourself

4) eta sobaka kusayetsya
   This dog bites

5) ženščina pričyosivayetsya
   The woman is combing her hair

6) on otravilsya
   He poisoned himself

7) mi vstretilis^y
   We met each other

8) grafik rabot narušalsya
   The work plan was being disturbed

9) lošad^y lyagayetsya
   The horse kicks

-163-

10) druzya obnyalis[γ]
The friends embraced each other

11) v obščestve čuvstvovalos[γ] liberal'noye tečeniye
Liberal trends of thought were felt in society

12) dom stroilsya
The house was being built

13) eta koška carapayetsya
This cat scratches

14) ivan vešalsya
Ivan tried to hang himself

15) rodstvenniki pocelovalis[γ]
The relatives kissed each other

16) poemy čitalis[γ] vsemi
The poems were read by everybody

17) eta materiya ne rvyotsya
This material will not tear

18) devuški dogovorilis[γ]
The girls reached an agreement

19) uroki vsegda pisalis[γ] nočyu
The homework assignments were always written during
the night

20) eta provoloka gnyotsya
This wire bends

217) <u>IRAQI ARABIC: VERBS</u> (elementary)

These sentences have a common constituent structure.
Represent it by a phrase marker. Comment on the structure
of the Arabic verbs and the word order.

1) l-walad y-šuuf l-beet
2) l-walad y-ḥibb l-binit
3) l-fallaaḥ y-naḍ̣ḍ̣if l-miḥraaθ
4) l-ʔab y-guṣṣ l-ḥabil
5) l-yanam y-aakul l-ḥašiiš
6) l-muʕallim y-saaʕid l-walad
7) l-muḥarrik y-mašša l-baabuur
8) l-qamar y-nawwar l-waaḥa
9) l-badu y-ṭaaʕim l-Jumal
10) l-muḥaami y-daafiʕ l-muJrim

l-	def.art.	ḥašiiš	grass
y-	pres.tense	muʕallim	teacher
walad	boy	-saaʕid	help
-šuuf	see	muḥarrik	motor
beet	house	-mašša	propel
-ḥibb	love	baabuur	steamship
binit	girl	qamar	moon
fallaaḥ	peasant	-nawwar	illuminate
-naḍ̣ḍ̣if	clean	waaḥa	oasis
miḥraaθ	plow	badu	bedouin
ʔab	father	-ṭaaʕim	feed
-guṣṣ	cut	Jumal	camel
ḥabil	rope	muḥaami	lawyer
yanam	sheep	-daafiʕ	defend
-aakul	eat	muJrim	criminal

218) **HEBREW: DIRECT OBJECTS** (elementary)

These sentences have a common constituent structure.
Represent it by a phrase marker. Comment of the structure
of direct objects in Hebrew.

1) ha-yeled ra?a et ha-kelev
2) ha-talmid siyem et ha-limudim
3) ha-yehudi biker et ha-arec
4) ha-ba?al maxar et ha-mexonit
5) ha-kelev axal et ha-basar
6) ha-eš saraf et ha-malon
7) ha-mabul hecif et ha-derex
8) ha-mešaret kibes et ha-kutonet
9) ha-xayat tafar et ha-beged
10) ha-ofe afa et ha-lexem

ha-	def.art.	saraf	burnt
et	(obj.)	malon	hotel
yeled	boy	mabul	flood
ra?a	saw	hecif	destroyed
kelev	dog	derex	road
talmid	student	mešaret	servant
siyem	finished	kibes	laundered
limudim	lessons	kutonet	shirt
yehudi	Jew	xayat	tailor
biker	visited	tafar	sewed
arec	Israel	beged	garment
ba?al	husband	ofe	baker
maxar	sold	afa	baked
mexonit	car	lexem	bread
axal	ate	eš	fire
besar	meat		

219) **SPANISH: DEFINITE ARTICLES** (elementary)

These sentences have a common constituent structure.
Represent it by a phrase marker. Comment on the structure
and position of the definite article in Spanish.

1) el muchacho mir-ó la fotografía
2) la señora compr-ó la leche
3) la vaca comi-ó la hierba
4) el hombre hall-ó el libro
5) el director escribi-ó la noticia
6) el terremoto derrib-ó la ciudad
7) la luna di-ó la luz
8) el coche entorpeci-ó la calle
9) la muchacha escuch-ó la conferencia
10) el carpintero construy-ó la casa

el	def.art.m.	noticia	notice
la	def.art.f.	·terremoto	earthquake
-ó	past tense	derrib-	destroy
muchacho	boy	ciudad	city
mir-	look at	luna	moon
fotografía	photograph	di-	give
señora	lady	luz	light
compr-	buy	coche	car
leche	milk	entorpeci-	block
vaca	cow	calle	street
comi-	eat	muchacha	girl
hierba	grass	escuch-	listen to
hombre	man	conferencia	lecture
hall-	find	carpintero	carpinter
libro	book	construy-	build
director	director	casa	house
escribi-	write		

220) FRENCH: ARTICLES (elementary)

These sentences have a common constituent structure.
Represent it by a phrase marker. Comment on the structure
and position of both definite and indefinite articles in
French

1) la mère prépar-ait le repas
2) une femme lav-ait l'-enfant
3) le client cherch-ait un garçon
4) un homme lis-ait un livre
5) un enfant mange-ait le pain
6) l'-amie fais-ait la vaiselle
7) l'-étudiante regard-ait un dessein
8) une étudiante regard-ait le dessein
9) le jardinier coup-ait l'-herbe
10) un gendarme conduis-ait la voiture

la~l'	def.art.f.	mange-	eat
le~l'	def.art.m.	pain	bread
un	indef.art.m.	amie	friend
une	indef.art.f.	fais-	do
-ait	past imp.	vaiselle	dishes
mère	mother	étudiante	student
prépar-	prepare	regard-	look at
repas	meal	dessein	drawing
femme	woman	jardinier	gardener
lav-	wash	coup-	cut
enfant	child	herbe	grass
client	customer	gendarme	gendarme
cherch-	look for	conduis-	drive
garçon	waiter	voiture	car
homme	man	livre	book
lis-	read		

221) GERMAN: PRONOUNS (elementary)

These sentences have a common constituent structure.
Represent it by a phrase marker. Comment on the place and
function of pronouns in German

1) das Kind sprich-t schnell
2) er is-t hier
3) der Kalb läuf-t frei
4) ein Säugling schläf-t viel
5) sie wein-t leise
6) er lach-t laut
7) eine Frau komm-t hervor
8) die Mutter sing-t schön
9) er spiel-t herum
10) der Mann lieg-t still

das	def.art.n.	sie	she
der	def.art.m.	wein-	cry
die	def.art.f.	leise	softly
-t	pres. tense	lach-	laugh
ein	indef.art.m.	laut	loudly
eine	indef.art.f.	Frau	woman
Kind	child	komm-	come
sprich-	speak	hervor	to here
schnell	fast	Mutter	mother
er	he	sing-	sing
is-	is	wohl	well
hier	here	spielt-	play
Kalb	calf	hierum	around here
läuf-	run	Mann	man
frei	freely	lieg-	lie
Säugling	infant	still	still
schlaf-	sleep	viel	much
viel	much		

222) **IRAQI ARABIC: TENSES** (elementary)

Represent the constituent structure of the following sentences. Comment on the verb tenses in Iraqi Arabic.

1) l-walad y-iḥči ʕarabi
2) l-walad raaḥ y-iḥčî ʕarabi
3) l-binit t-ruuḥ ʕa-l-beet
4) l-binit raaḥ t-ruuḥ ʕa-l-beet
5) r-riǰǰaal y-israb gahwa
6) r-riǰǰaal raaḥ y-išrab gahwa
7) l-mara t-ištiɣil bi-l-beet
8) l-mara raaḥ t-ištiɣil bi-l-beet
9) t-tilmiið y-idrus d-daris
10) t-tilmiið raaḥ y-idrus d-daris

l~r~t~d	def.art.	beet	house
y-	pres.m.	riǰǰaal	man
t-	pres.f.	-išrab	drink
raaḥ	(fut.)	gahwa	coffee
walad	boy	mara	woman
-iḥči	speak	-ištiɣil	work
ʕarabi	Arabic	bi-	in
binit	girl	tilmiið	student
-ruuḥ	go	-idrus	study
ʕa-	to	daris	lesson

223) IRAQI ARABIC: MODAL AUXILIARIES (elementary)

Represent the constituent structures of the following
sentences. Comment on the position and function of modal
auxiliaries in Iraqi Arabic. What form does the following
verb have?

1) l-walad y-idrus d-daris
2) l-walad raaḥ y-idrus d-daris
3) l-walad laazim y-idrus d-daris
4) l-walad mumkin y-idrus d-daris
5) l-walad y-imši ʕa-l-madrasa
6) l-walad raaḥ y-imši ʕa-l-madrasa
7) l-walad laazim y-imši ʕa-l-madrasa
8) l-walad mumkin y-imši ʕa-l-madrasa
9) l-binit t-imši ʕa-l-madrasa
10) l-binit laazin t-imši ʕa-l-madrasa

| laazim | necessary | imši | walk |
| mumkin | possible | madrasa | school |

-171-

224) **IRAQI ARABIC: VERB PHRASES** (elementary)
Represent the constituent structures of the following
sentences. Comment on the verb phrase in Iraqi Arabic. What
shape does each verb take?

1) l-fallaaḥ y-ištiɣil bi-l-mazraʕa
2) l-fallaaḥ y-igdar y-ištiɣil bi-l-mazraʕa
3) l-binit t-ištiri l-kitaab
4) l-binit t-riid t-ištiri l-kitaab
5) l-walad y-idrus bi-l-madrasa
6) l-walad y-ibtidi y-idrus bi-l-madrasa
7) l-mara t-iɣsil l-gamiiṣ
8) l-mara t-ibqa t-iɣsil l-qamiiṣ
9) l-muwǎẓ̌ẓ̌af y-iktib bi-l-qalam
10) l-muwaẓ̌ẓ̌af y-ḥawwil y-iktib bi-l-qalam

l-	def.art.	-iɣsil	wash
fallaaḥ	peasant	qamiiṣ	shirt
y~t	3rd.pers.	-ibqa	continue to
-ištiɣil	work	muwaẓ̌ẓ̌af	official
bi-	in	-iktib	write
mazraʕa	field	bi-	with
-igdar	be able to	qalam	pencil
binit	girl	-ḥawwil	try to
-ištiri	buy	-idrus	study
kitaab	book	madrasa	school
-riid	want to	-ibtidi	begin to
walad	boy	mara	woman

225) **LEBANESE ARABIC: VERB PHRASES** (elementary)

Represent the constituent structures of the following
sentences. Comment on the verb phrase in Lebanese Arabic.
What is the position and function of the b-prefix?

1)   l-walad b-y-idris d-dars
2)   l-walad b-y-i?dar y-idris d-dars
3)   l walad b-y-balliš y-idris d-dars
4)   l-walad b-y-ib?a y-idris d-dars
5)   l-walad b-y-i?dar y-balliš y-idris d-dars
6)   l-bint b-t-idris d-dars
7)   l-bint b-t-i?dar t-idris d-dars
8)   l-bint b-t-balliš t-idris d-dars
9)   l-bint b-t-ib?a t-idris d-dars
10) l-bint b-t-i?dar t-balliš t-idris d-dars

l~d	def.art.	walad	boy
b-	indic.	bint	girl
y-	pres.m.	-i?dar	can
t-	pres.f.	-balliš	begin
-idris	study	-ib?a	continue
dars	lesson		

-173-

226) IRAQI ARABIC: DEMONSTRATIVE (elementary)

Represent the constituent structures of the following
sentences. Comment on the shape, position and function of
the demonstrative adjective in Iraqi Arabic.

1) l-walad iJa
2) haaða l-walad iJa
3) l-binit iJa-t
4) haay l-binit iJa-t
5) ðaak r-riJJaal maat
6) ðiič l-mara maat-it
7) l-fallaaḥ šaaf haaða l-beet
8) l-muʕallima šaaf-it ðiič l-madrasa
9) haaða l-Jundi štara haay l-Jariida
10) haay l-ʔum yasal-it ðiič l-binit

haaða	this (m.sg.)	muʕallima	teacher
haay	this (f.sg.)	madrasa	school
ðaak	that (m.sg.)	Jundi	soldier
ðiič	that (f.sg.)	štara	bought
-t~-it	past f.	Jariida	newspaper
iJa	came	ʔum	mother
maat	died	yasal	washed
šaaf	saw	binit	girl
mara	woman	riJJaal	man
beet	house	fallaaḥ	peasant

-174-

227) **EGYPTIAN ARABIC: DEMONSTRATIVES** (elementary)

Represent the constituent structures of the following sentences. Comment on the shape, position and function of the demonstrative adjective in Egyptian Arabic. How does it differ from the demonstrative in Iraqi Arabic (see previous problem)?

1) l-walad da y-igi l-madrasa
2) l-bint di t-igi l-madrasa
3) l-muʕallim ḥa-y-saafir s-sana di
4) l-gamal da y-išrab may
5) l-mara di t-išrab ʔahwa
6) r-raagil da y-ḥibb l-mara di
7) l-fallaḥ da ḥa-y-ištiɣil hina
8) ṭ-ṭaaliba di t-idrus kitiir
9) ʔaḥmad y-ḥibb l-bint di
10) faaṭima t-ḥibb l-walad da

da	this (m.sg.)	walad	boy
di	this (f.sg.)	bint	girl
-igi	come(to)	mara	woman
madrasa	school	fallaaḥ	peasant
muʕallim	teacher	-ištiɣil	work
ḥa-	(future)	-idrus	study
saafir	travel	ʔaḥmad	Ahmad
sana	year	faaṭima	Fatima
gamal	camel	y-	pres.m.
-išrab	drink	t-	pres.f.
may	water	hina	here
ʔahwa	coffee	taaliba	student
raagil	man	kitiir	much
ḥibb	love		

228) LATIN: ADJECTIVES (elementary)

Represent the constituent structure of the following sentences by a phrase marker. Comment on the case and agreement between Latin nouns and adjectives.

1) serv-us bon-us es-t
2) puell-a bell-a es-t
3) templ-um magnific-um es-t
4) hort-us parv-us es-t
5) tog-a alb-a es-t
6) sign-um clãr-um est
7) gall-us fatu-us es-t
8) vi-a long-a es-t
9) for-um plēn-um es-t

-us	m.nom.sg.	vi-	road
-a	f.nom.sg.	long-	long
-um	n.nom.sg.	for-	forum
-t	pres.	plēn-	full
es-	be	parv-	small
serv-	servant	tog-	toga
bon-	good	alb-	white
puell-	girl	sign-	sign
bell-	pretty	clãr-	clear
templ-	temple	gall-	Gaul
magnific-	great	fatu-	stupid
hort-	garden		

229) <u>LATIN: CASE</u> (elementary)

Represent the constituent structure of the following sentences by a phrase marker. Comment on the use of the Latin cases relative to the verb.

1) serv-us puell-am vide-t
2) puell-a serv-um vide-t
3) serv-us hort-um vide-t
4) puell-a tog-am vide-t
5) serv-us tog-am lava-t
6) puell-a hort-um ama-t
7) pull-us aqu-am bibi-t
8) hirc-us cib-um edi-t
9) serv-us av-um adjuva-t
10) fili-a avuncul-um oscula-t
11) vacc-a vitul-um pari-t

-us	m.nom.sg.	fili-	daughter
-um	m.acc.sg.	avunvul-	uncle
-a	f.nom.sg.	oscula-	kiss
-am	f.acc.sg.	vacc-	cow
vide-	see	vitul-	calf
lava-	wash	pari-	bear
ama-	love	cib-	food
pull-	chick	edi-	eat
aqu-	water	av-	grandfather
bibi-	drink	adjuva-	help
hirc-	goat		

Represent the constituent structure of the statements and the questions. Comment on the position and function of the interrogative particle in Classical Arabic.

1) ḍarab-a ʔaḥmad-u zayd-an
2) hal ḍarab-a ʔaḥmad-u zayd-an?
3) samaʕ-a walad-un l-kalb-a
4) hal samaʕ-a walad-un l-kalb-a?
5) raʔa-ti l-bint-u bayt-an
6) hal raʔa-ti l-bint-u bayt-an?
7) qatal-a ṣ-ṣayyaad-u ʔasad-an
8) hal qatal-a ṣ-ṣayyaad-u ʔasad-an?
9) katab-a š-šaaʕir-u l-qaṣiidat-a
10) hal katab-a š-šaaʕir-u l-qaṣiidat-a?

-a	past m.	ṣayyaad-	hunter
-t	past f.	ʔasad-	lion
l~ṣ~š	def.art.	katab-	write
-u	nom.def.	šaaʕir-	poet
-a	acc.def.	qaṣiidat-	ode
-un	nom.indef.	samaʕ-	hear
-an	acc.indef.	walad-	boy
ḍarab-	hit	kalb-	dog
ʔaḥmad-	Ahmad	raʔa-	see
zayd-	Zeid	bint-	girl
hal	(question)	bayt-	house
qatal-	kill		

231) TURKISH: INTERROGATIVES (elementary)

Represent the constutuent structure of the statements and the questions. Comment on the shape and position of the interrogative particle in Turkish.

1) Ahmet kitap al-dı
2) Ahmet kitap al-dı mı?
3) Yabancı otel bul-du
4) Yabancı otel bul-du mu?
5) Asker düşman öldür-dü
6) Asker düşman öldür-dü mü?
7) Köpek su iç-di
8) Köpek su iç-di mi?
9) Kız şehir gör dü
10) Kız şehir gör dü mü?

dı~du~dü~di	past	ahmet	Ahmad
mı~mu~mü~mi	(ques.)	kitap	book
al-	buy	yabancı	foreigner
otel	hotel	öldür-	kill
bul-	find	köpek	dog
asker	soldier	su	water
düşman	enemy	iç-	drink
kız	girl	şehir	city
gör-	see		

232) ENGLISH: BASIC PHRASE STRUCTURES (elementary)

Represent the constituent structure of the following sentences.

1) She dreams
2) Peter slept
3) They have eaten
4) Paula is crying
5) He'll suffocate

6) Her eyes sparkle
7) The boy ran
8) My dog is barking
9) A girl sleeps
10) The students have been studying

11) My white rabbit died
12) The brave soldier was speaking
13) The strong wind has stopped
14) Her soft voice died out
15) The youngest child stutters

16) The big wolf from the black forest waited.
17) The musicians from Bremen played.
18) The clock on the wall ticked
19) The flames in the fireplace are crackling.
20) The people up in the hills have survived.

21) Cinderella prayed at the grave under the tree.
22) My little brother suffered at school for his foolishness.
23) She crouched over the stove in the corner.
24) His face glowed from the heat in the fireplace.
25) John spoke to the class in a low voice.

26) The young man walked her home.
27) They took the patient away.
28) My husband saw an accident this morning.
29) He believed her words completely.
30) The dog had frightened her badly.

31) His wife went with him gladly.
32) She must return to her office immediately.
33) He glanced at her curiously.
34) My older sister always prepared for the next day.
35) Leila wept silently in her bedroom.

36) Betty turned her face to the wall.
37) The nurse carried him to bed.
38) He watched her for a minute.
39) Thomas followed the boy with hesitation.
40) The policeman pushed him through the door.

41) John danced infrequently.
42) Her lips curved softly.
43) Ronnie is calling again.
44) They say that always.
45) She wept bitterly.

46) The unicorn is a mythical beast.
47) The yellow sun is bright and hot.
48) Her lips curved soft and full.
49) The sweater seems blue.
50) She was John's wife.

51) The little girl opened the door.
52) His wife dressed the children.
53) She felt little cold or dampness.
54) The prince was looking for a wife.
55) The plumber with twelve children won the Irish
    Sweepstakes.

56) My partner has forseen the danger of a serious crash.
57) The miser saw the error of his ways.
58) She is a child of the 30s.
59) I saw the white flowers in the meadows.
60) They admired his mane of white hair.

61) My grandfather is in the hospital.
62) He was browsing among the second hand books.
63) My uncle has been ill for many years.
64) We are flying at an unknown altitude.
65) The wife of a rich man was on her deathbed.

233) ENGLISH: SIMPLE SENTENCES (elementary)

Represent the constituent structures of the following sentences using phrase markers.

1) Her playing was an entertainment for our friends.
2) She sang "Yellow Rose of Texas".
3) Girls should sing hymns.
4) She was married to a former mathematical prodigy.
5) Mary worked as a dietician.
6) Ironical ovservations are a habit with him.
7) I arranged it.
8) I am at a crucial point.
9) Dotty was afraid.
10) The house was on fairly low-lying ground.

11) The pump had to work most of the time.
12) We had a dark rainy January.
13) Hugo and I felt gloomy.
14) The sound of the pump had replaced Dotty's piano-playing.
15) Its entire cost went onto our electricity bill.
16) Best thing could happen to it.
17) Hugo blew smoke in her face.
18) People around us were looking stern and gratified.
19) It was the silence.
20) The quarrel between us subsided in the excitement of moving.

234) ENGLISH: COMPLEX SENTENCES (NON-FINITE CLAUSES) (intermediate)

Identify the non-finite clauses and comment on their structure. What syntactic functions do they perform?

1) The best thing would be to tell everybody.
2) Leaving the room, he tripped over the mat.
3) Covered with confusion, I interrupted my lecture.
4) With the tree grown tall, we get more shade.
5) The best thing would be for you to leave the room.

6) Defeated, he slunk from the hall.
7) Her aunt having left the room, I declared my love for Celia.
8) Rather than have John do it, I'd prefer to give the job to Mary.
9) It would be better for me to disappear.
10) For her husband to carry the parcels was unbearable humiliation.

235) ENGLISH: COMPLEX SENTENCES (FINITE CLAUSES)
(intermediate)

Indicate the component parts of the following sentences. What syntactic functions do the finite clauses perform within the complex sentences?

1) That we need more equipment is obvious.
2) I know that she is nasty.
3) The point is that we're leaving.
4) He gave whoever it was a cup of cocoa.
5) Because the soloist was ill, they cancelled the concert.
6) They went wherever they could find work.
7) When I last saw you, you lived in Toronto.
8) I can't imagine what made him do it.
9) He didn't start to read until he was ten years old.
10) If you treat her kindly, she'll do anything for you.
11) If she was awake, she certainly heard the noise.
12) I lent him the money because he needed it.
13) Just as a moth is attracted by a light, so he was fascinated by Sheila.

Analyse each sentence into clauses. Identify their type
(head clause, subordinate clause). Identify the conjunctions
and identify their type (coordinating, subordinating). What
functions do the subordinate clauses perform within the
complex sentences?

1) I know I am.
2) Hugo said I ought to phone the landlady.
3) The truth was we both shrank from a confrontation
   with the proprietor.
4) In the middle of the night in the middle of a rainy
   week I woke up and wondered what had wakened me.
5) Just before Clea was born we took over a house in
   North Vancouver belonging to some friends who had
   gone to England.
6) When I got to Lydia's house she was frying chicken in
   the kitchen.
7) She kept her fork with her and laid it on the tablecloth
   where it left a greasy stain.
8) He suggested she move out.
9) I admitted that I didn't know.
10) She had insisted I call my husband and ask him to bring
    the documents over.
11) We had arranged to show some slides before we knew
    you were coming.
12) Those drones are the laziest devils you ever saw.

VI. SYNTACTIC PROCESSES

237) <u>SPANISH: OBJECTS</u> (elementary)

Comment on the relationship between sentences with an
object marker and those without.

1) el muchacho mir-a el retrato
2) el muchacho mir-a a la profesora
3) la chica am-a la gatita
4) la chica am-a a-l soldado
5) la madre hall-ó la escoba
6) la madre hall-ó a la niña
7) el padre vi-ó el coche
8) el padre vi-ó a la madre
9) el médico toc-a la herida
10) el médico toc-a a la enferma

el~l	def.art.m.	niña	girl
muchacho	boy	padre	father
mir-	look at	vi-	see
-a	pres.tense	coche	car
retrato	portrait	médico	doctor
a	(pers.obj.marker)	toc-	touch
la	def.art.f.	herida	wound
profesora	lady teacher	madre	mother
chica	girl	hall-	find
am-	love	-ó	past tense
gatita	kitten	escoba	broom
soldado	soldier	enferma	patient

238) <u>RUMANIAN: ARTICLES</u> (elementary)

Analyse the relationship between sentences with a definite
article and those with an indefinite article.

1) om-ul spal-ă cal-ul
2) copil-ul i-a ham-ul
3) un cal măninc-ă furaj-ul
4) un ţaran cumpar-ă un viţel
5) amic-ul ved-e un cîine
6) redactor-ul ar-e un dicţionar
7) un servitor deschid-e dulap-ul
8) ofiţer-ul be-a ceai-ul
9) un oficial traduc-e jurnal-ul
10) dulgher-ul fac-e un scaun

-ul	def.art.m.	cîine	dog
un	indef.art.m.	redactor	editor
-ă~-a~-e	pres.tense	ar-	have
om	man	dicţionar	dictionary
spal-	wash	servitor	servant
cal	horse	deschid-	open
copil	boy	dulap	cupboard
i-	take	ofiţer	officer
ham	harness	be-	drink
măninc-	eat	ceai-	tea
furaj-	fodder	oficial	official
ţaran	peasant	traduc-	translate
cumpar-	buy	jurnal	newspaper
viţel	calf	dulgher	carpenter
amic	friend	fac-	make
ved-	see	scaun	chair

239) **GERMAN: TENSE** (elementary)

Account for the relationship between sentences with a
present tense and those with a perfect tense.

1) er sieh-t das Kind
2) er ha-t das Kind gesehen
3) sie koch-t das Ei
4) sie ha-t das Ei gekocht
5) der Mann schreib-t einen Brief
6) der Mann ha-t einen Brief geschrieben
7) die Frau lies-t das Buch
8) die Frau ha-t das Buch gelesen
9) er sing-t ein Lied
10) er ha-t ein Lied gesungen

-t	pres.tense	geschrieben	written
das	def.art.n.	Frau	lady
der	def.art.m.	lies-	read
die	def.art.f.	Buch	book
ein	indef.art.	gelesen	read)
er	he	sing-	sing
sie	she	Lied	song
sieh-	see	gesungen	sung
Kind	child	Ei	egg
ha-	have (aux.)	gekocht	cooked
gesehen	seen	schreib-	write
koch-	cook	Brief	letter

240) <u>SPANISH: REFLEXIVES</u> (elementary)

Account for the relationship between sentences with a
reflexive pronoun and those without.

1) el muchacho lav-a el perro
2) el muchacho se lav-a
3) la chica mir-a el retrato
4) la chica se mir-a
5) el peluquero afeit-a a-l cliente
6) el peluquero se afeit-a
7) la mujer pein-a a la hija
8) la mujer se pein-a
9) el médico cur-a a-l enfermo
10) el médico se cur-a

-a	pres.tense	muchacho	boy
el	def.art.masc.	lav-	wash
la	def.art.fem.	perro	dog
se	(reflexive)	chica	girl
mir-	look at	pein-	comb
retrato	picture	hija	daughter
peluquero	barber	médico	doctor
afeit-	shave	cur-	cure
cliente	customer	enfermo	sick man
mujer	woman		

241) **FRENCH: INFINITIVE PHRASES** (elementary)

Account for the relationship between sentences with infinitive phrases and sentences without.

1) il achèt-e la maison
2) il veut achet-er la maison
3) il parl-e français
4) il préfèr-e parler français
5) il nag-e
6) il sai-t nag-er
7) il march-e vite
8) il sembl-e march-er vite
9) il condui-t la voiture
10) il peu-t condu-ir la voiture

il	he	nag-	swim
-e~-t	pres.tense	sai-	know
-er~-ir	infinitive	march-	walk
la	def.art.fem.	vite	fast
achèt-	buy	sembl-	seem
maison	house	condui-	drive
parl-	speak	voiture	car
français	French	peu-	can
préfèr-	prefer		

242) <u>LEBANESE ARABIC: POSSESSION</u> (elementary)

Account for the relationship between sentences with possessed nouns and sentences without possessed nouns.

1) ?aḥmad dihin l-baab
2) ?aḥmad dihin l-beet
3) ?aḥmad dihin baab l-beet
4) l-bustaan kaan kbiir
5) l-ḥayṭ kaan kbiir
6) ḥayṭ l-bustaan kaan kbiir
7) l-?ibin raaḥ ʕa-beeruut
8) l-waziir raaḥ ʕa-beeruut
9) ?ibin l-waziir raaḥ ʕa-beeruut
10) faaṭma šaaf-it l-mara
11) faaṭma šaaf-it š-šeex
12) faaṭma šaaf-it mart š-šeex

l~š	def.art.	mara~-t	wife
ʕa	to	šeex	sheikh
-it	past tense (fem.)	?ibin	son
dihin	painted	raaḥ	went
baab	door	ʕa	to
beet	house	beeruut	Beirut
bustaan	garden	waziir	minister
kaan	was	faaṭma	Fatima
kbiir	big	šaaf	saw
ḥayṭ	wall		

243) <u>LEBANESE ARABIC:RELATIVE CLAUSES</u>(intermediate)

Account for the relationship between sentences with
relative clauses and sentences without relatives clauses.

1) ?aḥmad šaaf l-walad
2) ?aḥmad šaaf-u
3) ?aḥmad šaaf l-bint
4) ?aḥmad šaaf-a
5) l-walad kaan hawn
6) l-walad illi ?aḥmad šaaf-u kaan hawn
7) l-bint kaan-it hawn
8) l-bint illi ?aḥmad šaaf-a kaan-it hawn
9) ?aḥmad šaaf l-wlaad
10) ?aḥmad šaaf-un
11) l-wlaad kaan-u hawn
12) l-wlaad illi ?aḥmad šaaf-un kaan-u hawn

-u	obj.pro.m.sg.	hawn	here
-a	obj.pro.f.sg.	wlaad	children
-un	obj.pro.pl.	šaaf	saw
illi	relative pro.	walad	boy
-it	past tense (fem.)	bint	girl
-u	past tense (pl.)		

244) <u>LEBANESE ARABIC: ADJECTIVE PHRASES</u>
(intermediate)

Account for the differences between predicate adjectives
and attributive adjectives in the following sentences. What
is the deep structure of attributive adjectives and what are
the transformations necessary for producing the surface
structure?

1) l-walad iža
2) l-walad kaan kbiir
3) l-walad l-kbiir iža
4) l-bint iž-it
5) l-bint kaan-it kbiir-i
6) l-bint l-kbiir-i iž-it
7) l-beet kaan ?adiim
8) šif-t l-beet l-?adiim
9) s-sayyaara kaan-it ždiid-i
10) šif-t s-sayyaara ž-ždiid-i

l~s~ž	def.art.	kbiir	big
-it	past tense (fem.).	šif-	saw
-i	fem.adj.	?adiim	old
-t	past 1st sg.	sayyaara	car
iža	came	ždiid	new
beet	house	kaan	was

245) SWAHILI: OBJECT MARKERS (elementary)

Account for the relationship between sentences with object markers and those without object markers.

1) m-toto a-li-soma ki-tabu
2) m-toto a-li-ki-soma
3) m-toto a-li-kula n-dizi
4) m-toto a-li-i-kula
5) m-toto a-li-paraga m-ti
6) m-toto a-li-u-paraga
7) m-tu a-li-chukua ji-we
8) m-tu a-li-li-chukua
9) m-ke a-li-piga m-toto
10) m-ke a-li-m-piga

m-	noun marker, m-class	-toto	child
ki-	noun marker, ki-class	-soma	read
n-	noun marker, n-class	-tabu	book
ji-	noun marker, ji-class	-chukua	carry
a-	sub. marker, m-class	-dizi	banana
-li-	past tense	-paraga	climb
-ki-	obj. marker, ki-class	-we	stone
-li-	obj. marker, ji-class	-kula	eat
-i-	obj. marker, n-class	-ti	tree
-m-	obj. marker, m(1)-class	-piga	beat
-u-	obj. marker, m(2)-class	-ke	wife

246) SWAHILI: ADJECTIVES (intermediate)

Account for the relationship between sentences with predicate adjectives and those with attributive adjectives.

1) Ki-su ni Ki-dogo
2) Ki-su Ki-dogo Ki-na-faa
3) vi-su ni vi-dogo
4) vi-su vi-dogo vi-na-faa
5) m-ti ni m-dogo
6) m-ti m-dogo u-na-faa
7) mi-ti ni mi-dogo
8) mi-ti mi-dogo i-na-faa
9) wa-tu ni wa-dogo
10) wa-tu wa-dogo wa-na-faa

Ki-	sg.marker, Ki-class	ni	is/are
vi-	pl.marker, Ki-class	-su	knife
wa-	pl.marker, m_1-class	-dogo	small
mi-	sg.marker, mi-class	-faa	be useful
m-	sg.n.marker, m_2-class	-ti	tree
u-	sg.v.marker, m_2-class	-tu	person
na	pres.tense marker	i-	pl.v.marker, m_2-class

247) FRENCH: NEGATIVE (elementary)

Account for the relationship between positive sentences and
the corresponding negative sentences.

1) je vois l'enfant
    I see the child

2) je ne vois pas l'enfant
    I don't see the child

3) j'ai vu l'enfant
    I have seen the child

4) je n'ai pas vu l'enfant
    I have not seen the child

5) je peux parler allemand
    I can speak German

6) je ne peux pas parler allemand
    I can't speak German

7) je suis heureux
    I am happy

8) je ne suis pas heureux
    I am not happy

9) je suis allé
    I have gone

10) je ne suis pas allé
    I have not gone

248)   <u>SPANISH: NEGATIVE</u> (intermediate)

Account for the relationship between positive sentences and
the corresponding negative sentences.

1)   veo algo
     I see something

2)   no veo nada
     I see nothing

3)   amo a alguien
     I love someone

4)   no amo a nadie
     I love no one

5)   canto siempre
     I always sing

6)   no canto nunca
     I never sing

7)   hay algún libro
     there is some book

8)   no hay ningún libro
     there is no book

249) SPANISH: SUBORDINATE CLAUSES (intermediate)

Account for the relationship between sentences with subordinate clauses and those without.

1) habla español
   he speaks Spanish

2) espero que hable español
   I hope that he speaks Spanish

3) tiene dinero
   he has money

4) dudo que tenga dinero
   I doubt that he has money

5) está aquí
   he is here

6) es mejor que esté aquí
   it is better that he be here

7) canta siempre
   she always sings

8) me gusta que cante siempre
   it pleases me that she always sings

9) vive en paz
   he lives in peace

10) !ojalá que viva en paz!
    may he live in peace!

250) <u>LATIN: SUBORDINATE CLAUSES</u> (intermediate)

Account for the relationship between sentences with finite verbs and similar sentences with infinitives.

1) Mīlitēs pugnant
   The soldiers are fighting

2) Canēs lātrant
   The dogs are barking

3) Custōdēs stant in templō
   The guards are standing in the temple

4) Uxōrēs lacrimant
   The wives are weeping

5) Hostēs properant
   The enemies are hurrying

1) Dīcit mīlitēs pugnāre
   He says that the soldiers are fighting

2) Dīcit canēs lātrāre
   He says that the dogs are barking

3) Dīcit custōdēs stāre in templō
   He says that the guards are standing in the temple

4) Dīcit uxōrēs lacrimāre
   He says that the wives are weeping

5) Dīcit hostēs properāre
   He says that the enemies are hurrying

251)   POLISH: DISJUNCTIVE QUESTIONS (intermediate)

Account for the relationship between declarative sentences
and the corresponding interrogative sentences.

Statements:

1)   Jones jest albo detektywem albo policjantem.
     Jones is either a detective or a policeman.

2)   Nasza June albo czyta książkę albo pisze list.
     Our June is either reading a book or writing a letter.

3)   Pan Kaler jest albo w biurze albo w domu.
     Mr. Caler is either in his office or at home.

4)   Maria ma albo lekcję muzyki albo randkę.
     Maria has either a music lesson or a date.

5)   Bydło hoduje się albo na mleko albo na mięso.
     The cow is grown either for milk or for meat.

Questions:

1)   Czy Jones jest detektywem, czy policjantem?
     Is Jones a detective or a policeman?

2)   Czy June czyta książkę, czy pisze list?
     Is June reading a book or writing a letter?

3)   Czy pan Kaler jest w biurze, czy w domu?
     Is Mr. Caler in his office or at home?

4)   Czy Maria ma lekcję muzyki, czy randkę?
     Does Maria have a music lesson or a date?

5)   Czy bydło hoduje się na mleko, czy na mięso?
     Is the cow grown for milk or for meat?

252) GERMAN: INDIRECT STATEMENTS (intermediate)

Make an analysis of the difference between direct statements and indirect statements in German. Fill in the blanks with the appropriate form of the verb in both sections and suggest transformations to account for the differences.

Direct Statements

1) Ich werde es vergessen
   I will forget it

2) Ich_____es versuchen
   I will look for it

3) Wir werden_____trinken
   We will drink it

4) _____werden es sehen
   We will see it

5) Wir_____es kaufen
   We will buy it

6) Ich_____nehmen
   I will take it

7) _____werde es machen
   I will do it

8) Wir werden es essen
   We will eat it

9) _____werde_____verlassen
   I will leave it

10) Ich_____bringen
    I will bring it

Indirect Statements

1) Er sagte, dass ich es vergessen würde
   He said I would forget it

2) Er sagte,_____ es versuchen würde
   He said I would look for it

3) Er sagte,_____ wir es trinken _____
   He said we will drink it

4) Er sagte, dass_____
   He said I would see it

5) Er sagte,_____ es_____
   He said we would buy it

6) Er sagte, dass ich es nehmen_____
   He said I would take it

7) Er sagte,_____wir_____machen___
   _____
   He said we would do it

8) Er sagte,_____ich_____
   He said I would eat it

9) Er sagte, _____wir_____es_____
   _____verlassen_____
   He said we would leave it

10) Er sagte,_____ würde
    He said I would bring it

253) <u>BULGARIAN: VERBAL TENSE</u> (elementary)

Account for the relationship between simple declarative sentences and the corresponding future, negative, interrogative, and negative-interrogative sentences.

(A)

1) az rabót$^\gamma$a
   I work

2) az xod$^\gamma$a
   I walk

3) az piša
   I write

4) az svir$^\gamma$a
   I play (music)

5) az gub$^\gamma$a
   I lose

(B)

1) az šče rabót$^\gamma$a
   I will work

2) az šče xod$^\gamma$a
   I will walk

3) az šče piša
   I will write

4) az šče svir$^\gamma$a
   I will play

5) az šče gub$^\gamma$a
   I will lose

(C)

1) az nʸama da rabótʸa
   I won't work

2) az nʸama da xodʸa
   I won't walk

3) az nʸama da piša
   I won't write

4) az nʸama da svirʸa
   I won't play

5) az nʸama da gubʸa
   I won't lose

(D)

1) rabotʸa li
   do I work?

2) xodʸa li
   do I walk?

3) piša li
   do I write

4) svirʸa li
   do I play?

5) gubʸa li
   do I lose?

(E)

1) az šče rabot^{y}a li
   will I work?

2) az šče xod^{y}a li
   will I walk?

3) az šče piša li
   will I write?

4) az šče svir^{y}a li
   will I play?

5) az šče gub^{y}a li
   will I lose?

(F)

1) az n^{y}ama li da rabot^{y}a
   won't I work?

2) az n^{y}ama li da xod^{y}a
   won't I walk?

3) az n^{y}ama li da piša
   won't I write?

4) az n^{y}ama li da svir^{y}a
   won't I play?

5) az n^{y}ama li da gub^{y}a
   won't I lose?

254) <u>CZECH: INFINITIVE CLAUSES</u> (intermediate)

Account for the relationship between infinitive sentences
and subordinate clauses in Czech.

<u>Czech infinitive clauses</u>

1) doktor se rozhodl višetřit yanu
   The doctor decided to examine Jana

2) eva xt^yela studovat filozofiyi
   Eva wanted to study philosophy

3) barbora odmi:tla vařit ob^yet
   Barbara refused to cook the lunch

4) yan b^yežel varovat sousedi
   Jan ran to warn the neighbours

5) liška se snažila xit^yit zayi:ce
   The fox tried to capture the hare

<u>Czech subordinate clauses</u>

1) přemluvila ysem doktora abi višetřil yanu
   I persuaded the doctor to examine Jana.

2) matka řekla ev^ye abi studovala filozofiyi
   Mother told Eva to study philosophy

3) muš fska:zal barboře abi uvařila ob^yet
   The husband sent a message to Barbara to cook the
   lunch

4) křičeli ysme na yana abi varoval sousedi
   We shouted at Jan to warn the neighbours

5) lofci podn^yecovali lišku abi xit^yila zayi:ce
   The hunters kept inciting the fox to catch the hare

255) CZECH: TENSE AND ASPECT (intermediate)

Account for the relationships between the sentences in sections A, B, C and D.

(A)

1) mariye xce či:st roma:n
    Maria wants to read a novel

2) kopa:č xce kopat strouhu
    The ditch-digger wants to dig a ditch

3) herečka xce hra:t ofeliyi
    The actress wants to play Ophelia

4) na:mořn^{y}i:k xce plout k ostrovu
    The sailor wants to sail to the island

5) muš xce psa:t dopis žen^{y}e
    The man wants to write a letter to his wife.

(B)

1) mariye čte roma:n
    Maria reads a novel

2) kopa:č kope strouhu
    The ditch-digger digs a ditch

3) herečka hraye ofeliyi
    The actress plays Ophelia

4) na:mořn^{y}i:k pluye k ostrovu
    The sailor sails to the island

5) muš pi:še dopis žen^{y}e
    The man writes a letter to his wife

(C)

1) mariye bude či:st roma:n
   Maria will read a novel

2) kopa:č bude kopat strouhu
   The ditch-digger will dig a ditch

3) herečka bude hra:t ofeliyi
   The actress will play Ophelia

4) na:mořⁿyi:k bude plout k ostrovu
   The sailor will sail to the island

5) muš bude psa:t dopis žen^ye
   The man will write a letter to his wife

(D)

1) mariye dočte roma:n
   Maria will finish reading a novel

2) kopa:č dokope strouhu
   The ditch-digger will finish digging the ditch

3) herečka dohraye ofeliyi
   The actress will finish playing Ophilia

4) na:mořⁿyi:k dopluye k ostrovu
   The sailor will reach the island

5) muš dopi:še dopis žen^ye
   The man will finish writing a letter to his wife

256) CZECH: NEGATIVE (elementary)

Account for the relationship between positive sentences and their corresponding negatives.

1) petr sta:l za dveřmi
    Peter stood behind the door

2) barbora pila mle:ko
    Barbara drank some milk

3) ivana zbožnʸovala filmove: hvʸezdi
    Ivana adored movie stars

4) yan obʸedval v restauraci
    Jan had his lunch in a restaurant

5) milan studoval hudbu
    Milan studied music

1) nʸigdo nesta:l za dveřmi
    Nobody stood behind the door

2) nʸigdo nepil mle:ko
    Nobody drank milk

3) nʸigdo nezbožnʸoval filmove: hvʸezdi
    Nobody adored movie stars

4) nʸigdo neobʸedval v restauraci
    Nobody had his lunch in a restauant

5) nʸigdo nestudoval hudbu
    Nobody studied music

257) CZECH: RELATIVE CLAUSES (intermediate)

Account for the relationships between the sentences in sections A, B and C, and explain the change in the order of elements.

(A) 1) to dʸéfče úhodʸilo toho múže
        That girl hit that man

2) ten múš pótporoval to dˠí:tˠe
   That man supported that child

3) ta dá:ma nósila tu páruku
   That lady wore that wig

4) ten máyitel pródal ten ópxot
   That owner sold that store

5) ta kárkulka pótkala toho vlka
   That Little Red Riding Hood met that wolf

(B) 1) to dˠéfče yey úhodˠilo
   That girl hit him

2) ten múš ye pótporoval
   That man supported it

3) ta dá:ma yi nósila
   That lady wore it (fem. inan.)

4) ten máyitel yey pródal
   That owner sold it (masc.inan.)

5) ta kárkulka yey pótkala
   That Little Red Riding Hood met him

(C) 1) múš có yey to dˠéfče úhodilo
   man that him that girl hit

2) dˠí:tˠe có ye ten múš pótporoval
   child that it that man supported

3) páruka có yi ta dá:ma nósila
   wig that her that lady wore

4) ópxot có yey ten máyitel pródal
   store that him (inan.) that owner sold

5) vlk có yey ta kárkulka pótkala
   wolf that him that Little Red Riding Hood met

258)   BASQUE: RELATIVE CLAUSES (intermediate)

Account for the relationship between sentences with main
clauses and sentences with relative clauses in Basque.

Main clauses

1) gizona ona da
   the man is good

2) sagarrak ontuak dira
   the apples are ripe

3) anderea serora da
   the lady is a nun

4) gizona zuhaitza da
   the man is mean

5) semea apheza du
   his son is a priest

6) liburu hau gurea da
   the book is ours

7) semea handia da
   his son is tall

8) arreba abogadu du
   his sister is a lawyer

Relative clauses

1) ona den gizona
   the man who is good

2) ontuak diren sagarrak
   the apples that are ripe

3) serora den anderea
   the lady who is a nun

4) zuhaitza den gizona
the man who is mean

5) semea apheza duen aita
the father whose son is a priest

6) hau gurea den liburu
the book that is ours

7) handia den semea
the son who is tall

8) arreba abogadu duena mutiko
the boy whose sister is a lawyer

259) ENGLISH: AUXILIARIES AND TENSE (intermediate)

Attempt to write a phrase-structure grammar for the verb phrases in the following sentences.

1) Amanda jogs.

2) The radicals protest again.

3) Amanda jogged in the park.

4) Paul has finished the work.

5) Amanda and Paul have written an essay.

6) The student had protested.

7) The professors had marked the exams.

8) Paul is jogging.

9) The mice are eating the crumbs.

10) The deer was running

11) The children were playing in the yard.

12) Paul has been exercising for two months.

13) The diplomats have been discussing the agreement.

14) Amanda had been jogging.

15) The rats had been contaminating our waters.

16) Paul will come soon.

17) Amanda and Paul will be exercise.

18) Ian would consider your suggestion.

19) The students would finish their studies.

20) The children will have been playing.

21) The mouse will have been eating the crumbs.

22) The doctor would have been prescribing aspirin.

23) The doctors would have been curing everybody.

260) <u>ENGLISH: NEGATIVE SENTENCES</u> (elementary)

Generate the following negative sentences.

1) You cannot choose your own name.

2) Lydia hasn't changed at all.

3) The coffee is not always bitter.

4) Children mustn't talk with their mouths full.

5) The tourists were not equipped with tape recorders.

6) The picture has not been hanging in the bedroom since Christmas.

7) The neighbours haven't been to their cottage yet.

8) Robert won't ever tan.

9) The weather is not getting better.

10) The men aren't expecting any trouble.

261) ENGLISH: QUESTIONS (elementary)

Generate the following interrogative sentences.

1) Has he had a letter from Lucy?

2) Are these women playing bridge this evening?

3) Must you go home now?

4) Can you pass me a slice of bread?

5) Has Laura a daughter?

6) Will the garden-party take place anyway?

7) Haven't you heard the news?

8) Isn't she a good-looking child?

9) Won't you help me?

10) Couldn't you have written at least a post card?

262) **ENGLISH: "DO" AUXILIARY** (elementary)

Generate the following sentences.

1) Did Laura brush her hair?

2) Don't you feel anything for them?

3) Does she see the tall dark fellow in the corner?

4) Do I still copy my mother's voice?

5) Does her upbringing make her wonder about this?

6) Doesn't Paul fancy her any more?

7) I do want to stay here and help you.

8) His followers do have faith in him.

9) Don't make any more mistakes!

10) Do visit us again!

263) **ENGLISH: TAG** (intermediate)

Generate the following sentences.

1) You will hear the bell, won't you?

2) She is a pretty good actress, isn't she?

3) Hugo does love his little sister, doesn't he?

4) The children didn't know her, did they?

5) My brother has gone home, hasn't he?

6) You were passing the shop yesterday, weren't you?

7) Mrs. Sheridan joined them, didn't she?

8) The telephone rings, doesn't it?

9) Mabel doesn't feel quite safe, does she?

10) His life won't be ruined so easily, will it?

264) ENGLISH: WH- QUESTIONS (elementary)

Generate the following wh-questions.

1) What does Lucy say?

2) Why had he not greeted my friend?

3) Where did Dr. Ferguson put the injection?

4) Which duck walked into the pond?

5) How is the patient doing?

6) Why are you crying?

7) Which pattern has Leila chosen?

8) What do you ever see in him?

9) Where are the eggs?

10) Who was Harold's favorite coach?

265) ENGLISH: PASSIVE SENTENCES (elementary)

Generate the following passive sentences.

1) Georgiana was led over the threshold of the laboratory.

2) The extensive apartments were occupied by Aylmer Enterprises.

3) Great wonders were achieved by our new cosmetic products.

4) The attempt should be made at whatever risk.

5) Until now he has not been made aware of her tyrannizing influence.

6) The window was begrimed with the smoke of the furnace.

7) This single imperfection can be removed easily by every young intern.

8) The portrait is being effected by rays of light.

9) Your life will be prolonged for years by this liquid.

10) In this small vial is contained a gentle yet powerful fragrance.

11) It is not well done.

266) ENGLISH: REFLEXIVE PRONOUNS (elementary)

Generate the following reflexive sentences.

1) Sylvia will speak up for herself.

2) Little John hurt himself badly.

3) The children felt sleepy and Sylvia herself felt sleepy.

4) The rabbit tore itself free.

5) We mustn't deceive ourselves.

6) You and Ernie mustn't deceive yourselves.

7) No one should fool himself.

8) I have never been there myself.

9) Aunt Frederica was beside herself with rage.

10) Would not her grandmother blame herself?

267) ENGLISH: RELATIVE CLAUSES (intermediate)

Generate the following sentences with relative clauses.

1) She was a woman who was able to keep things in order.

2) Mrs. Mooney, who took all the money, set up a boarding house in the nearest town.

3) The lady's son, who was clerk to a commission agent, had bad reputation.

4) Her eyes, which were gray, had a habit of glancing upwards.

5) This habit, which made her look like a little madonna, Chris disliked intensely.

6) Robert passed Jack, who was coming up from the pantry.

7) How many men that she knew would have done that?

8) John, whose eyes quickly scanned the tennis court, saw her immediately.

9) This horse is the animal which controls the others.

10) The cap that he held in his hand was dirty and torn.

268) <u>ENGLISH: ADVERBIAL CLAUSES</u> (intermediate)

Generate the following sentences with adverbial clauses.

1) The houskeeper gave her credit, as I had instructed.

2) When the table was cleared, she began her interview.

3) The old woman counted her cards before sending the servants up to their rooms.

4) His hand had been so unsteady that he had to stop shaving.

5) While he was sitting helplessly, Mary tapped at his door.

6) When Jack was dressed, he went over to her.

7) If you stop playing, you'll lead a very strenuous life.

8) Joe wasn't satisfied until the company finally paid him his back salary.

9) He sat in the bailiff's room because he wanted the job.

10) The green bushes bowed down as though they had been visited by archangels.

269) ENGLISH:VERB COMPLEMENT CLAUSES(intermediate)

Comment on the structure of the following sentences.

1) Polly decided when to be lenient and when to be stern.

2) She knew she would win.

3) Mother did not think that he could face the publicity.

4) He scarcely knew what he was eating.

5) Mary said that the missus wanted to see him.

6) The daughter wanted to prove how happy she was.

7) See if my coat needs pressing.

8) The cook asks if you have the bread for the sandwiches.

9) The children knew that she hadn't gotten the toys.

10) That is what you will do.

270) ENGLISH: SENTENCES WITH INFINITIVES

Comment on the following infinitive sentences.

1) City people yearn to live on a farm.

2) Kids like to eat.

3) We try to study the bees.

4) I hesitate to tell everybody.

5) I hasten to give you this good news.

6) Peter failed to pass the test.

7) The professor expected to win the Nobel prize.

8) We will all strive to do better next time.

9) I hate to lose.

10) We hope to arrive there tomorrow.

VII. SOUND CHANGE

271) OLD ICELANDIC (elementary)

In the following problem, explain the change or changes that Proto-Germanic */o:/ underwent in Old Icelandic.

	Proto-Gmc	Old Icelandic	
1)	fo:tiz	fö:tr	feet
2)	bo:kiz	bö:kr	books
3)	bo:ndiz	bö:ndr	inhabitants
4)	bo:tiz	bö:tr	compensations
5)	glo:θiz	glö:ᵭr	embers
6)	klo:wiz	klö:r	claws
7)	ro:tiz	rö:tr	roots
8)	θro:wiz	θrö:r	troughs
9)	o:θi	ö:ᵭi	fury
10)	o:skja	ö:skja	to wish
11)	do:maz	do:mr	court
12)	go:daz	go:ᵭr	good
13)	hlo:wan	hlo:a	to low
14)	fo:tum	fo:tum	feet (dat.)
15)	ho:faz	ho:fr	hoof
16)	hro:kaz	ho:fr	rook
17)	mo:θaz	mo:ᵭr	wrath

272) OLD ICELANDIC (elementary)

In the following problem, explain the change or changes that Proto-Germanic */a/ underwent in Old Icelandic.

	Proto-Gmc	Old Icelandic	
1)	armum	ɔrmum	arms (dat.)
2)	staθum	stɔᵭum	places (dat.)
3)	saku	sɔk	accusations
4)	salum	sɔlum	halls (dat.)

-221-

5)	landu	lɔnd	lands
6)	handu	hɔnd	hands
7)	barnum	bɔrnum	children (dat.)
8)	grabum	grɔfum	graves (dat.)
9)	manu	mɔn	manes
10)	nasu	nɔs	noses
11)	graban	grafa	to dig
12)	haban	hafa	to have
13)	armaz	armr	arm
14)	dagaz	dagr	day
15)	hwalaz	hvalr	whale
16)	swanaz	svanr	swan
17)	staθaz	staăr	place
18)	naglaz	nagl	nails

273) <u>SPANISH</u> (elementary)

In the following problem, explain the change or changes that earlier Vulgar Latin /a/ underwent in Spanish. Notice that the forms are presented in traditional orthography. The letter 'c' is pronounced [θ] before /i/ or /e/ in Spanish, otherwise [k] in both Spanish and Latin. Spanish 'qu' is pronounced [k].

	Vulgar Lt.	Spanish	
1)	caballariu	caballero	horseman
2)	area	era	threshing floor
3)	glarea	glera	graval
4)	caseu	queso	cheese
5)	basiu	beso	kiss
6)	cerasea	cereza	cherry
7)	sapiat	sepa	know (subjunctive)
8)	capiat	quepa	fit (subjunctive)
9)	porcariu	porquero	swineherd
10)	mansione	mesón	house

11)	campu	campo	field
12)	granu	grano	grain
13)	sale	sal	salt
14)	arbore	árbol	tree
15)	cantu	canto	I sing
16)	manu	mano	hand
17)	aqua	agua	water
18)	altu	alto	high
19)	saltare	saltar	to jump
20)	carru	carro	wagon

274) OLD HIGH GERMAN (elementary)

In the following problem, explain the change or changes that early Germanic */i/ underwent in Old High German. Notice that the Old High German is presented in a conventionalized orthography, in which the letter 'c' is pronounced [k].

	Early Gmc	OHG	
1)	wira	wer	man
2)	kwika	quec	alive
3)	libēn	lebēn	to live
4)	nista	nest	nest
5)	likkōn	leckōn	to lick
6)	spikka	spec	lard
7)	tikko	zecke	tick
8)	blika	blech	tin
9)	wiko	wehha	week
10)	nimiθ	nimit	he takes
11)	bitjan	bitten	to ask
12)	ist	ist	he is
13)	wisku	wisc	rag
14)	silubra	silbar	silver
15)	sibja	sippa	kinsman
16)	sitjan	siȝȝan	to sit
17)	hitjo	hiȝȝa	heat
18)	hrinθiz	rind	ox
19)	wristi	rist	instep

275) <u>MALTESE</u> (elementary)

In the following problem, explain the change or changes that the Old Arabic long vowel /aa/ underwent in Maltese. The consonants with a subposed dot (C̣) are laryngealized consonants, pronounced with the back of the tongue raised.

	Old Arabic	Maltese	
1)	kaan	kien	he was
2)	baab	biep	door
3)	faas	fies	axe
4)	Jaab	Jiep	he brought
5)	kaal	kiel	he ate
6)	laabis	liebes	dressed
7)	maat	miet	he died
8)	naas	nies	people
9)	naašif	niešef	dry
10)	taaJ	tieč	wedding
11)	ṭaar	taar	he flew
12)	ṣaab	saap	he found
13)	ṣaafi	saafi	clear
14)	ṣaam	saam	he fasted
15)	ḍaaq	daa?	he tasted
16)	daar	daar	house
17)	r̩aas	raas	head
18)	xaaṭ	haat	he sewed
19)	ḥaakim	haakem	governor
20)	naar̩	naar	fire

276) <u>RUMANIAN</u> (elementary)

In the following problem, explain the change or changes that Pre-Rumanian /ea/ underwent in modern Rumanian

	Pre-Rum.	Rumanian	
1)	featə	fatə	girl
2)	vearə	varə	summer
3)	measə	masə	table
4)	kəmeašə	kəmaše	shirt

5)	beala	bala	animal
6)	peara	para	pear
7)	peata	pata	kitchen
8)	feamen	famen	womanly
9)	vearga	varga	twig
10)	beata	bata	stripe
11)	seara	seara	evening
12)	kreasta	kreasta	crest
13)	kreada	kreada	believe
14)	neagra	neagra	black (fem.)
15)	nea	nea	snow
16)	šea	šea	seat
17)	šteaza	šteaza	splinter
18)	stea	stea	star
19)	teaka	teaka	sheath
20)	teara	teara	cloth

277) **RUMANIAN** (elementary)

In the following problem, explain the change or changes that Pre-Rumanian final */u/ underwent in modern Rumanian.

	Pre-Rum	Rumanian	
1)	nigru	negru	black
2)	makru	makru	thin
3)	kodru	kodru	forest
4)	lukru	lukru	gain
5)	duplu	duplu	double
6)	aspru	aspru	harsh
7)	intru	intru	inside
8)	vetlu	vekļu	old
9)	oklu	okļu	eye
10)	unglu	ungļu	angle

11)	vinu	vin	wine
12)	kɔrpu	korp	body
13)	fruktu	frupt	fruit
14)	ursu	urs	bear
15)	kulu	kur	ass
16)	pɔpulu	popor	people
17)	latu	lat	side
18)	umeru	umər	shoulder
19)	kampu	kämp	field
20)	kredu	kred	I believe

278) MALTESE (intermediate)

In the following problem, explain the change or changes undergone by the Old Arabic vowels when they are in the first syllable of these words. As in the earlier Maltese problem, a single vowel is short, a double vowel is long.

	Old Arabic	Maltese	
1)	naǯiif	ndayf	clean
2)	ḥisaab	hsiep	thought
3)	buḥayra	phayra	lake
4)	ṣabaaḥ	zbieh	pretty (pl.)
5)	salaam	sliem	peace
6)	ṭufuuliyya	tfuuliya	childhood
7)	makaan	mkien	nowhere
8)	munaǯǯaf	mnaddaf	cleaned
9)	musaafir	msiefer	departed
10)	šariik	šriik	partner
11)	taḥriik	tahriik	movement
12)	baṭṭiix	bettieh	watermelon
13)	barquuq	ber?uu?	apricot
14)	mismaar̩	musmaar	nail
15)	maskiin	miskiin	poor
16)	kibriit	kubriit	sulphur
17)	munxaar	munhaar	saw
18)	ḥusbaan	hozbien	calculation
19)	quddaam	?oddiem	before
20)	maʕruuf	maruuf	known

21)	miilaad	miliet	Christmas
22)	Jiiraan	Jirien	neighbors
23)	niiraan	nirien	flames
24)	buuṣuuf	busuuf	beetle
25)	mawluud	muluud	born

279) EGYPTIAN ARABIC (elementary)

In the following problem, explain the change or changes that
the Old Arabic long vowels underwent in Egyptian Arabic.

	Old Arabic	Egyptian Arabic	
1)	biːrna	birna	our well
2)	daːrkum	darkum	your (pl.) house
3)	banaːtha	banatha	her daughters
4)	fuːlna	fulna	our beans
5)	gamuːskum	gamuskum	your (pl.) buffaloes
6)	yiḥuːšni	yiḥušni	he prevents me
7)	tiːnha	tinha	her figs
8)	ṣuːfhum	ṣufhum	their wool
9)	waziːrna	wazirna	our minister
10)	filuːskum	filuskum	your (pl.) money
11)	biːru	biːru	his well
12)	zaːr	zaːr	he visited
13)	finJaːni	fingaːni	my cup
14)	quːm	ʔuːm	stand up!
15)	kitaːbak	kitaːbak	your book
16)	madiːna	madiːna	city
17)	kaθiːr	kitiːr	much
18)	waːḥid	waːḥid	one
19)	ṭariːq	ṭariː?	road
20)	ɣaːb	ɣaːb	he was absent

280) <u>LEBANESE ARABIC</u> (elementary)

In the following problem, explain the change or changes that
the Old Arabic short vowels underwent in Lebanese Arabic.

	Old Arabic	Lebanese	
1)	raʔs	ra:s	head
2)	biʔr	bi:r	well
3)	luʔluʔ	lu:lu	pearl
4)	yaʔkul	ya:kul	he eats
5)	Jiʔt	ži:t	I came
6)	faʔr	fa:r	rat
7)	ǎiʔb	di:b	jackal
8)	ziʔbaq	zi:baʔ	mercury
9)	šaʔn	(ʕa)ša:n	affair
10)	luʔm	lu:m	wickedness
11)	bint	bint	girl
12)	taḥt	taḥt	under
13)	ʕurs	ʕurs	wedding
14)	kalb	kalb	dog
15)	šaʕb	šaʕb	people
16)	baqar	baʔar	cattle
17)	lift	lift	turnips
18)	ʔili	ʔili	to me
19)	ʔuxti	ʔuxti	my sister
20)	muhim	muhim	important

281) SPANISH (elementary)

In the following problem, explain the change or changes that the initial clusters of Vulgar Latin underwent in Spanish. Notice that both the Vulgar Latin and the Spanish are presented in traditional orthography, which does not affect the solution to the problem.

	Vlg.Latin	Spanish	
1)	spissu	espeso	thick
2)	spica	espiga	ear of grain
3)	sperare	esperar	to hope
4)	stare	estar	to stand
5)	scala	escala	ladder
6)	scola	escuela	school
7)	scribere	escribir	to write
8)	squama	escama	scab
9)	stagnu	estaño	tin
10)	strictu	estrecho	narrow
11)	promptu	pronto	ready
12)	braca	braga	pants
13)	bruma	bruma	mist
14)	brachiu	brazo	arm
15)	tres	tres	three
16)	dracone	dragón	dragon
17)	crispu	crespo	wary
18)	granu	grano	grain
19)	fricare	fregar	to rub

282) LEBANESE ARABIC (elementary)

In the following problem, explain the change or changes that the final consonant clusters of Old Arabic underwent in Lebanese Arabic.

	Old Arabic	Lebanese	
1)	ʔaǩl	ʔaǩil	food
2)	ʔism	ʔisim	name
3)	qabl	ʔabil	before
4)	qaṣr	ʔaṣir	castle
5)	duhn	dihin	paint
6)	fiǩr	fiǩir	mind
7)	Jism	Žisim	body
8)	maṣr	maṣir	Egypt
9)	miθl	mitil	like
10)	ǯaqn	diʔin	chin
11)	bint	bint	girl
12)	xubz	xubz	bread
13)	ʕind	ʕind	with
14)	ʕabd	ʕabd	slave
15)	šaxṣ	šaxṣ	person
16)	Janb	Žamb	side
17)	ɣarb	ɣarb	west
18)	dars	dars	lesson
19)	bard	bard	cold
20)	ʔalquds	lʔuds	Jerusalem

283) **PORTUGESE** (intermediate)

In the following problem, explain the change or changes that Proto-Romance */n/ underwent in Portuguese.

	Proto-Rom.	Portugese	
1)	kantare	kãtar	to sing
2)	lɔnga	lõga	long
3)	infɛrnu	ĩfernu	hell
4)	dɛnte	dẽte	tooth
5)	ɔmine	ɔmẽ	man
6)	fine	fĩ	end
7)	tɛne	tẽ	he holds
8)	non	nõ	no
9)	kɥen	kẽ	who
10)	kun	kõ	with
11)	tɛnere	tɛr	to have
12)	vɛnire	vir	to come
13)	vena	veia	vein
14)	arena	areia	sand
15)	kena	seia	dinner
16)	luna	lua	moon
17)	ponere	por	to place
18)	femina	femea	woman
19)	katena	kadeia	chain
20)	panatarʲu	padeiru	baker

284) SPANISH (elementary)

In the following problem, explain the change or changes that Proto-Romance */p/, */t/, and */k/ have undergone in Spanish. Notice that the Spanish is given in traditional orthography, in which the letter 'c' is pronounced [k].

	Proto-Rom.	Spanish	
1)	tepidu	tibio	warm
2)	sapone	sabón	soap
3)	sapere	saber	to know
4)	ripa	riba	bank
5)	skopa	escoba	broom
6)	seta	seda	silk
7)	pratu	prado	meadow
8)	muta	muda	mute
9)	ɥita	vida	life
10)	natare	nadar	to swim
11)	fɔku	fuego	fire
12)	formika	hormiga	ant
13)	pakare	pagar	to pay
14)	frikare	fregar	to rub
15)	sekuru	seguro	secure
16)	hɔspite	huésped	guest
17)	kɔsta	cuesta	side
18)	muska	mosca	fly
19)	gustare	gustar	to please
20)	peskare	pescar	to fish

285) ITALIAN (elementary)

In the following problem, explain the change or changes that Proto-Romance */k/ and */g/ have undergone in Italian. Notice that the Italian is given in traditional orthography. The letter 'c' is pronounced [k], and the combination 'gn' is pronounced [ɲ̃].

	Proto-Rom.	Italian	
1)	nɔkte	notte	night
2)	lakte	latte	milk
3)	rɛktu	retto	upright
4)	strikto	stretto	narrow
5)	pɛktus	petto	chest
6)	tɛksere	tessere	to weave
7)	fraksinu	frassino	ash tree
8)	seksaginta	sessanta	sixty
9)	seksu	sesso	sex
10)	taksu	tasso	yew tree
11)	pugnu	pugno	fist
12)	pignu	pegno	pawn
13)	lignu	legno	wood
14)	signu	segno	sign
15)	kɔgnata	cognata	sister-in-law
16)	amiku	amico	friend
17)	sekuru	sicuro	sure
18)	negare	negare	to deny
19)	rogare	rogare	ask
20)	gola	gola	throat

286) MONTAGNAIS (elementary)

In the following problem, explain the change or changes that Proto-Algonquian */šK/ has undergone in Montagnais.

	Proto-Alg.	Montagnais	
1)	neškašya	nəxəši	fingernail
2)	neto:škwani	ntu:xən	elbow
3)	wete:šKani	ute:xan	his horn
4)	eškwete:wi	ixute:w	fire
5)	maškwehsyi	maxušu	grass
6)	neški:nšekwi	nissiši:kw	my eye
7)	aškipowa	assipu	he eats raw meat
8)	maškye:kwi	masse:kw	swamp
9)	ka:škipya:ta-	ka:ssipita-	he scratches it
10)	pa:škesikani	pa:ssikan	gun

287) SWAHILI (elementary)

In the following problem, explain the change or changes that Proto-Bantu */p/, */t/, and */k/ have undergone in Swahili.

	Proto-Ban.	Swahili	
1)	muɣokî	moši	smoke
2)	mukîpa	mšipa	vein
3)	muakî	mwaši	mason
4)	mupikî	mpiši	cook
5)	muandikî	mwandiši	writer
6)	pîtî	fisi	hyena
7)	mutetî	mtesi	quarrelsome
8)	mufuatî	mfuasi	follower
9)	-tîya	-sia	to leave
10)	kitîma	kisima	well
11)	-pîka	-fika	arrive
12)	mulapî	mlafi	glutton
13)	mulipî	mlifi	payer

14)	-pîna	-fina	pinch
15)	-pîta	-fita	hide
16)	-tatu	-tatu	three
17)	-ƙula	-ƙua	grow
18)	-pumula	-pumua	nest
19)	muƙila	mƙia	tail
20)	muti	mti	tree
21)	-pindua	-pindua	turn around

288) LATIN (elementary)

In the following problem, explain the change or changes that Proto-Indo-European */s/ has undergone in Latin. Notice that the Latin is presented in traditional orthography; this, however, does not affect the solution.

	Proto-IE	Latin	
1)	eusō	ūrō	I burn
2)	aj̣oses	āēris	metal (gen.)
3)	bhlōses	flōris	flower (gen.)
4)	disemō	dirimō	I separate
5)	esāt	erat	he was
6)	ƙu̯esur	queror	I complain
7)	ghesi	heri	yesterday
8)	ōses	ōris	mouth
9)	ōusā	ōra	edge
10)	sātis	satis	enough
11)	sacrodhōts	sacerdōs	priest
12)	salnes	salis	salt (gen.)
13)	gnēsƙō	nōscō	I know
14)	ghostis	hostis	enemy
15)	ƙatesna	catēna	chain
16)	ƙastrom	castrum	fort
17)	veidsō	vīsō	I inspect
18)	ƙu̯atso-	cāseus	cheese
19)	mej̣tsej̣	mīsī	sent

289) <u>ITALIAN</u> (elementary)

In the following problem, explain the change or changes that
Proto-Romance */k/ underwent in Italian. Notice that the
Italian is presented in traditional orthography, in which the
letter 'c' is pronounced [č] before 'e' and 'i', but is
pronounced [k] elsewhere.

	Proto-Rom.	Italian	
1)	kɛrvu	cervo	stag
2)	kɪlʲu	ciglio	eyelid
3)	kera	cera	wax
4)	dulke	dolce	sweet
5)	vikinu	vicino	neighbour
6)	pake	pace	peace
7)	voke	voce	voice
8)	kruke	croce	cross
9)	plakere	piacere	to please
10)	kivtate	città	town
11)	kapu	capo	head
12)	skala	scala	ladder
13)	kane	cane	dog
14)	karu	caro	dear
15)	kapɪllu	capello	hair
16)	muska	mosca	fly
17)	kaɥsa	cosa	cause
18)	vakka	vacca	cow
19)	kaballu	cavallo	horse
20)	kasa	casa	hut

290) <u>RUSSIAN</u> (elementary)

In the following problem, explain the change or changes in Russian of *K, coming from a variety of ancient sources, both words inherited from Proto-Slavic as well as borrowings from other languages. In some cases, the Proto-Slavic form is not available, and we provide a cognate form from another Indo-European language for guidance. Unless otherwise marked, the source is Proto-Slavic.

	Source	Russian	
1)	kendŏ	čádo	child
2)	krikēti	kričát^y	yell
3)	kēdŭ	čád	smoke
4)	rankŭkā	rúčka	hand (dim.)
5)	kel- (PIE)	čeló	brow
6)	kiauras (Lith.)	čúrka	chock
7)	vŭlkŭyĭ	vólčiy	wolf-like
8)	keik- (PIE)	čistiy	clean
9)	melkĭn	mléčnіy	milky
10)	kemerai	čémer	headache
11)	kem- (PIE)	čmél^y (dial.)	bumble bee
12)	kirvis (Lith.)	čérv^y (dial.)	worm
13)	melko	moloko	milk
14)	krikŭ (OCS)	krík	yelling
15)	kaulos (Lith.)	kavíl^y	grass
16)	rankā	ruká	hand
17)	vŭlkŭ	vólk	wolf
18)	okulus (Latv.)	okó	eye
19)	kamāne (Lith.)	komár	mosquito
20)	kori- (PIE)	koríca	cinnamon
21)	korauā (PIE)	koróva	cow
22)	kāl- (PIE)	kalúža	puddle

291) <u>RUSSIAN</u> (elementary)

In the following problem, explain the change or changes in Russian of the back consonants *x and *h, coming from a variety of ancient sources, both words inherited from Proto-Slavic as well as words borrowed from other languages. In some cases the Proto-Slavic form is not available, and we provide a cognate from another Indo-European language for guidance. Unless otherwise indicated, the source words are from Proto-Slavic.

	Source	Russian	
1)	teixīnā	tišiná	silence
2)	hiufo (OHG)	šip	thorn
3)	dŭxĭontŭ	díšut	they breathe
4)	helmaz (PGmc.)	šelóm	helmet
5)	xeladion (Gr.)	šalanda	river boat
6)	puxĭn-	pušnóy	furry
7)	olĭxīnā	olʸšína (dial.)	alder
8)	moruxĭk-	marúška	mark
9)	hiiri (Finn.)	šira	mouse
10)	bloxĭn-	blošínnıy	flea-like
11)	tixo	tíxo	silently
12)	těxa (OCS)	utéxa	joy
13)	dŭxŭ	dúx	spirit
14)	oxvŭ (PSl.)	oxóta	hunt, wish
15)	xardž (Turk.)	xarčı	provision
16)	pux-	púxlıy	chubby
17)	olĭxa	ólʸxa	alder
18)	bloxā	bloxá	flea
19)	xudŭ	xudoy	poor
20)	hŭbel (L.Gmc.)	xubli	woodshavings

292) <u>OLD CHURCH SLAVIC</u> (intermediate)

In the following problem, explain the change or changes in Old Church Slavic of *k, coming from a variety of sources, both words inherited from Proto-Slavic as well as borrowings. In some cases the Proto-Slavic form is not available, and we provide a cognate form from another Indo-European language for guidance. The source words below are Proto-Slavic unless otherwise indicated. (Note that OCS ě used to be pronounced as [ia].)

	Source	OCS	
1)	kainà (Lith.)	cěna	price
2)	skiedrà (Latv.)	cěditi	strain
3)	kailus (OPr.)	cělŭ	whole
4)	kaištu (Lith.)	cěsta	road
5)	kailo- (PIE)	cělovati	kiss
6)	kaipti (Lith.)	ocěpěněti	fear
7)	kaisar (Gk.)	cěsarĭ	emperor
8)	kai (Gk.)	cě	which
9)	rĭki	rĭci	say!
10)	kirikô (Goth.)	crĭki	church
11)	kuyati	kuyati	to murmur
12)	kaulā (PIE)	kila	knot
13)	kolso- (PIE)	klasŭ	ear (wheat)
14)	klād- (PSl.)	klada	block
15)	kāl- (PIE)	kalŭ	mud
16)	kalkalas (Lith.)	klakolŭ	bell
17)	klā- (PSl.)	klado	I place
18)	krūvà (Lith.)	krovŭ	roof
19)	taka (Aves.)	tokŭ	current
20)	rekǫ	rekǫ	I say

293) OLD CHURCH SLAVIC (intermediate)

In the following problem, explain the change or changes in Old Church Slavic of the back consonants represented as x, h and Kh in the ancient forms, coming from a variety of sources, both words inherited from Proto-Slavic as well as borrowings from other languages. In some cases the Proto-Slavic form is not available, and we provide a cognate form from another Indo-Eurpoean language for guidance. In the words below, the source word in Proto-Slavic unless otherwise indicated. (Note that OCS ě used to be pronounced [ja].)

	Source	OCS	
1)	heinä (Finn.)	sěno	garden
2)	hearm (OHG)	sramŭ	shame
3)	snŭxe	snŭsě	son's wife
4)	duxě	dusě	spirit
5)	duxi	dusi	spirits
6)	xoiro-	sěrŭ	grey
7)	hirvi (Finn.)	srŭna	doe
8)	heim (PGmc.)	sěmĭya	family
9)	hjarn (ON)	srěnŭ	white
10)	hiu- (OHG)	si	this
11)	duxŭ	duxŭ	spirit
12)	grěxovŭ	grěxovŭ	sin
13)	fauhô (Goth.)	puxŭ	fur
14)	puhati (SKt.)	puxati	to blow
15)	snŭxa	snŭxa	son's wife
16)	āhad- (Aves.)	xoditi	to go
17)	xoumeli (GK.)	xŭmelĭ	hops
18)	hlaiw (Goth.)	xlěvŭ	shed
19)	hulma (PGmc.)	xlŭmŭ	hill
20)	xōras	xira	weakness

-240-

294) OLD CHURCH SLAVIC (intermediate)

In the following problem, explain the change or changes in Old Church Slavic of the ancient velars *k, *g, *gʰ, coming from both words inherited from Proto-Slavic as well as from borrowings. In some cases, the Proto-Slavic form is not available, and we give a cognate form from another Indo-European language for guidance. In the sources below, the words are Proto-Slavic unless otherwise indicated. (Note that OCS ě used to be pronounced [i̯a]). On the basis of exercises 289-294 formulate a generalization on the development of PIE velars in OCS.

	Source	OCS	
1)	bogě	bozě	god (loc.sg.)
2)	k̈ërno (OG)	zrŭno	grain
3)	nogě	nozě	leg
4)	geiz (OG)	zayǫčĭ	hare
5)	gʰeim- (PIE)	zima	winter
6)	rogī	rozi	horns
7)	ginēn (OG)	zinǫti	yawn
8)	gem- (PIE)	zmii	snake
9)	giwèn (OHG)	zěvati	to yawn
10)	ginēn (OHG)	zinǫti	to gape
11)	bogu	bogu	god (dat.sg.)
12)	strig-	strigǫ	I shear
13)	gorgós (Gk.)	groza	storm
14)	gras (Goth.)	grozdĭ	cluster
15)	gǫdsli	gǫsli	psaltery
16)	gadŭ	gadŭ	snake
17)	gʰōlū (PIE)	glava	head
18)	gu̯olen (PIE)	golěni	bone
19)	agnís (Skt.)	ognĭ	fire
20)	pfluog (OHG)	plugŭ	plough

295) SPANISH (elementary)

In the following problem, explain the change or changes the Proto-Romance phoneme */ɛ/ underwent in Spanish. There are some secondary changes elsewhere in the problem that you should try to explain also. Notice that the Spanish is presented in standard orthography, in which the letter 'c' before 'e' or 'i' is pronounced [θ], but elsewhere is pronounced [k]. The letter combination 'ch' is pronounced [č]. The words are presented in alphabetic order of the English gloss, and must be grouped into the appropriate classes by the student.

	Proto-Rom.	Spanish	
1)	pulɛįu	poleo	acanthus
2)	profɛktu	provecho	advantage
3)	despɛktu	despecho	anger
4)	lɛktu	lecho	bed
5)	kɛku	ciego	blind
6)	pɛktu	pecho	chest
7)	vɛnįu	vengo	I come
8)	prɛmįa	premia	compensation
9)	fɛsta	fiesta	feast
10)	assɛktat	acecha	follow
11)	hɛrba	hierba	grass
12)	tɛnet	tiene	holds
13)	mɛle	miel	honey
14)	kɛntu	ciento	hundred
15)	fɛrru	hierro	iron
16)	pɛrdit	pierde	loses
17)	mɛdįu	medio	middle
18)	nɛrvįu	nervio	nerve
19)	apɛrtu	abierto	open

20)	prɛtʲu	precio	price
21)	sɛpte	siete	seven
22)	vɛntu	viento	wind
23)	matɛrʲa	madera	wood

296) ITALIAN (elementary)

In the following problem, explain the change or changes undergone by the Proto-Romance phoneme */ɛ/ in Italian. Notice that the forms are presented in standard orthography, in which the letter 'c' is pronounced [č] before 'e' or 'i', but [k] elsewhere, and the letter 'g' is pronounced [ǰ] before 'e' and 'i', but [g] elsewhere. When the combinations 'ci' or 'gi' are followed by another vowel, they are pronounced [č] and [ǰ], not [či] and [ǰi]. The combination 'sci' followed by another vowel letter is pronounced [š]. The combination 'gl' is pronounced [λ].

	Proto-Rom.	Italian	
1)	fɛra	fiera	beast
2)	mɛlʲu	meglio	better
3)	kɛku	cieco	blind
4)	pɛktu	petto	chest
5)	prɛssʲa	prescia	crowd
6)	desɛrtu	diserto	desert
7)	fɛsta	festa	feast
8)	pɛde	piede	foot
9)	gɛlu	gielo	frost
10)	fɛle	fiele	gall

11) lɛpre	lepre	hare
12) fɛnu	fieno	hay
13) tɛnet	tiene	holds
14) mɛle	miele	honey
15) kɛntu	cento	hundred
16) nɛskju	nescio	ignorant
17) fɛrru	ferro	iron
18) lɛve	lieve	light
19) pɛrdit	perde	loses
20) mɛdju	mezzo	middle
21) prɛtju	prezzo	price
22) sɛlla	sella	seat
23) sɛpte	sette	seven
24) kɛlu	cielo	sky
25) stɛrnutu	sternuto	sneeze
26) dɛke	dieci	ten
27) tɛmpu	tempo	time
28) tɛpidu	tiepido	warm

297) SPANISH AND ITALIAN (intermediate)

In the following problem, explain the change or changes that the Proto-Romance phoneme */ɔ/ has undergone in both Spanish and Italian. Notice that both languages are presented in standard orthography. Refer to problems 295 and 296 for the pertinent rules of pronunciation of these standard orthographies, and add that the letter combination 'ch' in Italian is pronounced [k]. Also note that the letter combinations 'ue' and 'uo' in Spanish and Italian respectively are diphthongs in which the 'u' represents a non-syllabic onglide, and the whole combination is only one syllable long.

	Proto-Rom.	Spanish	Italian	
1)	pɔdju	poyo	poggio	bench
2)	biskɔktu	bizcocho	biscotto	biscuit
3)	mɔrdit	muerde	morde	bites
4)	kɔrpu	cuerpo	corpo	body

5)	ɔssu	hueso	osso	bone
6)	kɔmputat	cuenta	conta	calculates
7)	pɔtet	puede	può	can
8)	mɔrit	muere	muore	dies
9)	ɔvu	huevo	uovo	egg
10)	ɔklu	ojo	occhio	eye
11)	ɔktu	ocho	otto	eight
12)	fɔku	fuego	fuoco	fire
13)	i̯ɔku	juego	giuoco	game
14)	hɔspite	huésped	ospite	guest
15)	fɔli̯a	hoja	foglia	leaf
16)	mɔdi̯u	moyo	mozzo	measure
17)	mɔvet	mueve	muove	moves
18)	nɔkte	noche	notte	night
19)	kɔksa	coja	cossa	thigh
20)	hɔdi̯e	hoy	oggi	today

298) RUSSIAN (intermediate)

In the following problem, explain the change or changes that have taken place between the earlier stage represented by Old Church Slavonic and the later stage represented by Russian in respect to the vowels /ĭ/ and /ŭ/.

	OCS	Russian	
1)	sŭnŭ	son	dream (nom.sg.)
2)	sŭna	sna	dream (gen.sg.)
3)	sŭnu	snu	dream (dat.sg.)
4)	sramŭ	sram	shame
5)	otĭcĭ	otec	father
6)	kŭto	kto	who
7)	kĭto	čto (arch.)	what
8)	mĭne	mne	me (dat.sg.)
9)	kŭnęzĭ	knyaz^y	duke
10)	dĭnĭ	den^y	day

11)	vĭdovica	vdovica	widow
12)	sŭlnĭce	solnce	sun
13)	kŭde	gde	where
14)	sŭto	sto	hundred
15)	pʸasŭkŭ	pesok	sand
16)	pʸasŭka	peska	sand (gen.sg.)
17)	pĭstrŭ	pestr	colourful
18)	pĭsĭ	pes	dog

299) RUSSIAN (intermediate)

In the following problem, given the Old Church Slavic form of the words, predict which vowel or lack thereof will occur in the Russian. Base your decision on what you know from the previous exercise,

	OCS	Russian	
1)	pĭni	p_ni	stumps
2)	zŭlo	z_lo	evil
3)	dŭva	d_va	two
4)	gŭnati	g_nat(i)	chase
5)	mŭxŭ	m_x_	moss
6)	sŭzŭvati	s_z_vat	invite
7)	tĭstĭ	t_st_	father-in-law
8)	uzŭkŭ	uz_k_	narrow (m.sg.)
9)	uzŭka	uz_ka	narrow (f.sg.)
10)	posŭlŭ	pos_l_	messenger

300) SLAVIC LANGUAGES (intermediate)

In the following problem, explain the change or changes that have occured with Proto-Slavic */or/ in the descendant Slavic languages. The English gloss represents only the approximate meaning common to all the languages in question.

	PSl.	OCS	Polish
1)	gordŭ	gradŭ	gród
2)	vornŭ	vrana	wrona
3)	borda	brada	broda
4)	porsen	prasę	prosię
5)	morz	mrazŭ	mróz
6)	gorx	graxŭ	groch
7)	storna	strana	strona
8)	storžĭ	stražĭ	stróż
9)	porxŭ	praxŭ	proch
10)	kortŭ	kratŭkŭ	krótki
11)	oržĭn	ražĭnŭ	rożen
12)	orvĭnŭ	ravinŭ	równy
13)	orb	rabŭ	rob
14)	orkyta	--	rokita
15)	orst-	rastǫ	wzrost
16)	orzū	razŭ	różny

	Czech	Russian	
1)	hrad	gorod	city
2)	vrána	vorona	crow
3)	brada	boroda	chin
4)	prase	porosa (arch.)	pig
5)	mráz	moroz	frost
6)	hrách	gorox	pea
7)	strana	storona	side
8)	stráž	storož	guard
9)	prach	porox	dust
10)	krátký	korotkiy	short

11) rožeń	rozon	spit
12) rovný	roven (arch.)	even
13) rob (arch.)	robota	slave
14) rokyta	rokíta	willow
15) rostu	rost	grow
16) rozličný	vrozn^y	various

301) SLAVIC LANGUAGES

In the following problem, explain the change or changes that have occured with the Proto-Slavic sequence */ol/ and */el/ in the various Slavic languages. The English gloss represents only the approximate meaning common to all the lanuages in question.

	Proto-Sl	OCS	Polish
1)	golva	glava	głowa
2)	dolgos	žlyabŭ	żłob
3)	poltŭno	platĭno	płotno
4)	polxŭ	plaxŭ	płochy
5)	moldvis	mladŭ	młody
6)	solviy	slaviy	słowik
7)	solma	slama	słoma
8)	soldŭ	sladŭkŭ	słodki
9)	soln-	slanŭ	słony
10)	volsŭ	vlasŭ	włos
11)	melko	mlěko	mleko
12)	pel-	plěti	pleč
13)	pelnú	plěnŭ	plenić
14)	pelva	plěva	plewa
15)	mel-	mlěti	mleć
16)	selz-	slězena	śledziona
17)	seldĭ	--	śledź
18)	selmen	slěme	ślemię
19)	velk	vlěkǫ	wlec
20)	šelmŭ	šlěmŭ	--

	Czech	Russian	
1)	hlava	golova	head
2)	žlab	žolob	gutter
3)	plátno	polotno	linen
4)	plachí	polox	fear
5)	mladý	molodoy	young
6)	slavík	solovey	nightingale
7)	sláma	soloma	straw
8)	sladký	solodkiy	sweet
9)	slaný	solonka	salt
10)	vlas	volos	hair
11)	mléko	moloko	milk
12)	pleti	poloty	weed
13)	plen	polon	capture
14)	pleva	polova	chaff
15)	mleti	molotyba	grind
16)	slezina	selezenka	spleen
17)	sled'	seledka	herring
18)	slémně (arch.)	solomya	strait
19)	vleku	voloč	drag
20)	šlem	šolom	helmet

302) ENGLISH (elementary)

In the following problem, rewrite the English forms in a phonemic transcription, and observe the phonemic alternations between the main stressed vocalic nucleus in the first column and the corresponding vocalic nucleus in the second column. Hypothesize a single vowel for both forms at an earlier stage of the language, and determine what sound changes have taken place in these vowels, and what conditioning factor was involved that led to the present alternation. The forms are arranged in alphabetical order, so it is up to the student to sort them out into suitable groups. In this and the remaining problems in this section, you might want to look up the etymology of the words in a dictionary either before or after you have done the problem.

1)	creep	crept
2)	dame	damsel
3)	five	fifteen
4)	float	flotsam
5)	goose	gosling
6)	house	husband
7)	kneel	knelt
8)	late	last
9)	lose	lost
10)	nose	nostril
11)	out	utmost
12)	wise	wisdom

303) ENGLISH (elementary)

In the following problem, again transcribe the words into a
phonemic transcription as in 302, and observe the phonemic
alternation between the main stressed vocalic nucleus in the
first column and the corresponding vocalic nucleus in the
second column. What conditioning factor is involved here?

1)	cape	capital
2)	crime	criminal
3)	globe	globular
4)	grade	gradual
5)	obscene	obscenity
6)	prove	probable
6)	school	scholarly
8)	severe	severity
9)	sole	solitude
10)	south	southerly
11)	vile	vilify

304) ENGLISH (elementary)

In the following problem, rewrite the forms in phonemic transcription. Observe the phonemic alternation between the main stressed vocalic nucleus in the first column and the corresponding vocalic nucleus in the second column. Hypothesize a single vowel for both forms at an earlier stage of the language, and identify the conditioning factor that was involved that is responsible for the alternation. Next consider the spellings of the vowels involved. What does this suggest? What conclusion can you come to by a comparison of the way the vowels are spelled and the way they are pronounced in modern English?

1)	creep	crept
2)	clean	cleanse
3)	deep	depth
4)	dream	dreamt
5)	feel	felt
6)	heal	health
7)	keep	kept
8)	kneel	knelt
9)	mean	meant
10)	steal	stealth

305) ENGLISH (elementary)

In the following problem, explain the change or changes that have taken place in the main stressed vowels from Old English to modern English. What is the conditioning factor for the differences between forms 1-6 and forms 7-12?

	OE	Later	Mn.Eng.
1)	gōsi	gōsi	geese
2)	tōθi	töθi	teeth
3)	mūsi	müsi	mice
4)	lūsi	lüsi	lice
5)	kunniŋ	künniŋ	king
6)	suni	süni	sin

7)	gōs	gos	goose
8)	tōθ	toθ	tooth
9)	mūs	mus	mouse
10)	lūs	lus	louse
11)	fōda	fod	food
12)	hūs	hus	house

306) <u>ENGLISH</u> (elementary)

In the following problem, explain the changes that have taken place in the phoneme /h/ between Old and modern English. Make sure that you transcribe the forms into a phonemic transcription. You are dealing with pronunciation in this problem, not spelling. Your conclusions may be different according to your dialect of English.

	<u>OE</u>	<u>MnEng.</u>
1)	hlūd	loud
2)	hlīd	lid
3)	hring	ring
4)	hræfn	raven
5)	hnutu	nut
6)	hnappian	nap
7)	hwīnan	whine
8)	hwæte	wheat
9)	hand	hand
10)	hēla	heel
11)	holin	holly
12)	helpan	help
13)	huntian	hunt

VII. RECONSTRUCTION

(In all the problems in Reconstruction, the English glosses represent only the approximate meaning common to all the languages in question.)

307) <u>ROMANCE I</u> (elementary)

In the following problem, reconstruct the first vowel, which also happens to be the stressed vowel, of the following words in Proto-Romance. Notice that in this and the following problems, the languages used in the reconstruction are presented in standard orthographies. In Rumanian, the letter 'ă' is pronounced [ə], the letter 'î' is pronounced [ɨ], the letter 'ş' is pronounced [š], and the letter 'ţ' is pronounced [c].

	Spanish	Sardinian	Rumanian	
1)	hilo	filu	fir	thread
2)	vida	bita	vită	life
3)	sí	si	şi	yes
4)	vino	binu	vin	wine
5)	día	díe	zi	day
6)	pino	pinu	pin	pine tree
7)	riba	riba	rîpă	bank
8)	río	riu	rîũ	river
9)	riso	rizu	rîs	laugh

308) ROMANCE II (elementary)

In the following problem, reconstruct the first vowel of the following words in Proto-Romance.

	Spanish	Sardinian	Rumanian	
1)	verde	birde	verde	green
2)	seco	sikku	sec	dry (masc.)
3)	pez	piske	peşte	fish
4)	teme	timi	teme	fear
5)	sed	sidis	sete	thirst
6)	cerco	kirku	cerc	circle
7)	dedo	didu	deget	finger
8)	cresta	krista	creastă	crest
9)	tema	tima	teamă	fear (subj.)
10)	seca	sikka	seacă	dry
11)	negra	nigra	neagră	black

309) ROMANCE III (elementary)

In the following problem, reconstruct the first vowel in the following words in Proto-Romance.

	Spanish	Sardinian	Rumanian	
1)	creo	kredo	cred	I believe
2)	mes	meze	mes	month
3)	seda	seda	--	silk
4)	pared	--	părete	wall
5)	tres	tres	trei	three
6)	crea	kreda	creadă	believe
7)	tela	tela	teară	cloth
8)	cera	kera	ceară	wax

310) ROMANCE IV (elementary)

In the following problem, reconstruct the first vowel of the
following words in Proto-Romance. In Spanish the letters
'ch' are pronounced [č].

	Spanish	Sardinian	Rumanian	
1)	hiel	fele	fiere	gall
2)	miel	mele	miere	honey
3)	pierdo	perdo	pierd	I lose
4)	hierro	ferru	fier	iron
5)	piedra	pedra	piatră	stone
6)	fiera	fera	fiară	wild
7)	yegua	ebba	iapă	mare
8)	hierba	erva	iarbă	grass
9)	lecho	lettu	--	bed
10)	pecho	pettus	piept	chest
11)	medio	mesu	miez	middle

311) ROMANCE V (elementary)

In the following problem, reconstruct the first vowel in the
following words in Proto-Romance.

	Spanish	Sardinian	Rumanian	
1)	vaca	baka	vacă	cow
2)	lago	lagu	lac	lake
3)	cabo	kabu	cap	head
4)	sal	sale	sare	salt
5)	parte	parte	parte	part
6)	hecho	fattu	fapt	fact
7)	leche	latte	lapte	milk
8)	pecho	pattu	--	tax

312) ROMANCE VI (elementary)

In the following problem, reconstruct the first vowel in the following words in Proto-Romance.

	Spanish	Sardinian	Rumanian	
1)	puerco	porku	porc	pig
2)	cuerpo	korpus	corp	body
3)	juego	Jogu	joc	game
4)	duelo	dolu	dor	pain
5)	nuestro	nostru	nostru	our
6)	suerte	sorte	soarte	luck
7)	puerta	porta	poartă	door
8)	duele	dole	doare	it hurts
9)	cuesta	kosta	coastă	rib

313) ROMANCE VII (elementary)

In the following problem, reconstruct the first vowel of the following words in Proto-Romance.

	Spanish	Sardinian	Rumanian	
1)	nos	nos	noi	we
2)	vos	vos	voi	you
3)	espinoso	ispinozu	spinos	thorny
4)	todo	tottu	tot	all
5)	sol	sole	soare	sun
6)	voz	boge	boace	voice
7)	hora	ora	oară	hour
8)	calor	kalori	căroare	heat
9)	jabón	sabone	săpun	soap
10)	monte	monte	munte	mountain
11)	pone	pone	pune	puts
12)	corona	korona	curună	crown

314) ROMANCE VIII (elementary)

In the following problem, reconstruct the first vowel of the following words in Proto-Romance.

	Spanish	Sardinian	Rumanian	
1)	gola	gula	gurằ	throat
2)	oso	ursu	urs	bear
3)	roto	ruttu	rupt	broken
4)	sordo	surdu	surd	deaf
5)	mosca	muska	muscằ	fly
6)	onda	unda	undằ	wave
7)	boca	bukka	bucằ	mouth
8)	gota	gutta	gutằ	drop

315) ROMANCE IX (elementary)

In the following problem, reconstruct the first vowel of the following words in Proto-Romance.

1)	luna	luna	lunằ	moon
2)	humo	fumu	fum	smoke
3)	espuma	ispuma	spumằ	foam
4)	crudo	krudu	crud	raw
5)	lumbre	lumene	lume	light
6)	muda	muta	mutằ	mute

316) INDO-EUROPEAN I (elementary)

In the following problem, reconstruct the initial consonant in the following words in Proto-Indo-European. In this and the following reconstruction problems, the cognate words in the other languages do not necessarily mean the same due to semantic change.

	English	Latin	Greek
1)	father	pater	patēr
2)	foot	pēs	pous
3)	for	per	peri
4)	fee	pecūs	pekō
5)	feather	penna	pteron
6)	foal	puer	pais
7)	full	plēnus	pleos
8)	fare	porto	poros
9)	flat	planus	platos
10)	fathom	patēre	patanē
11)	spike	spīca	spilos
12)	spurn	spernō	spairō
13)	(God)speed	spēr	--
14)	spy	specere	skopein
15)	sprout	sperma	spora
16)	spoon	sponda	spaθē

317) INDO-EUROPEAN II (elementary)

In the following problem, reconstruct the initial consonant in the following words in Proto-Indo-European.

	English	Latin	Greek
1)	thaw	tābēs	tēkein
2)	thin	tenuis	tanu-
3)	thresh	terere	terēdōn
4)	the	tam	to
5)	three	trēs	treis
6)	thou	tū	tu (Doric)

7)	through	trans	terθron
8)	thirst	torrēre	tersomai
9)	thumb	tumēre	tumbos
10)	threat	trūdere	--

11)	stand	stāre	statos
12)	staff	--	stephein
13)	sting	in-stig-are	stokhos
14)	stiff	stips	stibos
15)	straw	sternere	sternon
16)	star	stella	(a)ster
17)	strong	--	strangos

318) **INDO-EUROPEAN III** (elementary)

In the following problem, reconstruct the initial consonant
in the following words in Proto-Indo-European.

	English	Latin	Greek
1)	heave	capio	kōpē
2)	hole	cēlāre	kaluptein
3)	horn	cornū	keras
4)	heart	cor	kardia
5)	wheel	circulum	kuklos
6)	hound	canis	kuōn
7)	head	caput	kapia
8)	hen	canō	kanasso
9)	hear	cavēre	akouein

10)	shade	--	skotos
11)	shroud	scrotum	--
12	shine	scintilla	skia
13	shin	scindere	--
14)	shave	scabere	skaphe

319) <u>INDO-EUROPEAN IV</u> (elementary)

In the following problem, reconstruct the initial consonant of the following words in Proto-Indo-European. The Germanic cognates are Gothic unless otherwise indicated.

	Skt	Gk	Gmc (Gothic)	
1)	bʰātih	pʰanē	bandwa	light
2)	bʰadrah	--	batiza	good
3)	bʰanati	pʰēmi	bōn (OI)	speak
4)	bʰajati	pʰagein	--	partake
5)	--	pʰēyos	bōka	beech
6)	bʰrāter	pʰrātēr	brōθar	brother
7)	bʰarati	pʰerō	bāira	carry
8)	bʰūtih	pʰuō	būa (OI)	be
9)	bʰayatē	pitʰōn	bifa (OI)	fear
10)	bʰrūh	(o)pʰrūs	brūn (OI)	eyebrow
11)	bāhuh	pēkʰus	bōgr (OI)	elbow
12)	bādʰate	--	bida	push
13)	--	peitʰomai	baidjan	to force
14)	barhiš	--	bags	cushion
15)	badʰnāti	pentʰeros	bindan	bind
16)	bahu-	pakʰus	bingr (OI)	thick
17)	bardʰakah	pertʰō	bord (OI)	cut
18)	barhayati	--	bairgher	increase
19)	bōdʰati	peutʰomai	(ana)biudan	wake up
20)	bradʰnah	--	blinds	pale
21)	budʰnah	putʰmēn	bottom (Eng.)	ground

320) <u>INDO-EUROPEAN V</u> (elementary)

In the following problem, reconstruct the initial consonant in the following words in Proto-Indo-European.

	Skt	Gk	Gmc (Gothic)	
1)	dadʰāti	(e)tʰēka	dōn (OE)	do, place
2)	dʰāyaḥ	tʰēsato	daddjan	suck
3)	dʰamati	tʰemeros	daam (Norw.)	dust
4)	dʰanus	tʰenar	denn (OS)	flat

5)	dʰraṇati	tʰrēnos	drunjus	noise
6)	dʰrṣṇoti	tʰersos	(ga)dars	brave
7)	dʰavatē	tʰeō	dau (OS)	run
8)	dʰūmah	tʰūmos	dōmian (OS)	smoke
9)	--	tapʰos	(af)dōbn	astonish
10)	dahati	tepʰrā	--	burn
11)	dēhmi	teikʰos	digandin	knead
12)	dagʰnōti	takʰus	--	fast
13)	drapʰsah	trepʰō	derbi (OS)	coagulate
14)	--	tupʰoi	dowel (Engl.)	peg
15)	duhati	tukʰē	dang	press
16)	drāgʰatē	--	dracu (OS)	pain

321) INDO-EUROPEAN VI (elementary)

In the following problem, reconstruct the initial consonant
in the following words in Proto-Indo-European.

	Skt	Gk	Gmc (Gothic)	
1)	hēṣas	kʰaios	geirr (OI)	stick
2)	hamsah	kʰēn	gās (OI)	goose
3)	havate	--	guθ	call
4)	hadatē	kʰezo	gat (OS)	opening
5)	hinōti	--	gad (OS)	propell
6)	hēman	kʰeima	gōi (OS)	winter
7)	hari-	kʰolos	gulθ	yellow
8)	haryati	kʰairō	-gairns	joy
9)	hirah	kʰordē	gorn (OI)	intestine
10)	gabʰastih	--	gabei	take
11)	--	kepʰalē	gibla	summit
12)	gadʰyah	--	gadiliggs	join
13)	--	kantʰulē	gund	ulcer
14)	grha-	kortʰis	gards	house
15)	gūhati	--	gȳgr (OI)	conceal
16)	grabʰ-	--	grapa (ON)	grab

322) INDO-EUROPEAN VII (elementary)

In the following problem, reconstruct the dental consonant of the following words in Proto-Indo-European.

	Skt	Gmc (Gothic)	
1)	bʰrátar	bróθar	brother
2)	ántara	ánθar	other
3)	dánta-	túnθu-	tooth
4)	mántra-	máθla-	speech
5)	tátra	θáθro	there
6)	póteros (Gk)	hráθar	whether
7)	nítya-	níθjis	constant
8)	átati	áθnam	year
9)	áti	áθ(θan)	but
10)	páti-	(brúθ)faθs	husband
11)	pitár-	fádar	father
12)	matár-	módar	mother
13)	ketú-	háidu	appearance
14)	antár	úndar	under
15)	ātí-	ónd (ON)	duck
16)	catváras	fídwor	four
17)	çatá-	húnda-	hundred
18)	trtíya	θrídja-	third

323) SLAVIC I (elementary)

In the following problem, reconstruct the vowels of Proto-Slavic. Which language carries the original vocalic element?

	Ukr.	Rus.	Czech	Slovak	
1)	dilo	delo	dílo	dielo	work
2)	bida	beda	bída	bieda	misfortune
3)	biliy	beliy	bílý	bieli	white
4)	vira	vera	víra	viera	faith
5)	viter	veter	vítr	vietor	wind

6)	dívka	devka	dívka	dievka	girl
7)	rika	reka	říčka	rieka	river
8)	diža	deža	díže	dieža	container
9)	smix	smex	smích	smiex	laughter
10)	kvitka	cvetok	kvítek	kvietok	flower

324) SLAVIC II (intermediate)

In the following problem, set up a correspondence for vowels which have the nasal reflexes in Old Church Slavic (/ę/ and /ǫ/). Comment on the development of Old Russian /u/ and /ja/. The order of the forms is as follows: Old Church Slavic; Old Russian; Lithuanian; Other Indo-European: English gloss.

1) gǫsĭ; gus^Y; žasìs; gans (OHG): goose
2) kŭnęzĭ; knjaz^Y; --; kuning (OHG): nobleman
3) męta; mjata; minta; menta (Lat.): mint
4) desętĭ; desjat^Y; dešimtas; decem (Lat.): ten
5) pěnęzĭ; pěnjaz^Y; --; pfenning (OHG): coin
6) pamętĭ; pamjat^Y; atmintis; mens (Lat.): memory
7) svętŭ; svjat; šventas; swenta (O.Pruss.): saint
8) sěmę; sěmja; sémen-ys; sēmen (Lat.): seed
9) sǫtŭ; sut; --; sunt (Lat.) sind (German): they are
10) rǫka; ruka; rankà; rancko (O.Pruss.): hand
11) ǫgŭlĭ; ugl; ànglis; áŋgāras (Skt.): corner
12) ǫgŭre; ugre; unguras; ungarn (Germ.): Hungarians
13) dǫti; dut^Y; dumti; dumba (O.Norw.): blow
14) gǫba; guba; gum̃bas; kumb- (OHG): mouth
15) męso; mjaso; meisa; mensā (O.Pruss.): meat
16) agnę; jagnja; --; agnus (Lat.): lamb
17) lędviję; ljadveja; --; lentĭ (OHG): spoon
18) mǫka; muka; mánkan; mengian (O.Sax.): flour
19) mǫtiti; mutiti; --; manthatati (Skt.): stir up
20) grǫzĭ; gruz; gramzdau; --: mud
21) grobŭ; grub; grubùs; krampf (OHG): coarse

325) <u>SLAVIC III</u> (intermediate)

Old Church Slavic had two nasal vowels, /ę/ and /ǫ/. On the
basis of the forms in the other Slavic languages, fill in the
blank spaces in the Old Church Slavic forms below. The order
of the forms is: Old Church Slavic; Czech; Slovak; Serbo-
Croatian; Russian; English gloss. Refer to problem 331 if
necessary.

1) s_; se; sa; se; sja: self
2) p_tĭ; pět; pæt'; pět; pjat': five
3) r_ka; ruka; ruka; rúka; ruká: hand
4) r_k_; ruku; ruku; rûku; rúku: hand (gen.sg.)
5) p_tŭ; pátý; piaty; pěti; pjátyj: fifth
6) t_gn_ti; táhnouti; tahnut'; istégnuti; tjanút': to pull
7) j_zykŭ; jazyk; jazyk; jèzik; jazýk: tongue
8) d_bŭ; dub; dub; dúb; dub: oak
9) d_ba; dubu; duba; dúba; dúbu: oak (gen.sg.)
10) ženoj_; ženou; ženú; žènom; ženój: woman (inst.sg.)
11) j_dro; ja:dro; jadro; jézgra; jadró: kernel
12) s_tĭ; jsou; sú; su; --: they are
13) nes_tŭ; nesou; nesú; dònesū; nesūt: they carry
14) s_dŭ; soud; súd; súd; sud: court
15) im_; jméno; meno; ìme; ímja: name

326) PROTO-SLAVIC VERBAL STEM I (intermediate)

Find a one-stem reconstruction for every set of verbal forms, and comment on the changes the Proto-Slavic stem underwent in the infinitive. Next, find the Proto-Slavic suffix for the past tense. Which language preserves the ancient form? What changes did the other languages undergo? The suffix /-nou-~-nu-~-n-/ indicates momentary action. In what way does it influence the shape of the stem? The sign * at the end of a form indicates the cases where */e/ has gone to /o/ in Modern Russian. /ǯ/ indicates a prepalatal affricate. You should ignore occasional vocalic changes.

A) CZECH

	Inf.	1st pres.	Past.m.	
1)	pa:st^{y}i	pasu	pa:sl	pasture
2)	třa:st^y	třesu	třa:sl	shake
3)	ne:st^{y}i	nesu	nesl	carry
4)	le:st^{y}i	lezu	lezl	crawl
5)	ve:st^{y}i	vezu	vezl	bring
6)	bodnou-t^{y}i	bod-n-u	bodl	pierce
7)	pad-nou-t^{y}i	pad-n-u	padl	fall
8)	kra:st^{y}i	kradu	kradl	steal
9)	ve:st^{y}i	vedlu	vedl	lead
10)	me:st^{y}i	metu	metl	sweep

B) RUSSIAN

	Inf.	1st pres.	Past.m	
1)	pas^{y}t^{y}i	pasu	pas	pasture
2)	tr^{y}as^{y}t^{y}i	tr^{y}asu	tr^{y}as	shake
3)	n^{y}es^{y}t^{y}i	n^{y}esu	n^{y}es*	carry
4)	l^{y}es^{y}t^{y}i	l^{y}ezu	l^{y}es*	crawl
5)	v^{y}es^{y}t^{y}i	v^{y}ezu	v^{y}ez*	bring
6)	bod-nu-t^y	bod-n-u	bod-nu-l	pierce
7)	pas^{y}t^y	padnu	pal	fall
8)	kras^{y}t^y	kradu	kral	steal
9)	v^{y}es^{y}t^{y}i	v^{y}edu	v^{y}el*	lead
10)	m^{y}es^{y}t^{y}i	m^{y}etu	m^{y}el*	sweep

C) SERBO-CROATIAN

	Inf.	1st pers.	Past.m	
1)	pasti	pasem	pasao	pasture
2)	tresti	tresem	tresao	shake
3)	--	--	--	carry
4)	--	--	--	crawl
5)	--	--	--	bring
6)	bosti	bodem	bo	pierce
7)	pasti	padnem	pao	fall
8)	krasti	kradem	krao	steal
9)	povesti	pvedem	poveo	lead
10)	mesti	metem	meo	sweep

327) PROTO-SLAVIC VERBAL STEM II (intermediate)

Reconstruct as much of Proto-Slavic verb stems as you can. The order of the forms and the directions for working with the data are the same as in the previous problem.

A) CZECH

	Inf.	1st pers.	Past.m	
1)	mih-nou-ti	mi-h-n-u	mihl	flash
2)	moci	mohu	mohl	to be able
3)	sleh-nou-ti	slehnu	slehl	lay down
4)	sta:h-nou-ti	sta:h-n-u	sta:hl	tighten, pull
5)	st^{y}ih-nou-ti	st^{y}ih-n-u	st^{y}ihl	catch up
6)	pomoci	pomohu	pomohl	help
7)	pe:ci	peku	pekl	bake
8)	prote:ci	proteku	protekl	flow
9)	puk-nou-ti	puk-n-u	pukl	burst
10)	ři:ci	řek-n-u	řekl	say

-266-

B) RUSSIAN

Inf.	1st pers.	Past m.	
1) m^{y}ignut^y	m^{y}ignu	m^{y}ig	flash
2) moč	mogu	mog	to be able
3) sl^{y}eč	sl^{y}agu	sleg	lay down
4) t^{y}agat^y	t^{y}agaju	t^{y}agal	pull
5) das^{y}t^{y}ič	das^{y}t^{y}ig-n-u	das^{y}t^{y}ig	catch up
6) pamoč	pamagu	pamog	help
7) p^{y}eč	p^{y}eku	pek	bake
8) prat^{y}eč	prat^{y}eku	pratek	flow
9) pučit^y	jpuču	pučil	burst
10) atr^{y}ečs^{y}a	atr^{y}ekus^y	atr^{y}eks^{y}a	renounce

C) SERBO-CROATIAN

Inf.	1st pers.	Past m.	
1) mignuti	mignem	migao	flash
2) moği	mogu	mogao	to be able
3) sleği	sleb-n-em	slegao	lay down
4) steği	steg-n-em	stegao	tighten
5) dostiği	dostignem	dostigao	catch up
6) pomoği	pomognem	pomogao	help
7) peği	pečem	pekao	bake
8) proteği	protečem	protekao	flow
9) jpuği	puk-n-em	pukao	burst
10) reği	rek-n-em	rekao	say

Reconstruct as much of Proto-Austronesian as you can from
the following languages. The order of the forms is:
Sundanese; Old Javanese; New Javanese; Malay; Madurese:
English gloss

1) mataq; mata; mòtò; mata; matah: eye
2) manis; manis; manès; manes; manes: sweet, lovely
3) tumaq; tuma; tumò; tuma; tòmah: louse
4) taman; taman; taman; taman; taman: garden
5) raruq; laru; laru; laru; laròh: a potion
6) raris; --; larès; lares; larès: in demand
7) rurug; lurug; luróg; --; lòròk: go to war
8) kuraŋ; kuraŋ; kuraŋ; kuraŋ; kòraŋ: reduction
9) duqum; a-dŭm; dóm; --; dhuqum: to distribute
10) damar; damar; damar; damar; dhámar: lamp
11) kadaŋ; kadaŋ; kadaŋ; --; kadháŋ: kin
12) gandar; --; gandar; gandar; ghándhár: wooden shaft
13) ganjil; --; ganjél; ganjel; ghánjhil: uneven
14) tanjuŋ; tanjuŋ; tanjóŋ; tanjoŋ; tanjhuŋ: flower
15) panas; panas; panas; panas; panas: warm
16) bantal; bantal; bantal; bantal; bhántal: pillow
17) --; b-in-aŋsal; baŋsal; baŋsal; bháŋsal: building
18) harip; harəp; di-arəp-i; hadap; adáq: in front of
19) maruq; --; maru; madu; madu: fellow, wife
20) huraŋ; huraŋ; uraŋ; hudaŋ; odáŋ: shrimp
21) hirup; hurip; urép; hidop; òḍiq: to live

329) <u>AUSTRONESIAN LANGUAGES</u> II (intermediate)

Reconstruct the vocalic system of the Proto-Austronesian language. State the vocalic changes for each language and attempt to reconstruct each word in Proto-Austronesian. The order of the forms is the same as for the previous problem, except that Sundanese is the last of the languages instead of the first.

1) kita; kitò; kita; kèta; kitaq: I
2) baliraŋ; waliraŋ; baliráŋ; baleraŋ; --: suphur
3) gila; gilò; gila; gheláh; gilaq: shy, mad
4) lutuŋ; lutóŋ; lotoŋ; --; lutuŋ: monkey
5) kilaŋ; kilaŋ; kilaŋ; kèlaŋ; --: sugar, syrup
6) s-um-iŋgah; siŋgáh; --; sèŋghá; --: to avoid
7) ma-nuruŋ; suróŋ; soroŋ; soròŋ; suruŋ: to push
8) a-narima; tarimò; tarima; tarèma; tarimaq: to receive
9) tamiaŋ; --; tamiaŋ; --; tamiaŋ: bamboo
10) an-uluŋ; tulóŋ; toloŋ; tòlóŋ; tuluŋ: to help
11) a-pisah; pisah; pisah; pèsa; pisah: to separate
12) qupah; upah; opah; òpa; qupah: reward
13) --; tumpoq; tompoq; tòmpòq; tumpuk: small heap
14) galuga; galugò; galuga; ghálugháh; --: red dye
15) wulan; wulan; bulan; bulán; bulan: moon
16) wulu; wulu; bulu-bulu; buluh; buluq: hair

330) <u>PROTO-EASTERN OCEANIC</u> (intermediate)

Which consonants show systematic correspondences among the various languages? Present your findings in the form of a table. Fill in the missing forms, and point out which forms deviate from the general pattern. The order of the forms is as follows: Proto-Eastern Oceanic; Nggela; Fijian; Proto-Polynesian; English gloss.

1) zava; hava; cava; hafa: what
2) vizo; viho; vico; fiso: squirt out
3) zivo; hivo; civo; hifa: down
4) zaa; ha;_____ ; haa: what
5) tazi;_____ ; taci; tahi: sea
6) viza; ngiha; vica; fiha: how much
7) voze; vohe; voce; _____: paddle
8) zoKa; hoKa; coKa-; hoKa: spear
9) _____;hage-v; caKe-v; haKe: climb
10) zaŋa; hanga; caga; haŋa: span
11) ŋiza; ngiha; gica; anuha: when
12) Kesa; KaKesa; Kesa-v; Kesa: dye
13) misi; misimisi; misi-K; misi: suck
14) zala; hala; cala; hala: path
15) taŋi; tagi; tagi; taŋi: cry
16) i-sele; i-sele; i-sele; sele: Knife
17) zoKo; hogo; coKo; _____: fish
18) tazi; tahi; taci; tahina: sibling
19) Kanaze; Kanace; _____; Kanahe: mullet
20) mazu; mahu; macu; mahu: sated

331) MALAYO-JAVANIC GROUP (intermediate)

Reconstruct the consonants of each word in Proto-Malayo-Javanic. Discuss the tendencies of sound changes for each language. In the ancient Malay manuscripts words such as modern Malay /basar/, /karat/, /talog/, etc. are spelled **b.ss.r**, **k.rr.t**, **t.ll.g**, etc. The order of the forms is as follows: Sundanese; Javanese; Malay; Madurese: English gloss.

1) limaq; limó; lima; lémaq: five
2) mataq; mòtò; mata; mataq: eye
3) panas; panas; panas; panas: warm
4) batuq; watu; batu; pátò: stone
5) bentaŋ; lintaŋ; bintaŋ; bintaŋ: star
6) koneŋ; kunéŋ; kuneŋ; kònéŋ: yellow
7) taliq; tali; tali; talè: rope
8) kirit; karat; karat; karraq: cut
9) lisuŋ; lasóŋ; lesoŋ; lassòŋ: rice/mortar
10) laŋit; laŋét; laŋet; laŋŋèq: sky
11) birat; abòt; barat; barráq: heavy
12) bapaq; bapaq; bapaq; appaq: father
13) tiluq; talu; tiga; tallòq: three
14) kabeh; kabèh; semua; kabbhi: all
15) gariŋ; garéŋ; kareŋ; karréŋ: dry

-271-

332) TURKIC LANGUAGES I (intermediate)

On the basis of the data reconstruct the forms of the proto-language and formulate the sound changes. Do not look for conditioning factors in this exercise. The order of the forms is as follows: Azerbaijani; Turkish; Kumic; Tuvin; English gloss.

1) γaz-; Kaz-; Kaz-; Kas-: to dig
2) γal-; Kal-; Kal-; --: to stay
3) γar-; Kar-; Kar-; xar-: snow
4) γat-; Kat-; Kat-; Ka?t-: to add, mix
5) γač-; Kač-; Kač-; Kaš: to run
6) γoȷun-; Koȷun-; Koȷ-; xoȷ-: sheep
7) γol; Kol; Kol; xol-: hand
8) γul; Kul; Kul; Kul: slave
9) γuš; Kuš; Kuš; Ku?š: bird
10) γïz; Kïz; Kïz; Kïs: girl
11) γïl; Kïl; Kïl; xïl: hair
12) γïn; Kïn; Kïn; xïn: sheath
13) γïš; Kïš; Kïš; Kï?š: winter
14) gäl-; gël-; gël; Kël: to come
15) gir-; gir-; gir-; Kir-: to enter
16) göl; göl; göl-; xöl: lake
17) göȷ; gök; kök, gök; Kök: sky, blue
18) gör-; gör-; gör-; Kör-: to see
19) gün; gün; gün; xün: sun
20) güȷ; güč; güč; Küš: power

333) TURKIC LANGUAGES II (intermediate)

Observe some of the sound changes from Proto-Turkic to Turkmen and Yakutsk. On the basis of your observations reconstruct the missing forms of Proto-Turkic in the blank spaces. The order of the forms is as follows: Proto-Turkic; Turkmen; Yakutsk; English gloss.

1) Kä:n; gi:n^Y; Kiën^Y: wide
2) Kä:p; gä:p; Kiëp: form
3) Kä:č; gi:č; Kiësë: evening
4) ta:l; da:laK; ta:l; tear
5) ta:s; da:š; da:s: stone
6) _____; da:r; ta:r: narrow
7) tö:r; dör; tüör: to peck
8) _____; gö:K; Küöx: blue
9) Kü:č; güĵč; Kü:s: power
10) ti:š; di:š; ti:s: tooth
11) to:l; do:l; tuol: fill up

II. STRUCTURAL PHONOLOGY

75) CREE
Model Solution
a) Establishing the environments:

	#_V	V_#	C_V	V_V
[p]	1,4	2,5	3	
[b]				6,7,8,9,10

b)The status: The sounds [p] and [b] are in complementary distribution and therefor represent one phoneme.

c)Final statement:
/p/   → [b]/V_V
      → [p]/elsewhere

[b] occurs between vowels; [p] occurs elsewhere

(The allophone usually chosen for representation of the phoneme is the one with the more general or widespread distribution.)

76) BIBLICAL HEBREW
[f] occurs following vowels; [p] occurs elsewhere

77) BIBLICAL HEBREW
[θ] occurs following vowels; [t] occurs elsewhere

78) CREE
[d] occurs between vowels; [t] occurs elsewhere

79) BRAZILIAN PORTUGUESE
[č] occurs before the vowel [i]; [t] occurs elsewhere

80) BRAZILIAN PORTUGUESE
[J] occurs before the vowel [i]; [d] occurs elsewhere

81) KOREAN
   [š] occurs before the vowel [i]; [s] occurs elsewhere

82) CREE
   [ǰ] occurs between vowels; [č] occurs elsewhere

83) CREE
   [g] occurs between vowels; [k] occurs elsewhere. You
   will have observed by now that Cree does not have
   separate voiced and voiceless phonemes as does
   English in e.g. /p,b/, /t,d/, /k,g/, etc.

84) BIBLICAL HEBREW
   [k] occurs in initial position; [x] occurs elsewhere

85) GERMAN
   Model solution. This problem has to be done in two
   stages.

   a) Establishing the environments:

	V_V	Vu_V	C_V	V_C	#_V	#_C
γ	1,2,3,5 7,8,9,10	4,6				
g	11,14,15		12,18	13,19	16,17	20

   Sounds [γ] and [g] seem to contrast in the
   environment V_V. We will therefore consider the
   quality of the vowels found in this position, not just
   the presence or absence of a vowel.

   b) Adjusting the environment:

	a:_ə	u:_ə	o:_ə	a:_u	i:_ə	ö_ə	e:_ə
γ	1,2,3 10	5	7,8	9			
g					11	14	15

   c) The status: When the quality of the vowels is taken
   into account, it is found that the sound [γ] occurs

only after back vowels and the sound [g] occurs only after front vowels. The sounds [ɣ] and [g] are therefore in complementary distribution and represent one phoneme /g/.

c) Final statement:
/g/ → [ɣ]/ back vowel_V
→ [g]/ elsewhere

[ɣ] occurs after a back vowel when between vowels; [g] occurs elsewhere.

86) SERBO-CROATIAN
[ɕ] and [č] contrast; e.g. ćaća ~ čaša

87) TURKISH
[ɾ] occurs in final position; [r] occurs elsewhere

88) KOREAN
[r] occurs between vowels; [l] occurs elsewhere

89) LEBANESE ARABIC
[i] occurs in final position; [ɪ] occurs elsewhere

90) TURKISH
[i] occurs before a consonant followed by a vowel (CV); [ɪ] occurs elsewhere

91) POLISH
[ʒ] and [z] contrast; e.g. ʒvon ~ zvani

92) SPANISH
[ɛ] occurs before either [ɾ] or [x]; [e] occurs elsewhere

93) SLOVAK
[l] and [lʸ] contrast; e.g. lak ~ lʸak

94) LEBANESE ARABIC
[u] occurs in final position; [ʊ] occurs elsewhere

95) <u>TURKISH</u>
[u] occurs before a consonant followed by a vowel
(CV); [ʊ] occurs elsewhere

96) <u>SPANISH</u>
[b] occurs in initial position; [β] occurs between
vowels

97) <u>TURKISH</u>
[ǰ] and [ǰ] contrast; e.g. ačik ~ aǰi

98) <u>SPANISH</u>
[b] occurs after [m]; [β] occurs elsewhere. You
already know from problem 96 that [b] also occurs in
initial position.

99) <u>MALAY</u>
interpretation A is more suitable because Malay does
not favour consonantal clusters

100) <u>SLOVAK</u>
[v] and [ɥ] are allophones; [ɥ] occurs either in final
position or between a vowel and a consonant. [v]
occurs elsewhere; [f] belongs to a separate phoneme

101) <u>MALAY</u>
[t] and [tʸ] contrast; e.g. tarek ~ tʸarek. [ǰ] is a
free variant of [tʸ]

102) <u>CZECH</u>
[a] and [aː] contrast; e.g. lano ~ raːno ~ ranʸen

103) <u>JAPANESE</u>
[c] occurs before [u]; [č] occurs before [i]; [t]
occurs elsewhere

104) <u>SPANISH</u>
[ð] occurs between vowels; [d] occurs in initial
position

-277-

105) <u>GERMAN</u>

[ç] and [x] are allophones; [ç] occurs either after front vowels or after consonants. [x] occurs elsewhere; [š] belongs to a separate phoneme

106) <u>TURKISH</u>

[u] and [ü] contast; e.g. <u>usta</u> ~ <u>üst</u>

107) <u>MALAY</u>

[k] and [ʔ] are allophones; [ʔ] occurs in final position. [k] occurs elsewhere; [t] belongs to a separate phoneme

108) <u>SPANISH</u>

[g] occurs in initial position; [γ] occurs between vowels

109) <u>HUNGARIAN</u>

[n] and [nʸ] contrast; e.g. <u>panas</u> ~ <u>se:panʸa</u>

110) <u>SPANISH</u>

[g] occurs either in initial position or after [ŋ]; [γ] occurs elsewhere. You will have noticed that in Spanish all voiced stops and the corresponding voiced fricatives are allophones: voiced stops [b,d,g] occur in initial position or after nasals; the voiced fricatives [β,ð,γ] occur elsewhere.

111) <u>RUSSIAN</u>

[k] and [kʷ] are allophones; [kʷ] occurs before back rounded vowels [u] and [o]; [k] occurs elsewhere. [kʸ] belongs to a separate phoneme

112) <u>TURKISH</u>

[k] and [kʸ] are allophones; [g] and [gʸ] are allophones; both [kʸ] and [gʸ] occur next to front vowels

113) RUSSIAN
[xʷ] occurs before back rounded vowels; [xʸ] occurs before front vowels; [x] occurs elsewhere

114) CZECH
[ɽ̌] occurs either in final position or next to a voiceless stop; [ř] occurs elsewhere

115) HUNGARIAN
[a] and [a:] contrast; e.g. aga:r ~ a:g

116) RUSSIAN
There are two possibilities: a) that the sound [ɛ] is an allophone of the phoneme /e/, or that it is an allophone of the phoneme /æ/. The first hypothesis is the more likely since the phonetic similarity between [ɛ] and [e] is greater than the similarity between [ɛ] and [æ]. Therefore the preferred solution is: [ɛ] and [e] are allophones; [e] occurs before palatalized consonants (Cʸ); [ɛ] occurs elsewhere. [æ] belongs to a separate phoneme

117) CANADIAN FRENCH
[ü] occurs either in final position or before [v,z,ž,r]; [ʊ̈] occurs elsewhere

118) CANADIAN FRENCH
[u] occurs either in final position or before [v,z,ž,r]; [ʊ] occurs elsewhere

119) CANADIAN FRENCH
[i] occurs in final position; [ɪ] occurs before a consonant in final position

120) CANADIAN FRENCH
[i] occurs either in final position or before [v,z,ž,r] in final position; [ɪ] occurs elsewhere

121) <u>CANADIAN FRENCH</u>
[i] occurs either in final position or before [v,z,ž,r]
or in an open syllable (CV)

EXERCISES IN ENGLISH TRANSCRIPTION

The following transcriptions are done in the Smith-
Trager system and according to the pronounciation
given in the American Heritage Dictionary. Your
transcriptions may differ from these given here
depending on your dialect of English.

1) 1) sɔt
2) hud
3) loyd
4) mæs
5) fayt
6) fowm
7) reč
8) sey
9) tuwl
10) taym

11) lay
12) čik
13) lag
14) mawθ
15) naw
16) eyǰ
17) nad
18) dəz
19) put
20) leg

2) 1) truw
2) stik
3) prayd
4) klowz
5) blowk
6) drayv
7) stow
8) pliyz
9) strip
10) bril

11) kræm
12) freyd
13) fluwk
14) græs
15) kwik
16) slaym
17) twič
18) glib
19) fyuw
20) kriym

3)
1) strɔŋg
2) krimp
3) wɔkt
4) maynd
5) æsks
6) ečt
7) aylz
8) bowst
9) ləmpt
10) pæåz

11) wayvz
12) pænts
13) aks
14) kænt
15) Jagd
16) fort
17) owks
18) lilt
19) larJ
11) stæmps

4)
1) rékard
2) tǽtəl
3) gówiŋ
4) sítiy
5) háwzəz
6) áyviy
7) sówfə
8) sɔ́nə
9) gǽlənt
10) sówlow

11) tǽliy
12) fóybəl
13) líkər
14) kórəl
15) hǽsiy
16) súwtər
17) swíydiš
18) háwlər
19) mǽčəz
20) húkiŋ

5)
1) stréynJər
2) bándiJ
3) pánstər
4) ǽkšən
5) místəriy
6) mórtis
7) léŋθiy
8) gǽspiŋ
9) póršən
10) bréstwərks

11) dárknəs
12) sǽksən
13) láytliy
14) kíŋdəm
15) príysthud
16) gǽŋwey
17) óystər
18) prínsliy
19) mǽskiŋ
20) kárthwiyl

6) 1) riláy
2) imɪ́t
3) gitár
4) Kərǽl
5) rimówt
6) rilǽks
7) tənáyt
8) məríy
9) məláyn
10) pərúwz

11) miráž
12) əláwd
13) bəlúwn
14) riɟóys
15) rigéyl
16) rizɛ́nt
17) Kəláyd
18) rizúwm
19) sKidúw
20) ripɪ́yl

7) 1) Kwədríl
2) ɟentíyl
3) teKníyK
4) endíyr
5) ristréyn
6) Kartúwn
7) əbzálv
8) dispɛ́r
9) səpríym
10) bispówK

11) sərvéy
12) dispóyl
13) əbzárv
14) partéyK
15) məkláwd
16) distróy
17) Kartéyl
18) rispɛ́Kt
19) iKlíps
20) læmpúwn

8) 1) Kóraleyt
2) lǽŋgwišiŋ
3) prowsíydiŋ
4) prayvətíyr
5) hárpsiKord
6) hirówiK
7) pridíKšən
8) sæsKətúwn
9) brigədíyr
10) sərtətuwd

11) enčǽntəd
12) forbérəns
13) wárKmənšip
14) yúwnəvərs
15) KazmétiK
16) trænsléyšən
17) símbəlayz
18) rábəriy
19 páŋKčuwəl
20) məməfay

9) 1) rimárKəbəl
2) hælətówsis
3) bíbliyəfayl

11) sǽləmændər
12) sowšəlístiK
13) həbíčuwəl

-282-

4) kærizmǽtik
5) dikǽθlən
6) rowzəkrúšən
7) kǽpətəlayz
8) ripyúwdiyeyt
9) kǽləbowgiy
10) drǽmətərǰiy

10) 1) koriyágrəfiy
2) dikæpətéyšən
3) kwaləfəkéyšən
4) prinsəpǽlətiy
5) intərágətiv
6) hæbərdǽšəriy
7) indifǽtəgəbəl
8) mǽləprapizəm
9) rekənsiliyéyšən
10) trinətériyən

14) eysimétrik
15) gargǽnčuwən
16) hélikaptər
17) ínəveytiv
18) niyǽndərθal
19) mælaǰástəd
20) kampanséyšən

11) andərdivéləpt
12) prowdəktívətiy
13) ilektráləsis
14) impasəbílətiy
15) anprəféšənəl
16) dilǽpədeytəd
17) manəǰénəsis
18) ɔdatóriyəm
19) næšənəlayzéyšən
20) prezbətíriyən

III. PHONEMIC ALTERNATIONS

The following statements should be considered only as
hints toward a number of possible solutions within
various theoretical frameworks.

122) YORUBA
/m/ before /b/; /n/ before /d/; /ŋ/ before /k/.
Assimilation: the nasal assimilates to the position of
articulation of the following consonant.

123) LATIN
stem-final /g/ and /b/ become /k/ and /p/ when they
occur before the nominative singular inflection /-s/.
Stem-final /k/ and /p/ (as well as stem-final vowel)
are not affected. Assimilation: voiced /g/ and /b/
assimilate to the voicing of the following voiceless
/s/.

124) <u>ICELANDIC</u>

/e/ occurs before a following syllable containing /i/;
/a/ occurs elsewhere. Assimilation (umlaut): the vowel
of the stem assimilates to the front-back and
rounded-unrounded quality of the vowel in the
following syllable.

125) <u>SPANISH</u>

the stem vowel in examples 1-5 (underlying /ɛ/)
occurs as /ie/ when stressed; it occurs as /e/ when
unstressed. The stem vowel in 6-10 (underlying /e/)
does not diphthongize. Diphthongization.

126) <u>SPANISH</u>

the stem vowel in examples 1-5 (underlying /ɔ/)
occurs as /ue/ when stressed; it occurs as /o/ when
unstressed. The stem vowel in 6-10 (underlying /o/)
does not diphthongize. Diphthongization.

127) <u>GERMAN</u>

the stem-final voiced obstruants /b/, /d/, and /g/
become voiceless /p/, /t/, /k/ when they occur word-
final. The stem-final voiceless obstruants /p/, /t/,
/k/ are not affected. When only one of two contrasting
phonemes can occur in a certain position, the contrast
between them is said to be neutralized in that
position.

128) <u>TURKISH</u>

/t/ occurs following a voiceless consonant; /d/ occurs
elsewhere; e.g. <u>baš-ta</u> ~ <u>randevu-da</u>. Assimilation:
the consonant assimilates to the voicing or lack
thereof of the preceding consonant.

129) <u>TURKISH</u>

/e/ occurs following a front vowel of the root; /a/
occurs following a non-front vowel; e.g. <u>eš-ler</u> ~
<u>baš-lar</u>. Vowel harmony: a type of assmilation when
the vowel of a suffix assimilates to the place and
manner of the vowel of the stem.

130) <u>CREE</u>

/w/ occurs before a vowel, but disappears in final position preceded by a consonant; e.g. <u>atimw-ak</u>, <u>atimw-a</u> ~ <u>atim</u>. Deletion: the segment /w/ is deleted in word-final position following another consonant.

131) <u>CREE</u>

/t/ appears before a vowel, but disappears before a consonant; e.g. <u>nit-astotin</u> ~ <u>ni-či:man</u>. Deletion: the segment /t/ is deleted when followed by another consonant.

132) <u>AFRIKAANS</u>

/t/ occurs followed by a vowel, but disappears in final position whenpreceded by another consonant: e.g. <u>a:nraxt-ər</u> ~ <u>a:nrax</u>. This is the same process as in the preceding problem.

133) <u>PERSIAN</u>

/g/ occurs followed by a vowel, but disappears in final position preceded by a vowel: e.g. <u>bæččegan</u> ~ <u>bæčče</u>. Deletion: a segment /g/ is deleted in final position. This alternation, like many others in this section, are restricted to certain grammatical processes, and are not to be taken as general and universal rules in the languages concerned.

134) <u>MALTESE</u>

a cluster of identical consonants simplifies in final position; e.g. <u>mess-u</u> ~ <u>mes</u>. Geminate reduction: geminate consonants are reduced to single consonants in final position.

135) <u>GREEK</u>

/t,d,n/ occur before a vowel, but disappear when followed by /s/ in word-final position; e.g. <u>erot-os</u>, <u>elpid-os</u>, <u>hrin-os</u> ~ <u>ero-s</u>, <u>elpi-s</u>, <u>hri-s</u>. Deletion: a segment is deleted when followed by /s/.

136) CLASSICAL ARABIC

/w/ and /y/ occur before a consonant, but disappear in intervocalic position; e.g. qawl ~ qaala. Deletion: the segments /w/ and /y/ are deleted in intervocalic position.

137) IRAQI ARABIC

/a/ is inserted before a consonant in final position if the preceding vowel is also /a/; e.g. bayl-i ~ bayal. Epenthesis: a vowel is inserted between two consonants.

138) IRAQI ARABIC

/i/ is inserted before a consonant in final position if the preceding vowel is also /i/ and /u/ is inserted in the same position if the preceding vowel is /u/; e.g. bint-i ~ binit, xubz-i ~ xubuz. This is also epenthesis. Notice that the inserted vowel is like the vowel in the preceding syllable; this is a type of vowel harmony.

139) FIJIAN

the last consonant of a stem disappears in final position; e.g. lakov-a ~ lako. Deletion: a consonant is deleted in word-final position.

140) SWAHILI

/u/ occurs before a consonant; e.g. u-bale
/w/ occurs before a vowel; e.g. w-araka
/m/ occurs before /b/; e.g. m-bale
/n/ occurs before /d/; e.g. n-duvi
/ŋ/ occurs before /g/; e.g. ŋ-gimbi.
/ñ/ occurs before a vowel; e.g. ñ-araka

Assimilation: the nasal assimilates to the position of articulation of the following consonant. Palatalization: the nasal becomes palatalized before a vowel. Glide formation: the /u/ becomes /w/ before a following vowel.

141) **EGYPTIAN ARABIC**
/a/ occurs before a consonantal cluster; /aa/ occurs elsewhere; e.g. <u>šaf-na</u> ~ <u>šaaf</u>. Vowel shortening: a long vowel becomes short when followed by two consonants.

142) **EGYPTIAN ARABIC**
single vowel occurs before a consonantal cluster; two vowels occur elsewhere; e.g. <u>tag-na</u> ~ <u>taág</u>, <u>bir-na</u> ~ <u>biir</u>, <u>nur-na</u> ~ <u>nuur</u>; single vowel is either low or high, e.g. <u>bab-</u>, <u>bit-</u> ~ <u>beet</u>, <u>dur-</u> ~ <u>door</u>. Vowel shortening: a vowel becomes short when followed by two consonants; vowel raising: a mid vowel is raised to a high vowel when shortened.

143) **HUNGARIAN**
/e/ occurs following a front vowel; /o/ occurs following a non-front vowel; e.g. <u>ember-ek</u> ~ <u>dob-ok</u>. Vowel harmony: a vowel assimilates in place of articulation to the vowel of a preceding stem.

144) **HUNGARIAN**
/o/ disappears following a long vowel; e.g. <u>dob-ok</u> ~ <u>tanulo:-k</u>. Deletion: a vowel disappears in certain positions.

145) **SLOVAK**
long vowel ending occurs following a short vowel; short vowel ending occurs following either a long vowel or a diphthong; e.g. <u>krut-i:</u> ~ <u>ri:ʒ-i</u>, <u>biel-i</u>. This is a type if dissimation, in which a segment becomes unlike a neighbouring segment. In this case, the long vowel or diphthong in the stem calls for a short vowel in the inflection; a short vowel in the stem calls for a long vowel in the inflection.

146) <u>SLOVAK</u>

/iek/ occurs following a short vowel; /ok/ occurs following either a long vowel or a diphthong; e.g. <u>lat-iek</u> ~ <u>la:t-ok</u>, <u>čiel-ok</u>. This is another type of dissimilation, similar but not identical to the situation in the preceding problem. In this case, the inflection is either a diphthong, which is like a long vowel, or a short vowel.

147) <u>CZECH</u>

voiceless final consonant of the prepositions occurs before voiceless consonant; voiced consonant occurs elsewhere; e.g. <u>s tebou</u> ~ <u>z delegaci:</u>, <u>z ohn^Ye</u>. Assimilation: the consonant assimilates to the manner of articulation (voicing) of the following segment.

148) <u>HEBREW</u>

the final /t/ of the prefix changes places with the first consonant of the root if the consonant is a sibilant; e.g. <u>silek-histalek</u>, <u>šina-hištana</u> ~ <u>kibel-hit-kabel</u>. The process involved here is metathesis, when one segment changes places with another.

149) <u>FRENCH</u>

The feminine form has one more morpheme than the masculine. This feminine ending is traditionally regarded as /a/, which never shows up in pronunciation since it is deleted at the end of the word (e.g. /vɛrt-a/ fem., /vɛrt/ masc.). When it is not there, the final consonant of the base form (the masculine form) is also deleted. Deletion: the last segment of the word is deleted whether it is a vowel or a consonant.

150) <u>WELSH</u>

The morphemic difference must reside in the pronouns, however identical they look. One solution is to express them as /i/, /i-voicing/, and /i-spirantization/, with the effect on the following consonant, which happens to be the first consonant of

the following word. Another solution is to assume
that the pronouns have consonants at the ends: /i/
plus /voiceless consonant/, /i/ plus /voiced
consonant/, and /i/ plus /spirant consonant/. The
initial consonant of the following word assimilates to
the consonant at the end of the pronoun, after which
the consonant at the end of the pronoun is deleted.
Two processes: assimilation and segment deletion.
This process is also know as ~lenition" among
linguists who work with the Celtic languages.

151) POLISH
Polish has two nasal vowels, /õ/ and /ẽ/, which are
neutralized before a combination CV in final position.
In this position, only /ẽ/ can occur; e.g. /dõp/ -
/dẽbu/#; /Kẽs/ - /Kẽsa/#.

152) TURKISH
/a/ occurs if the last vowel of the stem is non-front.
/e/ occurs if the last vowel of the stem is front; e.g.
soy-mak ~ giy-mek. Vowel harmony, familiar from
previous problems in Turkish and Hungarian.

153) BULGARIAN
a vowel disappears before a sonorant followed by a
vowel. Deletion of a segment.

154) BULGARIAN
/K/ changes into /c/, /g/ into /z/, /x/ into /s/ before
a front vowel; e.g. rak-a ~ rac-i, vrag-a ~ vraz-i,
stomax-a ~ stomas-i. A consonant is always voiceless
in final position. Palatalization: a type of assimilation
when velar consonants are fronted to become palatal
consonants before a front vowel.

155) **FINNISH**

CC occur in an open syllable; a single consonant occurs in a closed syllable; e.g. kukka ~ kukan. This is known as consonant gradation, and is a type of syllable structure process in which a syllable changes structure (here from closed to open) in response to the structure of surrounding syllables.

156) **FINNISH**

CC occurs in a morpheme ending in an open syllable; a single consonant occurs in a morpheme ending in a closed syllable; e.g. menette-len ~ menetel-lä. Another example of gradation.

157) **FINNISH**

combination of a nasal and a stop occurs in an open syllable; two nasals occur in a closed syllable; e.g. huonomp-a ~ huonomm-an. This is a type of gradation combined with assimilation of the stop to the nasal. The same process occurs with other sonorants phonemes like /l/.

158) **CZECH**

/s/ occurs if the next morpheme begins with /tᵞ/; /t/ and /d/ occur elsewhere; e.g. met-u, met-e ~ me:s-tᵞi. Dissimilation: the segment becomes more unlike its environment.

159) **MODERN GREEK**

The first consonant of the prefix is a reduplication of the first consonant of a stem. Reduplication: all or a part of a morpheme is repeated in certain grammatical constructions.

160) **ENGLISH**

/ə/ occurs in unstressed position; e.g. /mórəl/ ~ /mərǽlətiy/. Vowel reduction: a type of weakening process.

161) **ENGLISH**

/š/ and /ž/ occur before underlying /i/; /t/ and /d/ occur elsewhere; e.g. /raleyt/ ~ /raleyšən/. Palatalization, a type of assimilation.

162) **ENGLISH**

/š/ and /ž/ occur before underlying /i/, /s/ and /z/ occur elsewhere; e.g. /reys/ ~ /reyšəl/

163) **ENGLISH**

clusters /gn/, /gm/, /mb/, /tn/, do not occur in final position; e.g. /signal/ ~ /sayn/. Segment deletion, a type of syllable structure process.

164) **ENGLISH**

/s/ occurs after a voiceless consonant; /iz/ occurs after a sibilant; /z/ occurs elsewhere; e.g. /wayfs/, /sistrz/, /bɔsiz/. The plural morpheme is basically /z/; it assimilates to the voicelessness of a preceding voiceless consonant. When it follows another sibilant, there is a process of segment insertion when the /i/ is placed between the two sibilants.

165) **ENGLISH**

/m/ occurs before a labial consonant; /n/ before a dental or alveolar; /ŋ/ before a velar; /l/ before /l/ and /r/ before /r/. Assimilation: the consonant of the prefix assimilates to the place and manner of the following consonant.

166) **ENGLISH**

suffix: /s/ occurs after a voiceless consonant; /iz/ occurs after a sibilant; /z/ occurs elsewhere; e.g. /pæθs/, /hawziz/, /huwvz/. The processes here are identical to those in problem 164, even though the morpheme here is the plural instead of the possessive. Notice that in the noun stems, the stem-final voiced spirant in the plural becomes voiceless in the singular. Assimilation and devoicing.

167) <u>ENGLISH</u>
see 166

168) <u>ENGLISH</u>
/t/ occurs after a voiceless consonant; /ɨd/ occurs
after /d/ or /t/; /d/ occurs elsewhere; e.g. /kept/,
/ædɨd/, /həgd/. Assimilation and segment insertion.

IV. MORPHOLOGY

In the following solutions, only the inflectional and
derivational morphemes will be listed except in the
model solutions, where all morphemes will be listed.

169) <u>EGYPTIAN ARABIC</u>
Model Solution:
Stems (past tense verbs): xabbar- told; ḥamal-
carried; xadam- served; šaf- saw; tabaʕ- followed;
raggaʕ- brought back
Object suffixes (conjunct pronouns): -ak you (masc.);
-ik you (fem.); -kum you (pl.); -hum them
Negative suffixes: ma ... -š not

170) <u>CZECH</u>
po- future; při- approximation; od- away; -u 1st
pers.sg.; -eš 2nd pers. sg.; -e 3rd pers. sg.; -eme 1st
pers. pl.; -ete 2nd pers. pl.; -ou 3rd pers. pl.

171) <u>LEBANESE ARABIC</u>
θ- 1st pers. sg.; t- 2nd pers. sg. masc.; t- ... -i 2nd
pers. sg. fem.; y- 3rd pers. sg. masc.; t- 3rd pers. sg.
fem.; n- 1st pers. pl.; t- ... -u 2nd pers. pl.; y- ... -u
3rd pers. pl.

172) <u>CREE</u>
ni- 1st pers.; ki- 2nd pers.; ni- ... -a:n 1st pers. pl.;
ki- ... -a:wa:w 2nd pers. pl.

173) SWAHILI

ni- 1st pers. sg.; u- 2nd pers. sg.; a- 3rd pers. sg.; tu-
1st pers. pl.; m- 2nd pers. pl.; wa- 3rd pers. pl.; -na-
pres.; -ta- future

174) SWAHILI

-na- pres.; -ta- future; -li- past; -me- perf.; -ni- me;
-ku- you; -m- him; -tu- us; -wa- you (pl.); -wa- them

175) HEBREW

-ti I; -ta you (masc.); -t you (fem.); -nu we; -tem
(masc. pl.); -ten you (fem. pl.).

176) HUNGARIAN

a) 1) 31; 2) 60; 3) 51; 4) 200; 5) 10,000 6) 1514; 7) 44;
8) 80; 9) 1848; 10) 27; 11) 100,000; 12) 33; 13) 19; 14)
22; 15) 69; 16) 75.
b) vowel harmony
c) ezerkilencsa:zn^{y}olcvanne:d^y; harmincöt; ezerke:t-
sa:zne:d^{y}venöt.

177) ITALIAN

-o 1st pers. sg.; -i 2nd pers. sg.; -a 3rd pers. sg.;
-iamo 1st pers. pl.; -ate 2nd pers. pl.; -ano 3rd pers
pl.; -ar- imperfect.

178) BULGARIAN

items 1-7: -0 nom. sg.; -ove nom. pl.; items 8-14: -ec
dimin. suffix; 0 nom. sg.; -c- dimin. suffix; ov-...-e
nom. pl.

179) LEBANESE ARABIC

-ni me; -ak you (masc.); -ik you (fem.); -n him; -a her;
-na us; -kun you (pl.); -un them.

180) CLASSICAL ARABIC

ʕ-L-M teach/learn; S-L-M hand over/obtain; S-L-F

-293-

lend/borrow; S-R-ʕ hasten/run; ð-K-R remember/
remind. Morphological processes: prefixation;
gemination; suffixation; vocalic alternation. The
gemination of the middle consonant of the stem can
also be considered infixation, since it comes in the
middle of a morpheme. Notice that the vowels vary in
a number of patterns. This is called "discontinuous
morphology", and is characteristic of the Semitic
languages.

181) <u>PERSIAN</u>

xah- future; -an inf.; na- negative; -am 1st pers. sg.;
-i 2nd pers. sg.; -ad 3rd pers. sg.; -im 1st pers. pl.;
-id 2nd pers. pl.; -and 3rd pers. pl.
xaham raŋ; xahand raŋ; naxahim raŋ.

182) <u>CREE</u>

-a pl.; ni- my; ki- your (sg.); o- his; ni- ... -ina:n our;
ki- ... iwa:w your (pl.); o- ... iwa:w their.

183) <u>EGYPTIAN ARABIC</u>

-t you (masc.); -ti ~ -tii you (fem.); -na ~ -naa we; -tu
~ -tuu you (pl.).
negative marker: ma- ... -š; objective markers: ha ~
haa her; ki ~ kii you (fem.); ni ~ nii me.

184) <u>BULGARIAN</u>

All items: -∅ sg.; -i pl.; items 11-20: suffix -in- in sg.

185) <u>PERSIAN</u>

-am 1st pers. sg.; -i 2nd pers. sg.; -id 3rd pers. sg.;
-im 1st pers. pl.; -id 2nd pers. pl.; -and 3rd pers. pl.;
mi- continuous action; na- negative.

186) <u>PERSIAN</u>

Inflections: see 185. mi- continuous action; be- may;
na- negative. Note that after the negative na-, the
be- is omitted.

187) **TURKISH**

-Ji/-Ji/-Ju/-Jü agent; -liK/-liK/-luK/-lüK abstract nouns, locality; -Je/-Ja/-če/-ča manner, relation; -siz/-siz/-suz/-süz negative.

188) **CREE**

wa:pa- see; Kanawe:li- Keep; -m- (indicates animate object); -ht- (indicates inanimate object); ni- I; Ki- you; 0- he; ni...a:w I-him; Ki...a:w you-him; 0...e:w he-him; ni...a:na:n we-him; Ki...a:wa:w you (pl.)-him; 0-...e:waK they-him.
ni...e:n I-it; Ki...e:n you-it; 0-...am he-it; ni...e:na:n we-it; Ki...e:na:wa:w you (pl.)-it; 0-...amwaK they-it. Further analysis is possible but not profitable at this level.

189) **CZECH**

I. Animate nouns ending with -š, -č, -ř, i.e. pre-palatal cons.; II. Animate nouns ending with other consonants. In I and II, accusative genitive; III Inanimate nouns ending with pre-palatal/palatal consonants; IV. Inanimate nouns ending with other consonants; III + IV accusative nominative.

190) **TURKISH**

1. eve; 2. ati; 3. gülün; 4. yoldan; 5. ičKiye; 6. odadan; 7. köprüyle; 8. paltonun; 9. Jeple; 10. Kitabi; 11. otobüsten; 12. KaraKol; 13. Kedinin; 14. parayla; 15. sürüye; 16. KoKuyu; 18. vatan; 19. güne; 20. horozu; 21. mefKinin; 22. elma; 23. Köylüyle; 24. piyangodan.

191) **HUNGARIAN**

-eK/-oK/-öK I; -s/-es/-as you (sg.); -0 he/she; -unK/ ünK we; -teK/-toK/-töK you (pl.); -neK/-naK they.

192) **CZECH**

The Key categories to different inflectional patterns are: gender (masc., fem., neuter); animate and case (nominative vs. dative); and number (sing. vs. pl). The plural ending depends on the category of animateness.

193) ENGLISH

Prefixes: an-, endr-, ba-, owt-, in; Deriv. suffixes: -liy, -nes, -šip, -ar, -ful, -iy, -les, -iš, -Kin, -riy, -an, -al, -ar, -iŋ; Inflex. suffixes: -s, -ad, -an.

194) ENGLISH

Group I: a) un-, non-, in-, dis-, a- (negative); b) un-, de- (reversative); Group II: a) mis-, mal-, pseudo-, (pejorative); b) arch-, sub-, over-, hyper- (degree); Group III: a) super-, sub-, inter-, under- (locative); b) ex-, fore-, pre-, post- (time).

195) ENGLISH

Occupational: 1, 4; Diminutive: 2, 7, 14, 16, 21, 26; Feminine: 5, 8; Member of a group: 6, 9, 23, 24, 27, 28; Abstract noun: 3, 10, 11, 15, 18, 19, 20, 22, 25, 29, 30; Action: 12; Adjectival: 13; Adverbial:17

196) ENGLISH

Deverbatives: 1, 5, 7, 8, 13, 14, 15, 19, 20, 22, 24, 27, 29; Denominatives: 2, 3, 4, 6, 9, 10, 11, 12, 16, 17, 18, 21, 23, 25, 26, 28, 30.

197) ENGLISH

Acronyms: 2, 17, 19, 39, 41, 46, 59; Derivatives: 1, 4, 5, 10, 11, 16, 22, 25, 29, 31, 34, 38, 40, 43, 44, 47, 55, 58; Conversions: 8, 12, 18, 49, 51, 54; Borrowings: 9, 13, 26, 33, 35, 37, 45, 48, 50, 52, 56; Compounds: 6, 20, 21, 23, 32, 42, 57, 60; Redupulicates: 3, 15, 27, 53; Clippings: 7, 14, 24, 28, 30, 36. (Laser: light amplification by stimulated emission of radiation; Radar: radio detecting and ranging)

198) ENGLISH

V → N: 1, 4, 5, 7, 8, 13, 16, 20, 22, 25, 28, 29; A → N: 2, 6, 27; N → V: 3, 10, 11, 14, 15, 17, 19, 23, 24, 30; A → V: 9, 12, 18, 21, 26.

199) **ENGLISH**
1) V + Subj; 2) V + Obj; 3) Obj + V; 4) Subj + V; 5) Adv
+ V; 6) N + N; 7) V + Subj; 8) N + N; 9) Obj + V; 10) Subj
+ V; 11) Adv + V; 12) Adv + V; 13) V + Obj; 14) V + Subj;
15) Adv + A; 16) A + N; 17) N + N; 18) Adv + V; 19) Obj
+ V; 20) Obj + V.

V. STRUCTURAL AND FUNCTIONAL SYNTAX

200) **MALAY**
Model solution:
Nouns: rumah house; bapa father; anak lelaki son;
perempuan girl; kakak sister
Verbs: lihat look; činta love; iɲin want; kahwin marry;
Jadi get; čadan decide; iŋkari disobey; ampun forgive;
bunuh kill; jerit scream; iŋgal leave
Adjectives: čantik beautiful; miskin poor; kaya rich;
marah angry
Adverbs: nasib baik luckily
Grammatical elements: ma-/mam-/maŋ-/man- continuous action or state; -ña possessive marker; itu
definite article; -kan transitive marker; saoraŋ
indefinite article; yaŋ adjective marker; (untuk)...i
infinitive; bar-, -kan reflexive markers (not obvious
from the sample); dan and.

201) **MALAY**
Sg. of nouns indicating persons - saoraŋ, pl. formed by
reduplication of the stem, e.g. murid-murid (pupils).
Sg. of nouns indicating animals - saekor, pl. indicated
by baŋak. Articles: saoraŋ a, one; itu the.

202) **LATIN**
Nominal suffixes: -a nom. sg.; -ae gen. sg.; -am acc.
sg.; -ae nom. pl.; -ārum gen. pl.; -ās acc. pl. Verbal
suffixes: -t 3rd pers. sg.; -nt 3rd pers. pl.; -mus 1st
pers. pl. Others: et and; -ne question marker.

203) <u>ESTONIAN</u>
<u>Nominal suffixes</u>: -ed/-ud plural; -it/-ut object; -il/
-el/-ul/-al on, at; -i/-u possess.; -i/-u/-a partitive;
-s/-is/-us in; -dega with. <u>Verbal suffixes</u>: -b 3rd
pers. sg.; -vad 3rd pers. pl. <u>Pronouns</u>: teisel/teised
other/others; ta she/he; mu my; tema her/his; meie
our; siin here. <u>Numerals</u>: üks one; kaks two; kolm
three. <u>Some stems</u>: poiss boy; kaan cover; isa father;
äri store; onutütar cousin; nukk doll; yutt story; on is/
are/has.

204) <u>BULGARIAN</u>
<u>Definite markers</u>: -at masc. sg.; -te masc. pl.; -ta fem.
sg. <u>Nominal suffixes</u>: -a nom. sg. fem.; -a gen. sg.
masc.; -i nom. pl. masc. <u>Prepositions</u>: na of/on; v in
(place); do in (direction).

205) <u>HEBREW</u>
<u>Pronouns</u>: ani I; ata you (masc.); at you (fem.); hu he;
hi she; anaxnu we; atem you (masc. pl.); aten you (fem.
pl.); hen they. <u>Verbal suffixes</u>: -∅ masc.sg.; -a fem
sg.; -im masc.pl.; -ot fem.pl. <u>Prefixes</u>: ba-/be- in.

206) <u>HINDI</u>
rahe progressive marker; kā possessive marker; -ta
pres. 3rd pers. sg. masc.; tī pres. 3rd pers. sg. fem.;
hai present tense marker/is; hãi present tense
marker/are; mẽ in; ko to; ke lie for; se from. Examples
of word order: 1) S + N + prep +V + prog. marker + hai;
8) S + Ind.O + Dir.O + V + hai; 22) S + Adv + Adj + hai.

207) <u>TURKISH</u>
-im/-üm I; -ik/-ɨk we; (y)-i/(y)-u/-(y)ɨ/-(y)ü acc.
definite; -ler/-lar pl.; bir indef. article.

208) <u>CLASSICAL ARABIC</u>
ʔal-/l- def. article; -u nom.; -a acc.; -i gen.(or prepositional); -hu ~ hi his; -hum ~ -him their (masc.); -hunna ~ -hinna their (fem.).

209) <u>CLASSICAL ARABIC</u>
l- def. article; -un nom. indef.; -an acc. indef. <u>Nominal suffixes</u>: -u nom.; -a acc. <u>Verbal suffixes</u>: -a 3rd pers. sg.; -ta you (subj. masc.); -ti you (subj. fem.); -naa we (subj.); -tum you (subj. pl.); -ka you (obj. masc.)⌐-ki you (obj. fem.); -kumu you (obj. pl.).

210) <u>CZECH</u>
<u>Masc. sg.</u>: -i: adj; -ø noun; -ø verb. <u>Masc. pl.</u>: -i: adj; -i noun; -i verb. <u>Fem. sg.</u>: -a adj; -a noun; -a verb. <u>Fem. pl.</u>: -e: adj; -i noun; -i verb; -l past tense.

211) <u>CZECH</u>
<u>Present participle</u>: -e masc. sg.; -i:c fem. sg.; -i:ce pl. <u>Past participle</u>: -lø masc. sg.; -la fem. sg.; -li pl.

212) <u>RUSSIAN</u>
Suffix -u indicates partitive – reference to unspecified quantity.

213) <u>GERMAN</u>
The prepositions govern the forms of the following noun phrases. Aus, bei, mit, nach, zu require <u>dem</u>; ohne, für, um, durch, gegen require <u>den</u>; während, anstelle, ausserhalb, zugunsten, anstatt require <u>des...es</u>.

214) <u>TURKISH</u>
S + (Time) + (Place) + (Dir. Obj.) + (Inf.) + V in 1, 2, 3, 4, 5, 6, 7, 8; (Ind.Obj) + Dir.Obj + V in 9, 10, 11, 15; S pron + Dir.Obj + Place + V in 12, 13; Place + Dir.Obj + V in 14.

215) <u>BASQUE</u>
-ak/-ek indicates the subject of transitive verbs.

216) RUSSIAN
The reflexive suffix indicates: a) Identity of Object
and Subject in 2, 3, 5, 6, 14; b) Reciprocity in 1, 7, 15,
18; c) Passive voice in 8, 11, 12, 16, 19; d)
Characteristic feature of the subject in 4, 9, 13, 17,
20.

217) IRAQI ARABIC
S: NP VP
NP: Art N
VP: V NP
V: Pers. Tense Marker VS

Art {l-}
N {walad, beet, ...}
p.t.m. {y-}
VS {-šuuf, -hibb, ...}

218) HEBREW
S: NP VP
NP: Art N
VP: V Ojb. Marker NP

Art {ha-}
N {yeled, kelev, ...}
V {raa, siyam, ...}
OM {et}

219) SPANISH
S: NP VP
NP: Art N
VP: V NP
V: VS Pers. Tense Marker

Art {el ~ la}
N {muchacho, fotografía, ...}
VS {mir-, compr-, ...}
p.t.m. {ó}

220) <u>FRENCH</u>
    S: NP VP
    NP: Art N
    VP: V NP
    V: VS Pers. Tense Marker

    Art {une ~ un, la ~ le}
    N {mère, repas, ...}
    VS {prépar-, lav-, ...}
    p.t.m. {-ait}

221) <u>GERMAN</u>
    S: NP VP
    NP: Art N/Pronoun
    VP: V Adv
    V: VS Pers. Tense Marker

    Art {das ~ der ~ die}
    N {Kind, Kalb, Frau, ...}
    Pro {er, sie, ...}
    VS {sprich-, is-, ...}
    p.t.m. {-t}
    Adv {schnell, hier, ...}

222) <u>IRAQI ARABIC</u>
    S: NP VP
    NP: Art N
    VP: Fut. Part. V NP/PP
    V: Pers. Tense Marker VS
    PP: Prep. NP

    Art {l-}
    N {walad, ʕarabi, ...}
    FP {raah}
    p.t.m. {y- ~ t- }
    VS {-ihci, -ruuh, ...}
    Prep {ʕa-, bi-, ...}

223) IRAQI ARABIC
S: NP VP
NP: Art N
VP: (Modal) V NP/PP
V: Pers. Tense Marker VS

Art {l- ~ d-}
N {walad, daris, ...}
Modal {raah, laazim, mumkin}
p.t.m. {y- ~ t-}
VS {idrus, imši}

224) IRAQI ARABIC
S: NP VP
NP: Art N
VP: (V_{aux}) V NP (PP)
V_{aux}: Pres. Tense Marker VS_{aux}
V: Pers. Tense Marker VS
PP: Prep N

Art {l-}
N {binit, kitaab, ...}
p.t.m. {y- ~ t-}
VS_{aux} {-igdar, -riid, ...}
VS: {-ištiri, -iɣsil, ...}
Prep {bi-}

225) LEBANESE ARABIC
S: NP VP
NP: Art N
VP: Mood (V_{aux} V NP
V_{aux}: Pers. Tense Marker VS_{aux}
V: Pers. Tense Marker VS

Art {1- ~ d-}
N {walad, dars, ...}
Mood {b}
p.t.m. {y- ~ t-}
VS$_{aux}$ {-i?dar, -ib?a, ...}
VS {idris}

226) IRAQI ARABIC
S: NP VP
NP: (Dem. Adj.) Art N
VP: V NP
V: VS Past

Dem. Adj. {haaða ~ haay, ...}
Art {1-}
N {madrasa, binit, ...}
VS {yasal, šaaf, ...}
Past {-θ ~ -it}

227) EGYPTIAN ARABIC
S: NP VP
NP: Art N (Dem. Adj.)
VP: V Adv
V: (Modal) Pers. Tense Maker VS

Art {1-}
N {walad, gamal, ...}
Dem. Adj. {da ~ di}
Modal {ha}
p.t.m. {y- ~ t-}
VS {-igi, saafir, ...}
Adv {hina, kitiir, ...}

228) LATIN
S: NP VP
NP: N
N: NS Case
VP: Adj. V
Adj: AS Case
V: VS Pers. Tense Marker

NS {serv-, puell-, ...}
Case {-us ~ -a ~ -um}
AdjS {bon-, bell-, ...}
VS {es}
p.t.m. {-t}

229) <u>LATIN</u>

S: NP VP
NP: N
N: NS Case
Case: Nom./Acc.
VP: N V
V: T₊S Pers. Tense Marker

NS {serv-, hort-, ...}
Nom. {-us ~ -a}
Acc. {-um ~ -am}
V₊S {vide-, lava-, ...}
p.t.m. {-t}

230) <u>CLASSICAL ARABIC</u>
S: (Q) VP NP
VP: V NP
V: VS Pers. Tense Marker
NP: NS Case

Q {hal}
VS {darab, katab, ...}
p.t.m. {-a ~ -t}
NS {?aḥmad, ?asad, ...}
Case {-u, -un, -a, -an}

231) <u>TURKISH</u>
S: NP VP (Q)
NP: N
VP: NP V
V: VS Past

Q {m1 ~ mu ...}
N {ahmed, asker, ...}
VS {al-, bul-, ...}
Past {d1 ~ du ...}

232) <u>ENGLISH</u>

1-5) {N/Pro} V_{it}; 6-10) Det N V_{it}; 11-15) Det A N V_{it};
16-20) Det (A) N PP V_{it}; 21-25) NP V_{it} PP PP; 26-30)
NP V_t NP Adv; 31-35) NP V_{it} PP Adv; 36-40) NP V_t NP
PP; 41-45) NP V_{it} (NP) Adv; 46-50) NP + V_{it} {Adj/NP};
51-55) NP + V + NP; 56-60) NP V_t NP 61-65) NP + V_{it}
+ PP

233) <u>ENGLISH</u>

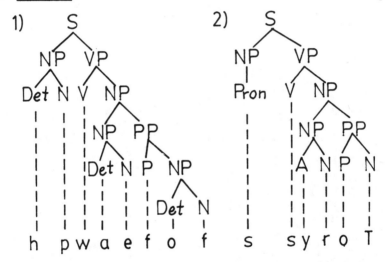

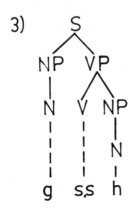

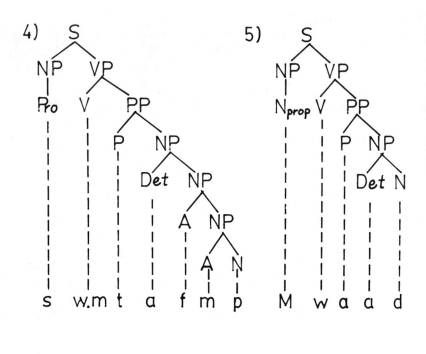

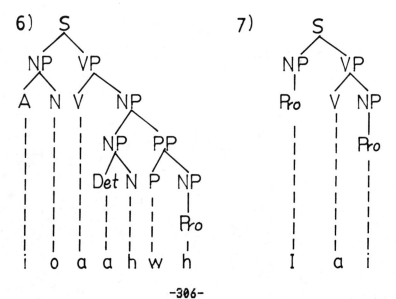

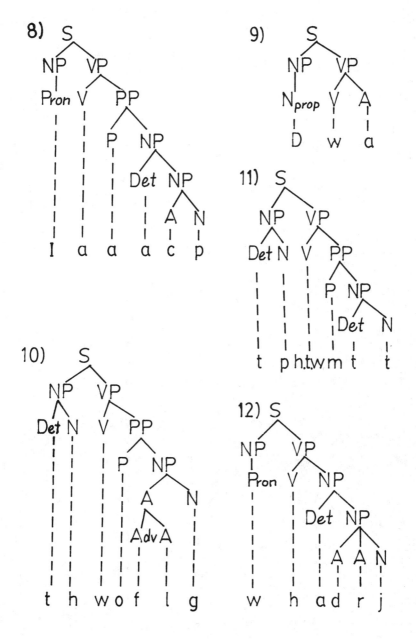

13)

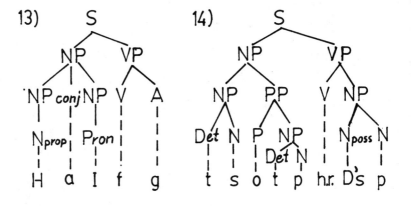

15)

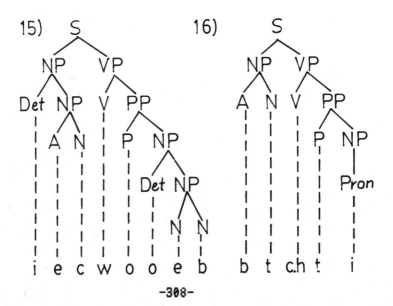

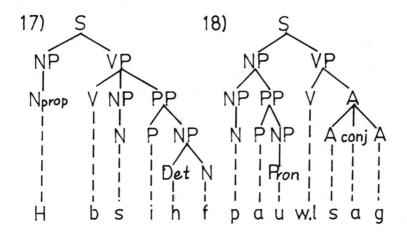

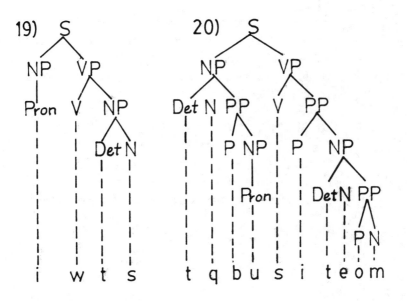

234) <u>ENGLISH</u>

A non-finite clause is a clause whose verbal element is an infinitive or a participle.
1) infinitive with <u>to</u> without subject; subjective complement. 2) -ing participle without subject; adverbial of time. 3) -ed participle without subject; adverbial of manner. 4) -ed participle with subject; adverbial of manner. 5) infinitive with <u>to</u> with subject; subjective complement. 6) -ed participle without subject; adverbial of time. 7) -ing participle with subject; adverbial of time. 8) infinitive without <u>to</u> with subject; adverbial of preference. 9) infinitive with <u>to</u> with subject; adjectival complement. 10) infinitive with <u>to</u> with subject; subject.

235) <u>ENGLISH</u>

Subordinate clauses function as: 1) subject; 2) direct object; 3) subjective complement; 4) indirect object; 5) adverbial (cause); 6) adverbial (place); 7) adverbial (time); 8) direct object; 9) adverbial (time); 10) adverbial (condition); 11) adverbial (condition); 12) adverbial (reason); 13) adverbial (manner).

236) <u>ENGLISH</u>

Functions of the subordinate clauses: 1) Object; 2) Object; 3) Subjective complement; 4) Not applicable; 5) Adverbial (time); 6) Adverbial (time); 7) Modifier; 8) Object; 9) Object; 10) Object, object; 11) Adverbial (time); 12) Modifier.

VI. <u>SYNTACTIC PROCESSES</u>

The following statements should be considered only as hints aiding in possible solutions within the framework of transformational generative theory.

237) **SPANISH**

$V N_{pers} \Rightarrow V a N_{pers}$

el muchacho mira la profesora

⇓

el muchacho mira a la profesora

238) **RUMANIAN**

Def Art N $\Rightarrow$ N Def Art

ul amic vede un caîne

⇓

amicul vede un caîne

239) **GERMAN**

hat Past Participle NP $\Rightarrow$ hat NP past Participle

er hat gesehen das Kind

⇓

er hat das Kind gesehen

240) **SPANISH**

$NP_1 V Np_1 \Rightarrow NP_1$ se V

el muchacho$_1$ lava al muchacho$_1$

⇓

el muchacho se lava

241) **FRENCH**

$N_1 V N_1 V \Rightarrow N V V_{infinitive}$

il veut [il achète la maison]

⇓

il veut acheter la maison

242) **LEBANESE ARABIC**

Art N Art N $\Rightarrow$ N Art N

?aḥmad diḥin l-baab l-beet

⇓

?aḥmad diḥin baab l-beet

243) **LEBANESE ARABIC**

$N_1 [N_2 V N_1] V \Rightarrow N_1$ illi N_2 V-pro

lwalad [?aḥmad šaaf lwalad] kaan hawn

⇩

lwalad illi ?aḥmad šaafu kaan hawn

244) <u>LEBANESE ARABIC</u>
Art N₁ [Art N₁ V Adj] ⇒ Art N₁ Art Adj
lwalad [lwalad kaan kbiir] iža

⇩

lwalad lkbiir iža

245) <u>SWAHILI</u>
PM tense VS NM NS ⇒ PM tense NM VS
mtoto alisoma kitabu

⇩

mtoto alikisoma

246) <u>SWAHILI</u>
N₁ [N₁ ni Adj] ⇒ N₁ Adj
kisu [kisu ni kidogo] kinafaa

⇩

kisu kidogo kinafaa

247) <u>FRENCH</u>
Neg V ⇒ ne V pas
Neg je vois l'enfant

⇩

je ne vois pas l'enfant

248) <u>SPANISH</u>
Neg V pro ⇒ no V Pro_{neg}
Neg veo algo

⇩

no veo nada

249) <u>SPANISH</u>
VS p.t.m._1 [VS p.t.m._2] ⇒ VS p.t.m._1 que VS p.t.m._2
subj
espero [habla español]

⇩

espero que hable español

250) LATIN
V [NP VS-ant] ⇒ V NP VS-are
dicit [milites pugnant] ⇒ dicit milites pugnare

251) POLISH
Q NP_1 V albo {NP_2/PP_1} albo {NP_3/PP_3} ⇒ Czy NP_1
V{NP_2/PP_1} Czy{NP_3/PP_2}
Q Jones jest albo dedektywem albo policjantem ⇒
Czy Jones jest dedektyvem czy policjantem

252) GERMAN
2) werde; 3) es; 4) wir; 5) werden; 6) werde es; 7) Ich;
9) ich, es; 10) werde es; 2) dass ich; 3) dass, würden;
4) ich es sehen würde; 5) dass wir, kaufen würden; 6)
würde; 7) dass, es, würden; 8) dass es essen würde; 9)
dass, es, würden; 10) dass ich es bringen.

NP_1 V {ich/wir} {werde/werden} + Pron + V inf ⇒ NP_1
V dass {ich/wir} Pron V inf {würde/würden}.
Er sagte [Ich werde es vergessen] ⇒ Er sagte dass
ich es vergessen würde

253) BULGARIAN
UF: (Neg) (Q) (Pro) (šče) V; C: Neg Pron ⇒ Pron n^yama
da V; D: Q Pron V ⇒ V li, etc.

254) CZECH
Infinitive: N_1 V_1past [N_1 V_2 N_2] ⇒ N_1 V_1past V_2inf
N_2
Barbora odmi:tla [barbora vaři: ob^yet]
⇓
barbora odmi:tla vaři: ob^yet

Subordinate: ...[$N_1$$V_2$ N_2] ⇒ ...abi θ V_2-past N_2
[barbora vaři: ob^yet] abi (u) vařila ob^yet

255) CZECH
A: N_1 Mod p.t.m. VS inf N_2; B: N_1 VS p.t.m. N_2; C: N_1
Mod p.t.m. VS inf N_2 D: N_1 {do-} VS p.t.m. N_2.

-313-

256) <u>CZECH</u>
Neg N V {PP/NP} ⇒ nigdo ne V {PP/NP}
petr sta:l za dveřmi
⇓
nigdo nesta:l za dveřmi

257) <u>CZECH</u>
Det N_1 V Det N_2 ⇒ Det N_1 Pron V
to d^{Y}éfče úhod^{Y}ilo toho múže
⇓
to d^{Y}éfče yey úhodilo

N_2 [Det N_1 V Det N_2] ⇒ N_2 co Pron$_2$ Det N_1 V
múš [to d^{Y}éfče úhod^{Y}ilo toho múže]
⇓
múš có yey to d^{Y}éfče úhod^{Y}ilo
An unstressed constituent always precedes a stressed constituent.

258) <u>BASQUE</u>
N_1 {A/N_2} V ⇒ {A/N_2} V -n N_1

259) <u>ENGLISH</u>
1) N_{prop} V Z_3; 2) NP_{pl} V Adv; N_{prop} V past PP; 4) N_{prop} have Z_3 V en NP; 5) N_{prop} Conj N_{prop} have V en NP; 6)NP_{sg} have past V en; 7) NP_{pl} have past V en NP; 8) N_{prop} be Z_3 V ing; 9) NP_{pl} be V ing NP; 10) NP_{sg} be past V ing; 11)NP_{pl} be past V ing PP; 12)N_{prop} have Z_3 be en V ing PP; 13) NP_{pl} have be en V ing NP; 14) N_{prop} have past be en V ing; 15) NP_{pl} have past be en V ing NP; 16) N_{prop} M V Adv; 17) N_{prop} Conj N_{prop} M V; 18) N_{prop} M past V NP; 19) NP_{pl} M past V NP; 20) NP_{pl} M havebe en V ing; 21) NP_{sg} M have be en V ing NP; 22) NP_{sg} M past have be en V ing NP; 23) NP_{pl} M past have be en V ing NP.

260) <u>ENGLISH</u>
Neg NP tense ({have/be/M})... ⇒ NP tense ({have/be/ M}) n't...

e.g. Neg the coffee Z_3 be always bitter
⇩
the coffee Z_3 be n't always bitter
The coffee isn't always bitter.

261) <u>ENGLISH</u>

Q NP tense (⟨have/be/M⟩)... ⇨ tense(⟨have/be/M⟩)
(n't) NP...
e.g. Q you θ M go home now
⇩
θ M you go home now
Must you go home now?

262) <u>ENGLISH</u>

Q NP tense V ... ⇨ tense do NP V ...
e.g. Laura past brush her hair
⇩
past do Laura brush her hair
Did Laura brush her hair?

263) <u>ENGLISH</u>

Tag NP_1 tense (⟨have/be/M⟩) {n't/θ} ... # ⇨ NP_1 tense
(⟨have/be/M⟩) {n't/θ} ... # tense (⟨have/be/M⟩) {θ/n't}
Pro_1
e.g. Tag she Z_3 be θ a pretty good actress #
⇩
she Z_3 be θ a pretty good actress # Z_3 be n't she
She is a pretty good actress, isn't she?

264) <u>ENGLISH</u>

A possible treatment is that one of the
transformations moves the unspecified constituent
(such as SOMEONE, SOMETHING) to the front and
attaches <u>wh-</u> to it.
e.g. Q Lucy Z_3 say SOMETHING
⇩

Z_3 Lucy say SOMETHING
$$\Downarrow$$
Wh-SOMETHING Z_3 Lucy say
$$\Downarrow$$
Wh-SOMETHING Z_3 do Lucy say
What does Lucy say?

265) ENGLISH
$NP_1 \ldots$ pass V_{tr} $NP_2 \Rightarrow NP_2$ be en V_{tr} by NP_1
e.g. NP_1 past pass occupy NP_2
$$\Downarrow$$
NP_2 past be en occupy by NP_1
The extensive apartments were occupied by Aylmer Enterprises.

266) ENGLISH
The reflexive transformation substitutes a pronoun for the NP which is identical in reference with the subject and adds self orselves to that pronoun.
e.g. Sylvia will speak up for Sylvia
$$\Downarrow$$
Sylvia will speak up for herself.

267) ENGLISH
This transformation substitutes the appropriate relativizer (who, whom, which, etc.) for the second NP
e.g. NP_1 past be NP_2 [NP_2 past be able ...] $\Rightarrow$
NP_1 past be NP_2who past be able...
She was a woman who was able...

268) ENGLISH
Sentences containing subordinate adverbial clauses are derived from deep structures in which the constituent Adv has been rewritten as a sentence.
e.g. SOMETIMES [Jack was dressed] he went over to her
$$\Downarrow$$
When Jack was dressed, he went over to her.

269) ENGLISH
Subject from an embedded clause becomes a constituent in the structure of a main clause.

e.g. He scarcely knew SOMETHING [he was eating]
⇩
He scarcely knew what he was eating.

270) ENGLISH
If the subject of the embedded clause is identical with
that of the main clause, then the second subject does
not appear in the surface structure.
e.g. City people yearn SOMETHING [City people live
on a farm]
⇩
City people yearn to live on a farm

VII. SOUND CHANGE

271) OLD ICELANDIC
1) o: > ö:/___C(C)i
2) z > r/i___#
3) i > 0/___r#

272) OLD ICELANDIC
1) a > ɔ/___C(C)u
2) u > 0/___#

273) SPANISH
1) a > e/___C(C) {e/i} V
2) {e/i} > 0/___V

274) OLD HIGH GERMAN
i > e/___C(C) {mid vowel/low vowel}

275) MALTESE
1) aa > aa/Ç
> ie/elsewhere
2) Ç > C

276) <u>RUMANIAN</u>
ea > a/labial C___

277) <u>RUMANIAN</u>
u > u/C {l/r} ___#
   > 0/C(C)___#

278) <u>MALTESE</u>
1) V > 0/___C {VV/VCC}
2) VV > V/___CVV

279) <u>EGYPTIAN ARABIC</u>
VV > V/___CC

280) <u>LEBANESE ARABIC</u>
V? > V:/___C

281) <u>SPANISH</u>
0 > e/#sC(C)V

282) <u>LEBANESE ARABIC</u>
0 > i/C___ {m/n/l/r}#

283) <u>PORTUGUESE</u>
1) e > 0/___#
2) V > Ṽ/___{m/n}{C/#}
3) n > 0/V___V

284) <u>SPANISH</u>
{p/t/k} > {b/d/g} /V___V

285) <u>ITALIAN</u>
{kt/ks/gn} > {tt/ss/gn [ññ̃]} /V___V

286) <u>MONTAGNAIS</u>
šk > ss/_{FV/y}
  > x/elsewhere

287) <u>SWAHILI</u>
{k/t/p} > {š/s/f} /___ʃ

-318-

288) LATIN
   s > r/V___V

289) ITALIAN
   k > č/___front vowel

290) RUSSIAN
   k > č/___front vowel

291) RUSSIAN
   {h/x} > š/___front vowel

292) OLD CHURCH SLAVIC
   k > c/___{ai/ei/i}

293) OLD CHURCH SLAVIC
   {x/h} > s/___front vowel

294) OLD CHURCH SLAVIC
   {k/g/gʰ} > z/___front vowel

295) SPANISH
   ε > e/___ {(C)(C)(i̯)/CC}
      > ie/elsewhere

296) ITALIAN
   ε > ie/___CV

297) SPANISH AND ITALIAN
   ɔ > o/___ {Ci̯/KC} in Spanish
      > ue/elsewhere in Spanish
      > uo/___CV in Italian

298) RUSSIAN
   1) ŭ > ∅/ {C___#/___CV} V ≠ ŭ, ɪ
      > o/elsewhere
   2) ɪ > ∅/ {C___#/___CV} V ≠ ŭ, ɪ
      > e/elsewhere

299) RUSSIAN
1) pni; 2) zlo; 3) dva; 4) gnati; 5) mox; 6) sozvat^y; 7) test^y; 8) uzok; 9) uzka; 10) posol

300) <u>SLAVIC LANGUAGES</u>
or ⟩ ra in OCS
    ⟩ ro in Polish
    ⟩ ro/#___ in Czech
    ⟩ ra/elsewhere in Czech
    ⟩ ro/#___ in Russian
    ⟩ oro/elsewhere in Russian

301) <u>SLAVIC LANGUAGES</u>
ol ⟩ la in OCS
    ⟩ lo in Polish
    ⟩ la in Czech
    ⟩ olo in Russian

el ⟩ lě in OCS
    ⟩ le in Polish
    ⟩ le in Czech
    ⟩ olo, ele in Russian

302) <u>ENGLISH</u>
ī ⟩ i/___CC
  ⟩ ay/elsewhere (five, wise)

ē ⟩ e/___CC
  ⟩ iy/elsewhere (creep, kneel)

ā ⟩ æ/___CC
  ⟩ ey/elsewhere (dame, late)

ɔ̄ ⟩ a/___CC
  ⟩ ow/elsewhere (float, nose)

ō ⟩ a/___CC
  ⟩ uw/elsewhere (goose, lose)

ɔ > ə/___CC
> aw/elsewhere (house, out)

Neither the quality of the original vowel nor its length is apparent from the data. However, you should have hypothesized six contrasting vowels and the conditioning factor. This set of changes took place in English during the 17th century, and is known as the Great Vowel Shift.

303) ENGLISH

The same six long vowels should be hypothesized here as in 302, but the conditioning factor is that the shortened vowel or monophthong occurs when followed by two more syllables: ī (crime, criminal); ē (obscene, obscenity); ā (cape, capital); ō (globe, globular); ō (school, scholarly); ū (south, southerly).

304) ENGLISH

In modern English the vowels in these words spelled "ee" and "ea" are pronounced identically. They also underwent the same changes during the Great Vowel Shift. The systematic difference in spelling indicates that at one time they were different vowels (ee = ē; ea = ɛ̄), and their equal historical development indicates that they fell together as one vowel (ē) before the Great Vowel Shift.

305) ENGLISH
1) back vowel > front vowel/___(C)C front vowel
2) i > ∅/___#
3) front rounded vowel > unrounded
Forms 1–6 had an i in the syllable following the affected vowel; forms 7–12 did not have this vowel. The fronting of the vowel under the influence of a following front vowel is called "umlaut".

306) ENGLISH
h > 0/#___l,r,n
  >h/#vowel or w
Basically, the h was retained word initial before a
vowel or before w; elsewhere it was lost. In many
dialects of English, it was also lost before w. Do not
confuse the modern orthographic sequence ''wh'' with
its pronounciation, which is /hw/.

VIII. RECONSTRUCTION

307) ROMANCE I

Sp	Sa	Rum
i	i	i
i	i	f/r___
*i		

308) ROMANCE II

Sp	Sa	Rum
e	i	e
e	i	ea/___C(C)a#
*ɪ		

309) ROMANCE III

Sp	Sa	Rum
e	e	e
e	e	ea/___C(C)a#
*e		

310) ROMANCE IV

Sp	Sa	Rum
ie	e	ie
ie	e	ia/___C(C)a#
e	e	ie/___ {č} [in Sp]
*ɛ		

311) ROMANCE V

Sp	Sa	Rum
a	a	a
e	a	a/___ {č} [in Sp]
*a		

-322-

312) ROMANCE VI

Sp	Sa	Rum
ue	o	o
ue	o	oa/___C(C) {FV/LV}#
*ɔ		

313) ROMANCE VII

Sp	Sa	Rum
o	o	o
o	o	oa/___C(C) {FV/LV}#
o	o	u/___n
*o		

314) ROMANCE VIII

Sp	Sa	Rum
o	u	u
*ʊ		

315) ROMANCE IX

Sp	Sa	Rum
u	u	u
*u		

316) INDO-EUROPEAN I

Eng	Lat	Gk
f	p	p
p	p	p/#s___
*p		

317) INDO-EUROPEAN II

Eng	Lat	Gk
θ	t	t
t	t	t/#s___
*t		

318) INDO-EUROPEAN III

Eng	Lat	Gk
h	c [k]	k
š <sk	c [k]	k/#s__
*k		

319) INDO-EUROPEAN IV

Skt	Gk	Gmc
bʰ	pʰ	b
b	p	b/#__V{Cʰ/rh/h}
*bʰ		

320) INDO-EUROPEAN V

Skt	Gk	Gmc
dʰ	tʰ	d
d	t	d/#__V{Cʰ/h}
*dʰ		

321) INDO-EUROPEAN VI

Skt	Gk	Gmc
h	kʰ	g
g	k	g/#__V{Cʰ/rh/h}
*gʰ		

322) INDO-EUROPEAN VII

Skt	Gmc
-t-	-θ-/V..._
-t-	-d-/__...V
*-t-	

323) SLAVIC I

Uk	Ru	Cz	Slovak
i	e	i	ie
*ie			

324) <u>SLAVIC II</u>
OCS back nasal ǫ is the reflex of the original
combination of back vowel plus nasal.
OCS front nasal ę is the reflex of the original
combination of front vowel plus nasal.

325) <u>SLAVIC III</u>
1) ę; 2) ę; 3) ǫ; 4) ǫ, ǫ; 5) ę; 6) ę, ǫ 7) ę; 8) ǫ; 9) ǫ; 10)
ǫ; 11) ę; 12) ǫ; 13) ǫ, 14) ǫ, 15) ę

326) <u>PROTO-SLAVIC VERBAL STEM I</u>
Reconstructed stems: 1) pas-; 2) tr^{y}as-; 3) nes-; 4)
lez-; 5) vez; 6) bod-; 7) pad; 8) krad-, ved-, met-
Changes in infinitive: {-d/-t} → s/-ti (dissimilation)
Past tense: suffix -l preserved in Czech
{sl/zl} → s; {dl/tl} → l in Russian
{dl/tl} → o in Serbo-Croatian

327) <u>PROTO-SLAVIC VERBAL STEM II</u>
1) mig-; 2) mog-; 3) sleg-; 4) tag-; 5) stig-; 6) pomog-
; 7) pek-; 8) protek-; 9) puk-; 10) rek-

328) <u>AUSTRONESIAN LANGUAGES I</u>
1) mataq; 2) manis; 3) tumaq; 4) taman; 5) laruq; 6)
laris; 7) lurug; 8) kuraŋ; 9) duqum; 10) damar; 11)
kadaŋ; 12) gandar; 13) ganjil; 14) tanjuŋ; 15) panas; 16)
bantal; 17) baŋsal; 18) hadəp; 19) maduq; 20) hudaŋ; 21)
hudip

329) <u>AUSTRONESIAN LANGUAGES II</u>
1) kitaq; 2) baliraŋ; 3) gilaq; 4) lutuŋ; 5) kilan; 6)
siŋgah; 7) suruŋ, 8) tarimaq; 9) tamiaŋ; 10) tuluŋ; 11)
pisah; 12) qupah; 13) tumpuq; 14) galugah; 15) bulan;
16) buluq

330) <u>PROTO-EASTERN OCEANIC</u>
4) Fiji: cā; 5) Nggela: tahi; 7) P-P: fohe; 9) P-E-O:
zake-v; 17) P-P: hoko; 19) Fiji:kanace
<u>Deviating form</u>: P-P: fiso, anuha; Ngg: ngiha, kanace

-325-

331) **MALAYO-JAVANIC GROUP**
1) l-m-q; 2) m-t-q; 3) p-n-s; 4) b-t-q; 5) b-nt-ŋ; 6) k-
n-ŋ; 7) t-l-q; 8) k-rr-q; 9) l-ss-ŋ; 10) l-ŋŋ-q; 11) b-
rr-q; 12) b-pp-q; 13) t-ll-q; 14) k-bb-h; 15) g-rr-ŋ

332) <u>TURKIC LANGUAGES I</u>
1) kaz; 2) kal; 3) kar/xar; 4) kat; 5) kač; 6) koi̯/xoi̯; 7)
kol/xol; 8) kul; 9) kuš; 10) kiz; 11) kil/xil; 12) kin/xin;
13) kiš; 14) gël; 15) gir; 16) göl; 17) gök; 18) gör; 19)
gün; 20) güč

333) <u>TURKIC LANGUAGES II</u>
6) ta:r; 8) kö:k

BIBLIOGRAPHY

Agard, Frederich, B.
1958   Structural Sketch of Rumanian. Language
        Monograph No. 28. Baltimore: Waverly Press.

Akhmatova, O.S., et al
1969   Russian-English Dictionary. Moscow: Sovetskaia
        enciklopedia.

Aquilino, Joseph
1959   The Structure of Maltese. Valetta: The Royal
        University of Malta.

Aronson, Howard I.
1968   Bulgarian Inflectional Morphophonology. The
        Hague: Mouton.

Bánhidi, Z., et al
1965   Learn Hungarian. Budapest: Tankönyvkiadó.

Bazterrica, I.
1968   Aditza. San   Antonio: Editorial   Montepio
        Diocesana.

Bender, Ernest
1967   Hindi   Grammar   and   Reader.   Philadelphia:
        University of Pennsylvania Press.

Betteridge, H.T., ed
1958   The New Cassell's German Dictionary. New York:
        Funk & Wagnalls.

Bidwell, Charles E.
1969   The Structure of Russian in Outline. Pittsburgh:
        University of Pittsburgh Press.

1962   An Alternative Phonemic Analysis of Russian.
        SEEJ 6:125-9.

Blanc, Haim
1964   Confessional Dialects in Baghdad. Cambridge,
        Mass.: Harvard University Press.

Bloomfield, Leonard
1946   Algonquian. Pp. 85-129 in Linguistic Structures of
        Native America. Viking Fund Publications in
        Anthropology 6. New York.

Bray, R.G.A. de
1951   Guide to the Slavonic Languages. New York: E.P.
        Dutton.

Bossou, J.E.
1964   Modern Mongolian. Uralic and Altaic Series, Vol.
        28. Bloomington: Indiana University Press.

Busuttil, E.D.
1950   Kalepin Malti-Ingliz. Il-Belt: Progress Press.

Cassidy, F.G., and R.N. Ringler, eds.
1971   Bright's Old English. New York: Holt, Rinehart
        and Winston.

Collins, S.J.
1962   Small English-Tonga Dictionary. London:
        Longmans.

Comrie, Bernard
1981   Language Universals and Language Typology.
        Oxford: Basil Blackwell.

Dunn, C.J., and S. Yanada
1968   Teach Yourself Japanese. London: The English
        Universities Press.

Ellis, C. Douglas
1983   Spoken Cree. Edmonton: University of Alberta
        Press.

Erwin, Wallace A.
1969   A Basic Course in Iraqi Arabic. Washington:
        Georgetown University Press.

Fasmer, M.
1971   Etimologicheskii Slovar' russkogo iazyka. I-IV.
        Moscow: Progress.

Geraghty, Paul A.
1983   The History of the Fijian Languages. Honolulu:
        University of Hawaii Press.

Gili Gaya, Samuel, ed.
1953   Dictionario general ilustrado de la lengua
        española. Barcelona: Editorial Spes.

Gimson, A.C.
1967   An Introduction to the Pronunciation of English.
        London: Edward Arnold.

Goodwin, William
1898   A Greek Grammar. London: Macmillan.

Gordon, E.V.
1968   An Introduction to Old Norse. Oxford: Oxford
        University Press.

Guralnik, D.B., ed.
1970   Webster's New World Dictionary of the American
        Language. Second College Edition. New York:
        World Publishing Co.

Guthrie, Malcolm
1967   Comparative Bantu. Farnborough: Gregg.

Gvozdev, A.N.
1967   Sovremennyj russkij literaturnyj jazyk, I. Moscow:
        Prosveschchenie.

Hale, William G., and Carl D. Buck
1966   A Latin Grammar. University, Alabama: University of Alabama Press.

Hall, Robert A.
1976   Proto-Romance Phonology. New York: Elsevier.

Hoa, Nguyen Dinh
1965   Speak Vietnamese. Saigon: Ministry of Education and Culture.

Javarek, V., and M. Sudjic'.
1963   Teach Yourself Serbo-Croat. London: English Universities Press.

Jones, D., and D. Ward
1969   The Phonetics of Russian. Cambridge: Cambridge University Press.

Kautzsch, E., ed.
1960   Gesenius' Hebrew Grammar. Oxford: Oxford University Press.

Khanh, Le-Ba, and Le-Ba Kong
1975   Vietnamese-English Dictionary. New York: Frederick Ungar.

Kluge, Friedrich
1967   Etymologisches Wörterbuch der deutschen Sprache. Berlin: De Gruyter.

Kornrumpf, H.J.
1963   Methuen's Universal Dictionary, Turkish-English, English-Turkish. London: Methuen.

Kučera, H.
1961   The Phonology of Czech. The Hague: Mouton.

Kuno, Susumu
1973   The Structure of the Japanese Language. Cambridge, Mass.: MIT Press.

Kurz, Josef, and Petr Jan, eds.
1982   Srbsko-Charvátsko-Český   Slovnik.   Prague:
        Academia.

Lambton, A.K.S.
1963   Persian   Grammar.   Cambridge: Cambridge
        University Press.

1979   Persian   Vocabulary.   Cambridge: Cambridge
        University Press.

Lapesa, Rafael
1955   Historia de la lengua española. Madrid: Escelicer.

Lewis, Charlton T., and Charles Short.
1975   A Latin Dictionary. Oxford: Oxford University
        Press.

Lewis, G.L.
1971   Turkish. Teach Yourself Books. London: St. Paul's
        House.

Liddell, H.G., and W.S. Scott
1975   An Intermediate Greek-English Lexicon. Oxford:
        Oxford University Press.

Lockwood, W.B.
1977   Indo-European Philology. London: Hutchinson.

Lunt, H.G.
1974   Old Church Slavonic Grammar. 6th ed. The Hague:
        Mouton.

Mansion, J.E.
1978   Harrap's   New   Shorter   French   and   English
        Dictionary [revised]. London: George G. Harrap.

Marchand, J.W.
1961   Applied   Linguistics   German: A   Guide   for
        Teachers. Boston: D.C. Heath.

Mardin, Yusuf
1961   Colloquial Turkish. London: Routledge and Kegan.

Marinova, M., et al.
1964   Bulgarski ezik. Sofia: Narodna prosveta.

Martin, S.E.
1954   Korean Morphophonemics. W.D. Whitney Linguistic
        Series. Baltimore: Linguistic Society of America.

Mathews, R.H.
1979   Chinese-English Dictionary. Cambridge, Mass.:
        Harvard University Press.

Menéndez Pidal, R.
1952   Manual de gramática histórica española. Madrid:
        Espasa-Calpe.

Meyer-Lübke, W.
1972   Romanisches Etymologisches Wörterbuch.
        Heidelberg: Carl Winter Universitätsverlag.

Miklosich, F.
1886   Etymologisches Wörterbuch der Slavischen
        Sprachen. Wien: W. Braumüller.

1973   Vergleichende Grammatik der Slavischen Sprachen,
        I. Osnabruck: Biblio Verlag.

Milner, G.B.
1956   Fijian Grammar. Suva: Government Press.

Mitchell, T.F.
1956   An Introduction to Egyptian Colloquial Arabic.
        Oxford: Oxford University Press.

Morris, William, ed.
1971   The American Heritage Dictionary of the English
        Language. New York: Houghton Mifflin.

Nasr, Raja T.
1966   Colloquial Arabic. Beirut: Librarie du Liban.

Navarro Tomas, T.
1953   Manual de pronunción espanõla. Madrid: Revista
       de Filología Española.

N'diaye, G.
1970   Structure du dialecte Basque de Maya. The Hague:
       Mouton.

Niederman, M.
1953   Précis de phonétique historique du latin. Paris:
       Klincksieck.

Nothofer, Bernd
1975   The Reconstruction of Proto-Malayo-Javanic. The
       Hague: Martinus Nijhoff

Ohala, Manjari
1983   Aspects of Hindi Phonology. Delhi: Motilal
       Banarsidass.

Oinas, F.J.
1966   Basic Course in Estonian. Bloomington: Indiana
       University Press.

Oleksy, W.
1979   Questions in English and Polish. Semantics and
       Pragmatics. Edmonton: Linguistic Research.

Országh, L.
1969   Magyar-Angol Szótár, I-II. Budapest: Academy of
       Science.

Papp, F.
1969   Reverse-Alphabetized   Dictionary   of   the
       Hungarian Language. Budapest: Academy of
       Science.

Perrott, D.V.
1969   Teach Yourself Swahili. London: The English
        Universities Press.

Pokorný, J.
1959   Indogermanisches Etymologisches Wörterbuch, I-
        II. Bern: Francke Verlag.

Preobrazhensky, A.G.
1951   Etymological Dictionary of the Russian Language.
        New York: Columbia University Press.

Prokosch, E.
1938   A Comparative Germanic Grammar. Baltimore:
        Linguistic Society of America.

Quirk, R., and S. Greenbaum
1973   A University Grammar of English. London:
        Longman Group.

Reif, Joseph, and Hanna Levinson
1965   Hebrew Basic Course. Washington: Foreign
        Service Institute.

Rowlands, Evan
1969   Teach Yourself Yoruba. London: The English
        Universities Press.

Russo, Joseph L.
1929   Elementary Italian Grammar. New York: D.C.
        Heath.

Saint-Jacques, B.
1971   Structural Analysis of Modern Japanese.
        Vancouver: University of British Columbia
        Publishing Center.

Schuchardt, H.
1947   Primitiae Lingvae Vasconum. Salamanca:Colegio
        Trilingüe de la Universidad.

Shcherbak, A.M.
1970   Sravnitel'naja fonetika tjurkskix jazykov.
        Leningrad: AN SSSR.

Shevelov, G.Y.
1964   A Prehistory of Slavic. Heidelberg: Carl Winter
        Universitätsverlag.

Smith, C. Alphonso
1896   Anglo-Saxon Grammar and Exercise Book. New
        York: Allyn and Bacon.

Stanislawski, J.
1970   Wielki Stownik Polsko-Anglielski. Warsaw: State
        Publishing House.

Swift, Lloyd B., and Selman Ağrali
1966   Turkish Basic Course. Washington: Foreign
        Service Institute.

Tovar, A.
1957   The Basque Language. Philadelphia: University of
        Pennsylvania Press.

Trubachev, O.N., ed.
1974   Etimologicheskij slovar' slavjanskix jazykov, I-VI.
        Moscow: Nauka.

Urkizu, P.
1978   Lengua y literatura vasca. San Sebastian: Luis
        Haranburu.

Vago, R.M.
1980   The Sound Pattern of Hungarian. Washington:
        Georgetown University Press.

Vaillant, A.
1974   Grammaire comparée des langues slaves. Paris:
        Editions Klincksieck.

Vasilenko, I.A.
1965   Istoricheskaia grammatika russkogo iazyka,
        Sbornik uprazhneuii. Moscow: Prosveshchenie.

Wehr, Hans
1961   A Dictionary of Modern Written Arabic.
        Wiesbaden: Otto Harrossowitz.

Zelizniak, A.A.
1963   Lingvističeskie zadači. Pp. in Issledovanija po
        strukturnoj tipologii. Moscow: AN SSSR, Institut
        slavjanovedenija.

INDEX OF LANGUAGES
(Numbers indicate exercise number)

Javanese, Old: 328, 329
Korean: 16, 81, 88
Kumic: 332
Latin: 123, 202, 228, 229, 250, 288, 316, 317, 318
Lithuanian: 324
Madurese: 328, 329, 331
Malay: 99, 101, 107, 200, 201, 328, 329, 331
Maltese: 134, 275, 278
Montagnais: 286
Nggela: 330
Persian: 133, 181, 185, 186
Polynesian, Proto-: 330
Polish: 91, 151, 251, 300, 301
Portuguese: 283
Portuguese, Brazilian: 79, 80
Rumanian: 55, 56, 58, 238, 276, 277, 307, 308, 309, 310, 311,
    312, 313, 314, 315
Russian: 9, 10, 11, 14, 111, 113, 116, 212, 216, 290, 291, 298,
    299, 300, 301, 323, 326, 327
Russian, Old: 324
Sanskrit: 319, 320, 321, 322
Sardinian: 307, 308, 309, 310, 311, 312, 313, 314, 315
Serbo-Croatian: 86, 325, 326, 327
Slavic, Old Church: 292, 293, 294, 300, 301, 324, 325
Slavic, Proto-: 300, 301
Slovak: 93, 100, 145, 146, 323, 325
Spanish: 4, 27, 31, 34, 35, 38, 39, 40, 46, 47, 62, 92, 96, 98,
    104, 108, 110, 125, 126, 219, 237, 240, 248, 249, 273, 281,
    284, 295, 297, 307, 308, 309, 310, 311, 312, 313, 314, 315
Spanish, Castillian: 29, 36, 37
Sundanese: 328, 329, 331
Swahili: 140, 173, 174, 245, 246, 287
Turkic, Proto-: 333
Turkish: 87, 90, 95, 97, 106, 112, 128, 129, 152, 187, 190, 207,
    214, 231, 332
Turkmen: 333
Tuvin: 332
Ukranian: 323
Vietnamese: 5, 68
Welsh: 150
Yakutsk: 333
Yoruba: 122

This book was produced using the Gutenberg Sr Word
Progessing Programme on an Apple II+ micro-computer, and
was printed on an Apple Imagewriter.

In the BENJAMINS PAPERBACKS series the following volumes have been published thus far:

1. MEY, Jacob: *Whose Language: A Study in Linguistic Pragmatics.* Amsterdam, 1985.
2. COLLINGE, N.E.: *The Laws of Indo-European.* Amsterdam, 1985.
3. WODAK, Ruth & Muriel SCHULZ: *The Language of Love and Guilt. Mother-daughter relationships from a cross-cultural perspective.* Amsterdam, 1986.
4. LUELSDORFF, Philip: Constraints on Error Variables in Grammar: Bilingual Misspelling Orthographies. Amsterdam, 1986.
5. COWAN, William & Jaromira RAKUŠAN: *Source book for Linguistics.* Philadelphia/Amsterdam, 1985 (Second revised edition 1987).
6. SCAGLIONE, Aldo: *The Liberal Arts and the Jesuit College System.* Amsterdam, 1986.
7. SALMON, Vivian & Edwina BURNESS (comps.): *A READER IN THE LANGUAGE OF SHAKESPEAREAN DRAMA.* Amsterdam, 1987.